Fighting Pollution and Climate Change

An EPA Veteran's Guide
How to Join in Saving Our Life on Planet Earth

Richard W. Emory, Jr.

https://www.richardwemoryjr.com
https://www.fightingpollutionbook.com
or Google "fighting pollution and climate change"
Richard W. Emory, Jr.

http://www.booklocker.com

BookLocker
Saint Petersburg, Florida

*Michael Morrill,
With best wishes,
as we still have a planet to save!
Richard Emory*

ISBN 978-1-64438-069-7

Printed on acid-free, crème paper.

Library of Congress Control Number: 2019918191
Library of Congress Cataloguing-in-Publication Data
Emory, Jr., Richard W., 1941–
Fighting Pollution and Climate Change: An EPA Veteran's Guide
How to Join in Saving Our Life on Planet Earth / Richard W.
Emory, Jr.

BookLocker.com, Inc.
2020

First Edition

Disclaimer

This book is not approved, endorsed, or authorized by the U.S. Environmental Protection Agency, and the retired badge pictured on the cover does not imply any official authority then or now. While Richard Emory was never a federal Special Agent, he is proud to personally own and in retirement possess honorary EPA gold badge number 2, portrayed on the book cover. It was awarded at the conclusion of his service as nationwide legal advisor to EPA's Special Agents, numbering about 100 brave men and women investigating the worst (intentional and sometimes with a dead-body count, thus criminal) cases of pollution. Not to be confused with or worn as a credential, this commemorative badge is permanently mounted on a plaque bearing these words: "For outstanding service as Acting Director of the Criminal Enforcement Counsel Division of the Office of Criminal Enforcement…, by providing sound legal advice and national management to achieve a fair and effective program of environmental criminal enforcement."

Acknowledgments and Dedication

I want to thank Monty Helfgott, who so generously gives of his time to lead a memoir writers' club in our Florida retirement community. Without him I would not have begun and reached the finish line for an undertaking as big as a book. Without the assistance of another neighbor, the computer genius Alan Paderewski, these words would not have been possible. I have been greatly assisted by Jane Crosen of Crackerjack Editorial Services, www.mainemapmaker.com. She very professionally edited my text, and then as a new friend believing that my book should be read, she did much more to help in my search for a publisher. I thank Torsten Muller of Artwize, at roadiecraft @icloud.com, for the artistry of the dynamic and colorful cover, and I thank Todd Engel of Engel Creative, at engel@att.net, for completing the final design layout. I thank my friend Matt Kahn for his professional rephotographing of my snapshot from 1974 that appears on the back of the cover. My excellent website designer is Crystal Narayana at web@crystalnarayana.com. My cousin Ben Emory, conservationist and author of *Sailor for the Wild*, is the person most responsible for keeping my spirits up by helping me helping me with suggestions as to content, leads to a publisher who would not ignore or dismiss a first-time author, and marketing assistance. And my lifelong friend, Sam Hopkins, has done the same.

Special thanks go to Richard H. Mays, one of the finest EPA lawyers and human beings I have ever met, and to Richard Condit, Mick Harrison, and Joanne Royce of the Government Accountability Project. Special thanks also to Jeff Ruch who founded and led the Public Employees for Environmental Responsibility, now led by Tim Whitehouse who earlier worked with me inside EPA. GAP, PEER, and similar organizations deserve our support. They are vital to protecting honest civil servants who would "take care that the laws [of the United

States] be faithfully executed" from being crushed by powerful interests and their politicians who would deny Americans "equal justice under law." Thanks to Durwood Zaelke, who from his International Network for Environmental Compliance and Enforcement (INECE) was a great NGO partner helping EPA and our Dutch partners with foreign assistance. And he was first to provide generous words of endorsement, which I am proud for all to see on my book's cover. I am very grateful to Richard Sanderson, Michael Alushin, and Robert Heiss. These leaders in the civil service made possible the 17 years I enjoyed working in EPA's mission of foreign assistance to other nations that would join with EPA in working to save our planet.

I thank those who reviewed portions of my book for publication, including Natalie Meier Bhandari, Angela Bularga, Alan Ross, Harvey Spitz, Terry Sullivan, Elliot Weinstock, and especially Whitney Emory Yeager who reviewed it all. None of these good people are responsible for my words.

I dedicate this book to my wife Donna, our three children, and to our seven grandchildren: Sam, Cole, Madeleine, Emilia, Haven, Reis, and Elle. Their generation will have the burden of saving human habitat and life on Earth. The failure of too many of my generation to recognize the dangers of fossil fuels, that became clear by the 1980s and in our lifetime, will be a blot on human nature as long as humanity survives. This may not be much longer, but today's younger generations will see the perils when wading in seawater in their city streets, pounded by worsening storms, and elsewhere suffering fire and drought. Some of the best will seek relevant educations and find the many opportunities in the work of climate protection and adaption to rebuild so many cities inland on higher ground. I do predict that—to protect their grandchildren yet to be born—our grandchildren will pull humanity back from the brink.

Finally, I dedicate this book to the brave pollution fighters within the U.S. government who have remained at posts during

2017–2021. In these years, a willfully ignorant President and his conniving cronies tried their best to dismantle pollution control and natural resource protection in America, and to accelerate the oncoming climate chaos. If life on Earth is to continue, EPA, NOAA, DOI, FEMA, and many parts of the federal government must be revitalized, enlarged, and strengthened. Internationally, the United Nations Environment Programme (UNEP) and governments at all levels and in all places must be resourced and repurposed to do the growing work of adaptation and mitigation. The World Trade Organization (WTO) must elevate its values to put the planet first, no longer allowing profits from dirty, lowest-cost production methods and the shipping of carbon-intensive products. Non-governmental organizations, provided they are working in the public interest, must again be welcomed as partners by the national government. And the innovative private sector must be incentivized and rewarded with profits in a global free market redesigned to correct for the present market's failure to quickly bring on clean technologies.

To the new pollution fighters of the future, my wish of course is that I could continue on among you. But each person's allotted time here is limited. What I can do is hope that this book will provide some help along the way, and that you will feel my hopeful spirit guiding you on to save our little planet from human denial and procrastination.

Contents

Introduction

I WRITE THIS BOOK BASED ON MY FIRM BELIEF that the United States Environmental Protection Agency (EPA) as soon as possible must be revived and then greatly strengthened if humanity is to avoid climate chaos and mass extinction. While I seek to motivate and enlist pollution fighters, young and old, this book is also both a critique and a paean, mostly a song of praise for what the Agency once was and must become again if humanity is to survive on this planet. EPA brought clean air to America, climate change is just another air-pollution problem, and EPA must lead the world in stopping it. I do not hesitate to state lessons learned that today's leaders and our posterity should know and act upon without repeating mistakes or wasting any more time.

This book is to demonstrate to any person how you too may join in. While my path was the law, there are so many, many fields of science and engineering where you can make a big contribution. Artists, writers, economists, law-enforcement officers, policy makers, political leaders—all are needed. If you can identify your skills and train yourself to use them, and if your passion is protecting the public health, natural resources, or any part of our little planet, your career will be as full of joy as was mine. All fields will eventually intersect with the law, so it will be useful that you read here the story of a pollution-fighting lawyer. If you are an older person, a mature citizen already concerned about our planet and perhaps even a leader in your sphere of influence, you too—especially and right now—are needed as a pollution fighter.

Fighting Pollution and Climate Change: An EPA Veteran's Guide How to Join in Saving Our Life on Planet Earth is mostly issues-based. Some chapters are mostly about science and technology, and how they intersect with economics, public policy, and law.

The first chapter will look at human-caused extinctions facing wildlife, and following chapters will cover toxic-waste dumping of hazardous chemicals, man-made holes in the ozone layer needed to protect us from the sun, the unnatural pesticides and other contaminants that we allow and even choose to put in our food supply, and the climate chaos that we are bringing upon ourselves. These chapters will focus on solutions no less than problems. The last chapter presents the solutions to protect our climate.

Alternating chapters are partially autobiographical, but only as an organizing framework useful to covering the issues while demonstrating the human side of public service. My life of working through recent environmental history, as a state, national, and international pollution fighter, should be instructive to new environmental protectors. The first half of my public service, at both the state and national levels, was to enforce science-based pollution-control laws—crime fighting. As a "happy warrior," I found it thrilling to work to take criminals down and off the field. In the second half of my career, often as a teacher I worked internationally in USEPA's mission of foreign assistance. Despite heavy challenges, most of the time it was a pleasure to have the honor to represent our nation.

While parts of this book may be ponderous, other parts should be fun. While making links to recent events and to history, I hope to entertain you with stories of some adventures, including official assignments to work in Paris and to teach in Germany. In most planet-protection work, there indeed is much "joy" to be found by any person who loves our Earth.

Chapter 1—Extinctions, Past and Present

OUR PLANET IS LOSING ITS LIFE. The Earth's climate is now deteriorating rapidly, and disaster—even human extinction—is now coming into view in the not very distant future. The cause is one more, man-made, air-pollution problem now threatening even the planet's most invasive species, us. The geochemical dynamic for extinction is explained in the science book *Under a Green Sky,* by Peter D. Ward (Harper Collins, 2008). The book's subtitle reads: "Climate change, the mass extinctions of the past, and what they tell us about our future." Professor Ward describes how, in four of Earth's extinctions during the last half-billion years, excess carbon dioxide starting at the level of 1,000 parts per million (ppm) caused the oceans to become poisoned with deadly hydrogen sulfide. He tells us that this chemical, being emitted from the sea as gas, turned the sky permanently green and killed most life on land.[1]

Paleontologists and geologists confirm that since life on Earth began about 500 million years ago there have been five mass extinctions.[2] They tell us that there are accurate and close correlations to be made between global average temperature, sea-level rise, atmospheric CO_2, and mass extinctions. Man-made air pollution is the cause of climate change leading to the mass extinction that may end the gradual sixth extinction now happening and accelerating. If we continue with business as usual burning fossil fuels, leaking methane and refrigerants, and in other ways also thoughtlessly damaging the climate, possibly in about 200 to 250 years we will have so poisoned the sea and the air that it does seem that humanity will join in the sixth extinction.

To set the stage for this book about fighting climate pollution, this first chapter is much about the life our planet has already lost and is losing now at the hand of man, that part of the sixth extinction caused by bullets, poisons, traps, and man's other physical tools of kinetic death. Any day now, the gillnets of Mexican fishermen could drown the last of the vaquitas, doll-faced porpoises only about five feet long. If they are not yet extinct, now perhaps only about ten remain alive. The smallest of all cetaceans, an adorable elf of a whale, today the vaquita is about to become a myth and a memory.

Preventing such tragedies is the job of wildlife officers, who like pollution-control officers share the large field of natural-resource and environmental protection. But it is pollution fighters, both volunteers and employed, and not wildlife officers, who can prevent the completion of the sixth extinction by controlling and ending climate-killing air pollution. Accompanying them will be many other professions, especially engineers of all types needed to build the new, clean-energy sources and to relocate so many cities to higher ground inland.

I did not know about climate change before I was well into my career at the U.S. Environmental Protection Agency. I never imagined that I would become, even briefly, the nation's top lawyer for federal investigations of pollution crime. But the foundations for my life as a pollution fighter began 50 years earlier in the 1940s, when I was a child living on the coast of Maine.

At the sounding of the horn, some women—permanent residents of our little town—grabbed their sharpest knives and rushed out their front doors. In the street they were joined by hungry cats, and excited children like me, eight years old and attracted to commotion. We all rushed down the road to the harbor to see coming in from the sea the sardine transport boat arriving at what we called "the fish factory." Being halfway "down east" in Brooklin, Hancock County, Maine, these town women anticipated a rare payday.

After being lifted out of the hold of the transport boat, the little fish would travel down a long, watery sluice roofed over to keep out the gulls. Their cries were loudly calling their companions, arriving now in numbers enough to have eaten the entire catch, but only the boldest came in under the roof. Standing along the sluice, the aproned women sliced, sorted, packed, and threw enough scraps about so the town cats never left hungry. The smells, sights, and sounds—squawking, meowing, heavy motors running, the women talking and their knives flashing as they worked, water rushing down the sluice—were irresistible to me and the other town children there too. Then the sardine carrier's hold was emptied, all was packed, and "the fish factory" became empty and silent.

The women returned to their homes. They put some cash in their dresser drawers and resumed preserving summer fruits and vegetables to keep in their cellars against the long, lean winter to come. In late August, the evenings became chilly and dark early, and in the night sky we might see glimmers of the *aurora borealis* that we called the "northern lights." All too soon it would be September, and I would be taken 600 miles south to my parents' home in Baltimore. There during another long school year in a big city, I would be wanting and waiting to return to my small town by the cold sea.

Finally, June would come again, and we summer people would reappear in town. Until July, most mornings our harbor would be unseen until the sun could burn off the fog. Another summer had come to the coast of Maine, and then would come another, but the big sardine boat never returned. Sometime in the1950s, the fish factory was sold to become a boatyard for building and repairing the yachts and small pleasure boats of summer that were replacing year-round working boats. A way of life was shifting because of new realities. Fish-factory jobs were surely tough, low-paying, and intermittent, and in 2010 the last Maine sardine factory closed. Whether the year-round people of the town considered this change to be for the better or worse, I cannot say. To me the arrival of the sardine boat is a shimmering memory of big excitement during carefree and glorious summer days. But a way of life was ending, and in 1959 my childhood would end too.

Long since I was so lucky to have been a summer child living in my grandmother's home on the Maine coast, I have wondered—did the sardines disappear from overfishing, did foreign countries catch and can them for less, or was it because the East Coast market taste shifted to lobster and tuna? Today, I contemplate the fish factory as a mystery of nature in relation to the impact of man. Now we know that around the world many fisheries have been exploited to the point of commercial extinction. Man-made plastics are being eaten by and killing marine animals, birds, and fish, and scientists say that in a few decades there will be a greater weight of plastics than fish in the sea. Maine lobsters, while still plentiful and very profitable with many customers now in China, are beginning to shift their range northward to Canadian waters because of the warming of Maine waters. This warming also is impairing the soft-shell clams by bringing in invasive green crabs and milky ribbon worms. These predators, along with toxic red tides until now rarely occurring in New England waters, are reducing clam harvests needed for fried clams, chowder, buckets of "steamers," and clambakes on the shore. As the climate changes, it is possible in future decades that the lobsters and clams may disappear like the sardines. In 50 years, for today's children now on the Maine coast, digging at low tide for clams, like seeing lobster boats going and coming—these too may become just shimmering memories of a colorful way of life gone by.

I did not know it at the time, but about 100 miles south of my grandmother's house on the Maine coast, from the early 1950s, lived Rachel Carson. Here she was quietly writing her book *Silent Spring,* published in 1962, which opened many eyes and caused her to be seen by many as the mother of modern environmentalism or ecology. While she was an oceanographic scientist who understood what she was seeing, and I was an unknowing child, it happened that separately yet in the same years we each liked wading into tidepools to lift the seaweed to reveal little hidden creatures and smell the salty brine. We each liked peering down from a rowboat to see the life on the bottom of a harbor, and picking up starfish and sea urchins at low tide. We each liked walking among the whispering spruce and fir trees of a little island, hearing the waves splatter on the rocks of its windward shore.[3] While she was coming to the end of her life's work, as a child and then a teenager I too was absorbing the magic of the Maine coast, forming lifelong interests and values that would lead to my own life's work. Always remembering the legacy of Rachel Carson, and in the hope that others will do the same, this book is in part the story of how a person may well follow along her path in life.

Rachel Carson wrote about science clearly and simply, and often almost poetically. Here are some of her words:

> It is a wholesome and necessary thing for us to turn again to the earth and in the contemplation of her beauties to know the sense of wonder and humility.

> Those who dwell among the beauties and mysteries of the earth are never alone or weary of life.

> In every out-thrust headland, in every curving beach, in every grain of sand there is the story of the earth.

Rachel Carson understood and loved the sea, which covers 70 percent of the surface of the Earth. I also love the sea, yet my book due to length limitations does not give the sea the full exploration it deserves. The decline of the health of the sea is caused by human attitudes and behavior mostly occurring on the land, so I have made the 30 percent that is land the locus of this book, knowing that all things eventually flow into the sea.

Fortunately, steering in Rachel Carson's wake is Peter Neill, a thinker who writes with passion and eloquence about saving the world's oceans and water sources:

> ...I hear it again and again...presentation of the overwhelming problem[s of the sea] followed by silence, not solutions. It is as if we are sailing along the edge of an abyss; we have the skill perhaps to keep going, to extend our way for a time, until we fall off into darkness, or we can apply that skill to our ship and change course, away in a new direction. It is dangerous and uncertain, but I submit that we have no choice but to set forth.[4]

As you will read in a following chapter, with her life and message Rachel Carson inspired good people and good laws that certainly have saved some endangered species. But since she died in 1964, too little has been done to limit wildlife depletions and extinctions that man is causing on sea and land all around the world. The North Atlantic subspecies of the largest whale in the sea, the so-called "right whale," today is threatened by ship strikes and fishing nets off Maine and the Canadian Maritime Provinces. The National Oceanic and Atmospheric Administration describes this whale as almost extinct. It may soon join its cousin the tiny vaquita, all extinguished at the hand of man. For so many more species, mass extinction is now in sight because of the climate chaos coming. And yet the U.S. Department of the Interior has neglected to place humanity officially on its endangered species list.

As we begin to address the fate of all life on our planet, let us consider these questions posed to us by Rachel Carson:

> ... to open your eyes... ask yourself—What if I had never seen this before?

> What if I knew I would never see it again?

Before we consider, in another chapter to follow, how human carelessness with air pollution now threatens humanity, we will first look into extinctions facing wildlife. Humanity has been causing Earth's sixth extinction, with species exterminations accelerated since perhaps 11,000 years ago at the ending of the last ice age. To begin tracing the history of the sixth extinction, let us visit the North Sea, where fishermen today in their nets may pull in not just sardines, but femurs four feet long and other gigantic bones raised from the seafloor. Woolly mammoths and mastodons were hunted and eaten by our prehistoric ancestors, but here they did not eat them all. During the last ice age, when sea levels were much lower, today's seafloor between England, the Netherlands, and Norway was dry; this area was called "Doggerland." Whether drowned slowly by the sea rising as the planet warmed, or by a seismic sea wave when Norwegian submarine mountains collapsed, some mastodons or woolly mammoths drowned naturally as Doggerland became the Dogger Bank, today a place for commercial fishing. But human appetites are not to be underestimated.

Like the town cats scurrying to the arrival of the sardine boat in Maine, early Europeans too were usually cold and always hungry. They probably did eat every last giant ox—the auroch—famously painted in the caves of Lascaux in France. Of course, they were just early and unwitting followers of today's stylish "paleo" or "Atkins" diet! In North America, humans arriving from Asia ate all the camels, zebras, and horses. Yes, there were indigenous horses long before the arrival of Spanish *conquistadors* whose mounts escaped and repopulated the American West. Once extinct on continents, some species survived on islands. But, with the invention of high-seas vessels, then came sailors. Seventeenth-century Dutchmen landing on the island of Mauritius found the dodo bird, a 50-pound flightless pigeon, so curious it walked up to greet the sailors coming ashore with firearms and appetites. Roasted dodo birds tasted so delicious after too many fish dinners on sailing ships. So the sailors ate them all. In the last 400 years, more than 500—some say 800—extinctions of animals, and more than 600 extinctions of plants, have been documented, and the pace of extinctions is accelerating.

European settlers arriving in North America shot all the Carolina parakeets and all the passenger pigeons. It is an amazing feat that relatively few hunters could kill about four billion passenger pigeons. They shot them as cheap food for themselves and their slaves and because they were pests to farmers' crops. Like the cavemen in who sketched the auroch, we can thank John James Audubon who in the 19th century arrived in the U.S. just in time to paint some of the last of these birds that we will never see alive.

In the American "Wild West," adventuring hunters and settlers almost exterminated the American bison...we call it the "buffalo." Nineteenth-century European-Americans shot them for their skins and even for sport, sometimes from windows of the first steam trains, often leaving their bodies to rot on the ground. This was government policy as part of the ethnic cleansing to starve and remove the Native Americans living on the Great Plains east of the Rocky Mountains. To quote U.S. Army General Philip Sheridan: "Let them [white adventurers and settlers] kill, skin, and sell until the last buffalo is exterminated...to bring lasting peace and allow civilization to advance." White men killed perhaps as many as 50 million buffalos, leaving only about 2,000 surviving.

During the 19th century in the far northwest in today's State of Washington, Chief Seattle led the Duwamish and Suquamish tribes. He worried about the invasive white men taking the salmon, trees, and lands of his native people, reportedly saying:

> What is man without the beasts? If all the beasts were gone, men would die from a great loneliness of spirit. For whatever happens to the beasts, soon happens to man. All

things are connected.... Whatever befalls the earth, befalls the sons of the earth. My people resemble the scattering of trees—fallen—on a storm-swept plain.[5]

We are fortunate today to have the example of a very energetic young gentleman from New York, who while adventuring in the 1880s in the Wild West, had observed the disappearance of buffalos, other wild game, and even their habitats to the overgrazing of cattle. He then became alarmed by the disappearance in Florida of plumed wading birds, harvested for their feathers that sold by weight exceeding the price of gold in New York City, London, and Paris. "TR" or "Teddy" Roosevelt in his day became world famous for many reasons, including his well-publicized refusal to shoot a lame old bear held captive on a rope. This image took shape as a stuffed toy, the "Teddy Bear," that became the enduring symbol of a child's natural love for animals. Theodore Roosevelt would be the first to put high on the national agenda the conservation of natural resources.

In 1900, Roosevelt helped Congressman John Lacey pass the first federal law to protect birds and game animals shipped in interstate commerce. Officers began seizing bird feathers and skins, and the "Lacey Bird and Game Act of 1900" saved many wildlife species (of both plants and animals) from extinction by outlawing their harvesting, hunting, and interstate shipping to market. But illegal taking ("poaching") and transporting across state lines continued, so beginning in 1901 Roosevelt, by then the President, protected about 230 million acres as national wildlife refuges, national forests, and national monuments, including lands that became many of the first national parks. Only on federally protected lands could the birds and animals live entirely safe from hunters.

While Teddy Roosevelt showed us the way forward within the U.S., we should remember the careless behavior of our ancestors.

And we should be aware that today it is modern buyers often from supposedly sophisticated nations who continue pushing wildlife toward extinction. The Lacey Act has since been updated beyond interstate trade to also apply to international black marketers and traffickers. It prohibits the import into the U.S. of animals and plants (whether live, dead, or made into products) that are either on the U.S. list of endangered species, or even if they are only protected by laws in their home countries that may be far away. This is a far-reaching and very powerful law, enthusiastically enforced by the officers of the U.S. Fish and Wildlife Service of the Department of the Interior. But alone it cannot save many species native to foreign lands.

As the first three examples of "charismatic megafauna"—big, appealing, or fascinating mammals—that are in big trouble today, consider tigers. Their habitat is steadily lost to human settlements that eliminate as food their natural prey. But worse is "poaching" to obtain tiger pelts, teeth, and claws as marketable decorative items. Tiger bones are harvested for use in traditional medicines by Asian consumers who wrongly believe they can treat ulcers and burns, rheumatism, heart ailments, liver disorders, fever—and that they can somehow strengthen human bones. Whiskers are thought to magically treat toothaches. Eating a tiger penis is said to be aphrodisiac. So today fewer than 2,500 breeding adult tigers are left in the wild, and their numbers are declining. Extinction in the wild is clearly in view for tigers.

The rhinoceros also has been hunted, some subspecies to extinction, others to the brink. After a rhino is killed, the horn is removed and smuggled to Asia, where many believers in traditional medicine imagine that pulverized horn is a magical pharmaceutical to cure almost any ill. Reports are that rhino horn may be sold for as much as $65,000 per kilo. In truth, rhino horn is just keratin, and an ill person by consuming his own toenails would improve his health no less than by consuming rhino horn.

For African elephants, it is the same, tragic story. After killing an elephant and removing just its massive tusks, in Japan, China, and throughout Southeast Asia they are carved into statues, trinkets, and adornments that can be very beautiful. These are often sold in luxury hotels where prices may be quoted in U.S. dollars. For decorative items made from the bodies of many endangered species, China has been the biggest market and the U.S. is second. The international market for tiger and elephant products has its parallels in the market for so-called "blood diamonds" mined by warlords in Africa, and in the U.S. market for narcotics from the murderous syndicates of Latin-American drug traffickers.

I am sure that my readers all love most animals, but lest we good citizens feel too self-righteous about whatever we are doing to save wildlife, let us realize that the popular demand in our supposedly civilized nations causes crime and official corruption here and in many troubled and distant countries. Buyers may be our friends and neighbors, and they may make their purchases on the Internet. The International Fund for Animal Welfare (IFAW) reported that the U.S. is responsible for more than two-thirds of all Internet trade in illegal wildlife, ordering online and importing almost ten times more than the next two countries—the U.K. and China. The global value of all illegal wildlife trade is estimated to be $10 to $20 billion annually, and after narcotics, wildlife is the world's third largest illegal trade.

In 1973, to protect wildlife the world signed the Convention on International Trade in Endangered Species of Flora and Fauna (CITES). This treaty addresses international sales by attempting to separate harvesters and poachers on one continent from their customers far away in other countries. Guards in the field attempting to protect wildlife at the source are soldiers in a war with organized local outlaws who supply international cartels. Now the criminals come with their own helicopters and night-vision goggles for aiming their automatic weapons. A World

Wildlife Fund survey found that two-thirds of all guards have been attacked by poachers, who do not hesitate first to kill the guards and then to kill animals (*fauna*) to supply markets in wealthy nations far across sea. Despite the best efforts of many good people, as wildlife numbers continue to decline, we cannot say that CITES has not been a failure.

So imagine yourself in the native market examining those nice tortoise shells, or a reptile-skin belt. Often it will not be obvious that a polished and charming tourist curio is even made from fragments of a dead, protected animal. As a tourist who does not want to become also a criminal, you must know with absolute certainty what dead animal it really is made of, and also that it is not illegal. Of course, the friendly shopkeeper will assure you that your purchase is from a legal variety. But in any case, how can you be sure? Why would you believe this? Only a scientist or trained officer—who can talk the language of taxonomy from top to bottom, from the phylum, class, order, family, genus, all the way down to the subspecies at the bottom—will know for sure. What are we tourists to do? The best advice is that you cannot possibly know the truth. Unless you are extremely knowledgeable as an expert, don't even think about buying anything dicey to bring home. Tourists returning to the U.S. will be greeted by experts in uniform who very well know the biological and botanical taxonomy. The officers of the U.S. Fish and Wildlife Service are very good at spotting illegal imports. In the spirit of Teddy Roosevelt, you will find the U.S. government very serious about CITES enforcement. Even if you can convince the arresting officer that you are an innocent tourist who was duped by a slippery salesman far away, federal agents will seize your items and you will pay a large fine.

Endangered plants (*flora*) are also protected by CITES and the Lacey Act. The actual CITES list is very long and very complicated, and among these are many subspecies of corals. Beyond harvesting for souvenirs, corals are diminished by fishing using dynamite, anchoring boats on reefs, and land-based pollution. But corals' biggest problem by far is carbonic acid and heat from carbon dioxide emissions—yes, global warming. Of all CO_2 and heat from burning fossil fuels that man has pumped into the air, about 92 percent of this is then absorbed into sea. We can be happy that the sea is so dense and absorbent, because if all this heat were to stay in the air, average global air temperature would exceed 120°F and on land we would be dying like flies. Instead of us, first to go are the corals in the sea. Now almost everywhere, corals are showing signs of "bleaching" into skeletons that soon will crumble into sand. At the present rate of decline, very soon, perhaps by 2030 and probably by 2050, scientists now tell us that 90 percent of coral reefs will be gone, and without this habitat, the reef fish disappear too. Our great-grandchildren probably will never snorkel to see beautiful reefs with colorful fish. This loss is likely to be inevitable, one might say "baked in," as mankind's first, complete destruction of a global ecosystem.

Now let us all leave the reef and come back into port to stand with the customs and wildlife officers catching professional smugglers of live animals. In freight shipments, officers have found live fish in waterproof sacks, baby birds stuffed in plastic tubes, turtles in snack-food boxes, and pythons in garden pots. In luggage they have found spiders hidden in film canisters, bird and reptile eggs hidden in clothing, and snakes coiled in stockings. Worn under clothing, officers have found live lizards taped to the chest, and even pygmy monkeys worn inside a man's undershorts! Perhaps this last example was a career highlight for the arresting officer, and it does seem amusing. But the penalty for such clandestine, commercial smuggling is up to 20 years in U.S. federal prison.

For an officer inspecting imports, most of the time the job is frustrating and may seem almost impossible. Contraband can be hidden almost anywhere—imagine a few hundred locked shipping containers on just one pier, or a land port of entry with dozens of large trucks impatiently lined up for clearance. The list of illegal goods is long, and it includes trafficked people who may be close to death. Officers surprised by animals in luggage or containers may receive scratches, bites, stings, and poisonings. Other cargoes are far more threatening. Consider the challenge of sampling canisters that may be under pressure or drums of chemicals, which may or may not be properly labeled with a skull and crossbones and other warnings that a cause of death is within. Contents may be pesticides or gases that can destroy the stratospheric ozone layer, prohibited not by CITES but by other global environmental treaties. Everyday bolt-and-lock cutters will not open a steel container, and without an environmental technician on site wearing a chemicals hazmat or "moon" suit and able to use technical sampling equipment, no customs officer can be expected to open and inspect toxic shipments alone.

Officers looking for wildlife may find almost any of a huge number of species. Their similar identities and varied legal status can be confusing, as many are protected yet have close relatives or look-alike varieties that are more common and legal. Some trade is unregulated, some is banned, and some is allowed but only if permitted. Where a species is only protected at the option of its nation of origin, legality often depends on whether it was taken or harvested lawfully in that faraway exporting nation. What actually happened there usually cannot be known by officers at the place of import, and they have to rely on permits that assure proper sourcing. Wildlife permits, like human passports, can vary from country to country. Yet unlike human passports, wildlife permits present in varied formats and in unfamiliar languages. Like passports, permits may look good but be falsified at the place of issuance or *en route*. A post may have short staffing, little training, and supervisors pressuring to clear shipments quickly to keep international trade moving.

Upon seizing a live specimen, the next problem is how to keep it alive. Without an established relationship with a nearby zoo that can help, officers at a port of entry may find it impossible to provide the needed special food, water, and temperature in a safe space to a huge variety of animals, often very young ones. The sorrow of watching them die in custody is one more burden. To conclude this overview of the work of our customs and wildlife officers at ports and borders, it is clear that they have difficult jobs, and the many honest officers deserve our respect and cooperation.

We turn now from smuggling to consider a different problem: the fate of warm-blooded aquatic mammals in the context of today's globalization and free-trade deals. Seals are "sea dogs," closely related to our tail-wagging pets who are "man's best friend." And dolphins also seem to want to talk with us; they may nuzzle us if we choose to swim among them; they seem almost human. Seals and dolphins chasing tuna on the high seas are routinely caught in the purse-seining nets of industrial-scale, large fishing boats. The marine mammals are pulled aboard with the tuna fish, and then as so-called "by-catch" they are cut up as bait or thrown dead back into the sea. Because they are too numerous to face extinction as a species, the treaty CITES does not protect dolphins, porpoises, and seals.

Without available international law to help, the U.S. government unilaterally has used the nation's wildlife laws that began under Teddy Roosevelt and since have been expanded to protect marine mammals and a longer list of other declining species including sea turtles and albatrosses. U.S. laws apply to American citizens abroad and to violators of any nation who come within U.S. territorial jurisdiction. U.S. laws prohibit import of U.S.-protected species that may come from anywhere in the world, even the high seas far beyond U.S. territorial waters and including the Pacific Ocean off Mexico. Applying this law in the 1990s, the federal government banned imports of tuna caught improperly, and dolphin deaths dropped 97 percent. And to provide to tuna-fish consumers information and confidence that catching our tuna did not harm dolphins, the U.S. government required cans of tuna to bear a label certifying that the contents were dolphin-safe.

The U.S. law worked, but it was no match for the commercial forces of globalization operated by the World Trade Organization (WTO). The WTO ruled that the unilateral U.S. laws violated the WTO treaty's free-trade rights of Mexican tuna fishermen. To apply U.S. national laws to protect species not on the CITES list, like seals, dolphins, and many others, the WTO ruled that U.S. would have to pay punitive monetary compensation to Mexico. So today, in the name of free trade, "sea dog" and "Flipper"—as by-catch—still are slaughtered unnecessarily in very high numbers. Unwilling to withdraw from the WTO, the U.S. cannot and does not apply its wildlife laws to prevent dolphin-deadly tuna imports, or require the former consumer-information labeling rule. Similar WTO rulings have impaired the U.S. fight against many other products. For example, while the U.S. would discourage youthful smoking, today the U.S. is blocked from banning foreign imports of candy-flavored tobacco products targeting even children. Any State, such as New York, that may ban them may be exposed to jeopardy under international law; this is an issue for the future.

In Europe beginning in the late 1980s, near panic arose over the "mad cow" scare involving exported cattle. A person eating a contaminated steak within a year could like the cow also be dead of a degenerative brain disease. If an American reads the news and is a careful food shopper, more recently they may be wary of contaminated medical drugs, foods, and even baby formula exported from named foreign countries well known to be careless about the fate of consumers across the sea. Now food-safety protesters have joined environmentalists in protesting a variety of insults to drugs and food, including imported honey found to be contaminated with lead and strange antibiotics, and even to not contain much actual honey. So the U.S. and European nations enacted laws requiring country-of-origin labeling, so-called "COOL rules," to warn consumers by naming and exposing the offending exporting country or countries in the news. But at the request of product manufacturers and commercial interests, in the name of free trade the WTO struck down COOL rules. Now shoppers cannot have labels to identify reckless source countries, and being denied this consumer information, we cannot save ourselves from putting fearsome products into our bodies.

There has been a reaction. Starting in the 1990s, often well-educated young professionals have been marching in the streets at meetings of the WTO in Europe and in Seattle, Québec, and Washington, D.C. Carrying provocative signs, some even calling the WTO the "World Terrorist Organization," they are making the news. These young "greens" are protesting that too many free-trade agreements too often shelter the lowest-cost and dirtiest production, allow the destruction of natural resources and the environment, and beyond this that the WTO shelters trade in products directly dangerous to our food and the public health. But we have seen that things can go very badly in the streets. Black-suited, masked anarchists may infiltrate a legitimate protest, using the event to break into shops, loot, throw stones, and bring down a police response even upon the mass of well-intentioned and peaceful protesters.

We should put lawless anarchists in jail and not let them distract or keep us from seeing that there is a legitimate tension or conflict between free-trade "protectionism" and planet protection. Nations often do try to block foreign competition for illegitimate reasons, and as the WTO works globally to deregulate and facilitate international trade, certainly it is not all bad. The WTO is useful to strike down protectionist laws that only for economic reasons would unfairly shelter domestic manufacturers. The U.S. government has often benefited by using the WTO to force open foreign markets that should not be closed to competing and safe products from the U.S. The world needs a WTO to strike down false or bogus environmental, food-safety, and labor laws that are not science-based or needed but in fact are disguised protectionism.

While the WTO too frequently disregards and invalidates even legitimate labor and environmental protections, CITES is effective where a species is endangered and listed by CITES. CITES does explicitly authorize nations to block trading of species that face extinction. And being a treaty, CITES may checkmate the WTO. In addition to CITES, other environmental treaties also authorize (if not require) trade sanctions at national discretion or option. Applying international law in the ports and on the borders or frontiers of the world, to protect wildlife and the environment, national officers can and do routinely close borders against trafficking. To compel compliance by an exporting nation, an importing nation may sometimes impose a broader trade sanction or restriction on other, even unrelated products. While recognizing the benefits of free trade, we may regret trade sanctions, yet using this tool is much better than environmental disaster, or species extinction, or poisoning consumers. There is no other peaceful tool, and a trade war is better than a shooting war.

To discipline evasive or outlaw nations whose conduct is very threatening to the good order of the world, trade sanctions have been and should be expanded to block visas for offending oligarchs, prohibit tourists coming to or from rogue nations, block international banking transactions, and prohibit landings of their ships and planes. This is no different from the teacher keeping the bully in during recess to the playground, or the referee putting an athlete in the penalty box for too many fouls on the sports field. If we were paying attention in kindergarten and high school, we would have learned the rules that are effective to create a fair and level international playing field. In a future chapter, lest humanity be added to the list of extinct species, we will consider that a future climate treaty must not only authorize but require trade sanctions that cannot be defeated by fossil-fuel interests influencing the WTO.

So as not to end this chapter in despair, the good news is that finally—at least for African elephants—new tools are at hand. Now drones are used to overfly areas where elephants roam to see poachers in action. To find where unseen poachers have been killing elephants, technicians are matching the DNA of tusks seized in Southeast Asia to the DNA in feces or scat collected from many places in Africa where elephants roam. These are the places where rangers in Africa will then know to watch for the poachers. The best news of all is that in October 2016 the Parties[6] to CITES finally, and before it would have been too late, voted to require all Parties to close their domestic ivory markets and carving shops. China agreed, and there are reports that in 2017 China actually did this. If so, we can thank China for a big step to save elephants. Finally, there is another effective tool, although the responsible U.S. federal agencies for more than 30 years have mostly neglected to set up, advertise, and use it. To bring forth informants, the U.S. Congress since 1987 has authorized and funded cash rewards to any persons—including foreigners—who provide information about wildlife traffickers and even corrupt foreign officials bribed to look the other way. This tool needs only the right leadership to be taken off the shelf and put into use as a powerful means to develop intelligence about many wildlife criminals, and to bring U.S. justice to more of them.

Any individual wanting to help address a global problem may support an involved, international, non-governmental organization (NGO). Your annual contribution will bring to you an informative e-letter or magazine as you support their work. In addition to the previously mentioned International Fund for Animal Welfare (IFAW), one may consider the International Union for the Conservation of Nature (IUCN, also called the World Conservation Union) and the World Wildlife Fund (WWF, also called the World Wide Fund for Nature). Organizations that are more "activist" include Friends of the Earth (FOE), Greenpeace, Sea Shepherd International, TRAFFIC, and the Environmental Investigations Agency (EIA). Despite its official-sounding name, EIA is an NGO operating globally with offices in London and Washington, D.C. In my international work for USEPA, I came to really admire their law-enforcement focus and courage to do undercover private investigations, perilous work done face-to-face with international environmental criminals in unsafe, distant places. I also admire TRAFFIC, a bigger NGO focusing on CITES that is on the ground with a worldwide network monitoring the wildlife trade.

The opposite of an endangered species is an invasive species, including humans. Being extraordinarily invasive ourselves, we even collect other invasive species as pets until they get too big or eat too much. Then into ill-prepared environments we release exotics like the Burmese python, Nile monitor lizard, giant and toxic "bufo" toad, walking and armored catfish, feral house cats and pigs. These are some of the more than one-quarter of all animal wildlife that is exotic in Florida, which also has one of the world's highest concentrations of exotic plants. Like humans, exotics overpopulate and in one way or another destroy native species. Yet there is one small part of this big problem that we can control by having a good time! Consider the gorgeous lionfish, colored orange and yellow and trailing many spectacular, antenna-like spines. Native to the Indian and Western Pacific oceans, it was probably released into the Atlantic

Ocean by Florida fish hobbyists who emptied their aquariums when their lionfish grew too numerous or large. On an excursion swimming off a beach or from a dive boat in the Florida Keys or the Caribbean, today you do not see many cardinal fish, parrot fish, damselfish, angelfish, "Nemo" the clownfish, and other harmless beauties. Most of these pretty reef fish have been eaten by lionfish. With venomous spines, their only natural predator may be a big fish with a strong stomach, the grouper.

But groupers have long been on our restaurant menus, and we the people (descended from those hungry cavemen of prehistory) have already eaten most groupers. So it seems only fair that we ravenous humans should replace the grouper as the worst nightmare of the lionfish. If you are on a tropical excursion and want to help, many fishing and dive boat captains will ask you to kill all the lionfish that you may hook or spear. The crew will bring them aboard and then ashore where lionfish are appearing on menus in local restaurants where we tourists are the top-tier predators. Their venomous spines are easily removed, and there is no possible danger in eating the flesh. So order a lionfish! The flesh is delicious, and lionfish is coming now even to some food markets, at least in Florida. Ask for it, and eat some more. Raise your glass of white wine in a toast to health of Nemo, the cute clownfish. You really will be saving Nemo by eating the lionfish.

We have been tracing various aspects of the man-made sixth extinction, now in progress, that began perhaps 11,000 years ago with the ending of the last ice age.[7] Right now—today—we, the most invasive species, are causing other species to become extinct at between 100 to 1,000 times the natural rate before man dominated the planet.[8] The ultimate question is, will humanity actually become extinct in a few hundred years? Barring a catastrophic impact by a large asteroid or a global nuclear war, my personal opinion is that humanity probably will continue to exist indefinitely. As the last chapter in this book will describe, we already today have all the new technologies and proven government policies to speed the switch to climate-friendly energy that can keep humanity off the sixth extinction list. Already we see an advance guard of today's young "greens," organizing in groups with colorful names like "Extinction Rebellion." Regularly now they are marching and carrying signs like "The Seas Are Rising, And So Are We," "We Are The Tide Coming Up And In," and "There Is No Planet B." It will be a very close call, but there should be enough time for a majority of our descendants—who too many, too soon will be wading into catastrophic sea-level rise—to make controlling political decisions to act in time to save their children from climate chaos and extinction. While too many of my generation and those presently in power are either ignorant or willfully failing to act, I do believe that humanity has a future.

Those of us who are grandparents can start the process. To end this chapter where we began, recall the conservationist Teddy Roosevelt. Let us be sure that each new grandchild—who at bedtime naturally may be quite wild—has a Teddy Bear to hug and learn to love wild animals and all of nature. Let us also read to them, helping them to learn to be thoughtful and to care also for the future of the world's most invasive species.

---

1. Science journalist Peter Brannen followed up with his less technical book *The Ends of the World* (Harper Collins 2017) subtitled "... lethal oceans and our quest to understand Earth's past mass extinctions." Short of extinction, the extent of the devastation about to befall civilization is described in recent books, including *The Uninhabitable Earth: Life After Warming*, by David Wallace-Wells (Tim Dugan Books, 2019), and *This Is the Way the World Ends: How Droughts and Die-Offs, Heat Waves and Hurricanes Are Converging on America*, by Jeff Nesbit (St. Martin's Press, 2018).

2. The previous five mass extinctions in the last 500 million years are summarized in a one-page table in an addendum at the end of this book.

3. From Rachel Carson's first book written in 1941, she presented the mysteries of the sea in clear and beautiful words that millions of thinking people have loved. *Seaweed Chronicles: A World at the Water's Edge*, by Susan H. Shetterly (Algonquin Books, 2018), is similarly lyrical and learned. Like Rachel Carson, Shetterly describes the intertidal and subtidal zones, the fascination of their flora and fauna, and their importance to the business and people who depend on them. While considering so much the oceans have to teach us, her book is also enlivened by adventures meeting delightful, often quirky characters living on the coast.

4. In his important book, *The Once and Future Ocean: Notes Toward a New Hydraulic Society* (Leete's Island Books, 2015), Peter Neill comprehensively tells how in modern times we have brought the sea to the point of exhaustion, and offers some solutions. The quotation is from his page 25.

5. Chief Seattle (ca. 1786–1866) was tall, an orator, and a natural leader. French missionaries converted him to Roman Catholicism, and in his later years he was a philosophical and benevolent man who tried to accommodate his people peacefully to the ways of the arriving settlers. However, his exact words of more than 140 years ago have been obscured and are disputed, lost to time and the reconstructions and imaginations of publishers of many differing versions.

6. Nations that sign and then ratify a treaty are called "Parties," just like the parties to a marriage or other legal contract. An amendment or supplemental agreement may be called a "Protocol." Many names of treaties bear the French synonym, "Convention." Parties are obligated to enact national laws and establish enforcement programs sufficient to meet their treaty obligations to all other Parties. Effective national implementation of treaties is essential, because with few exceptions (such as the conventions for chemical and nuclear weapons) there is no international body with personnel authorized to inspect or conduct other implementing actions.

7. To fully explore the sixth extinction, consider a wonderful travel and adventure book by Elizabeth Kolbert. Already in 2005 she had won the Journalism Award from American Association for Advancement of Science. She then visited some of the world's most remote and interesting outposts of science, and her resulting book, *The Sixth Extinction: An Unnatural History* (Henry Holt and Company, 2014), in 2015 won the Pulitzer Prize in general nonfiction. Do read her book, she makes science fun.

8. It should be understood that the great majority of species becoming extinct are insects. One expert supporting this assertion is Edward Osborne "E. O." Wilson, a retired Harvard professor of entomology considered to be the intellectual father of biodiversity. He has published best-sellers and twice won the Pulitzer Prize. In his book *The Future of Life* (Abacus, 2002), he predicts that half of all species on Earth, most of which are insects including beneficial ones, will be extinct in 100 years if present trends continue.

Chapter 2—*Semper Paratus* in the Coast Guard

A READER WHO IS A MILITARY VETERAN, assuming no irreparable injury was suffered, will probably agree that military service teaches valuable lessons while quickly transforming a young person into an adult. It will expose you to Americans from all parts of the country, help you to achieve success in whatever endeavor follows military service, and it may lead to a career in national service that can take many forms. My journey in environmental protection began in military service in 1963. Even though I saw no work of pollution control,[2] the Coast Guard was foundational to my becoming a pollution fighter for the USA. To this day I sometimes remember and see myself young again as I was in the U.S. Coast Guard, called out for search and rescue, speeding through the sea. After a glance aft to see our national flag fluttering in the breeze, I would peer forward over the waves for the trouble ahead.

The trouble ashore that I faced in June 1963 was burnout from constant studying and memorizing in college. I knew that after graduation I needed a "gap year" where the only book to contemplate would be the *Coast Guardsman's Manual.* So as not to be drafted and sent to Vietnam,[1] I joined the Reserves. For so many lessons in self-reliance and team building that are essential for success in both corporate America and big-government America, I can only thank the Coast Guard. To achieve the Coast Guard's motto of *Semper paratus*, I became always ready for action.

For today's young people making a career in the Coast Guard, your role will include catching vessels of any size polluting the air and water in coastal and ocean waters. During my EPA career, the Agency's website featured pictures of fugitives on a most-wanted list—and most of the wanted were foreigners who had worked on polluting ships. Consider this pollution investigation that occurred during the 1990s. On a cruise ship after dinner, a young couple stood at the ship's rail, in the moonlight seeing and photographing many plastic bags floating away from the ship. Ashore after their cruise, they reported this to the Coast Guard. The ship's officer said that it could only have been rogue crewmen acting without authority to open a door in the side of the ship where the trash and garbage were stored just above the waterline. The Coast Guard investigators then went down to see the door, but they could not open it. The crewmen there told the Coast Guard that for safety at sea the door could only be opened upon orders when unlocked electronically by a switch on the bridge of the ship where the ship's officers ruled. Therefore, the cruise line itself was responsible, it paid a huge fine to the government, and from this money the Department of Justice awarded to the young couple an informant's bounty of hundreds of thousands of dollars.

Many Coast Guard cases involve such law-enforcement detective work to fight pollution, which can be exciting and fun. In addition, while business as usual continues to pollute the air that is destroying our climate, the role of life-saving will grow as more and more Americans are needing the Coast Guard to rescue them from savage storms and rising seas. You will never be bored in the Coast Guard. What follows is my story of entry in public service, where I found adventure and purpose that years later would lead to my fulfilling career at the U.S. Environmental Protection Agency. If you prefer to skip the rest of this chapter, a sometimes amusing and perhaps exciting story that is a digression from serious environmental protection, do proceed directly to the next chapter on chemical control focusing on pesticides.

In June 1963, skinnier than I was strong, I reported for duty at boot camp in Cape May, New Jersey. Soon enough I found myself ordered by our company's petty officer to do push-ups, wearing my white sailor suit, with my hands in mud. "Faster, faster. Stay on an even keel, or you are lower than whale shit!" he would yell, and then my arms failed and I fell flat into the muddy water. Another uniform to wash. In the middle of many nights in the barracks, while I was sleeping in my top bunk, our petty officer would turn on all the lights and yell, "Air raid! All hands take cover!" With all 100 other young men, we would jump down to the floor to crawl under our bunk beds and shelter our heads with our arms. Next would come the command, "Fire and flood in the main engineroom! Abandon ship!" All of us would leap up onto our top bunks and pretend to paddle away from a burning and sinking Coast Guard Cutter. Yet from such foolishness would come many lessons for success out in the real world.

After graduating *magna cum laude* in May 1963 from Yale and so becoming a certified thinker, by July in my first weeks of basic training I was being taught not to think about anything independently. Instead, I was taught to follow all orders without questioning their wisdom. The first three months of basic training were tough, with physical exercises and repeated passages through, under, and over an obstacle course copied from the U.S. Marines. Humiliating and senseless orders were given intentionally just so trainees would become obedient. One military order—that we could not swim from the ocean beach—was a possibly dangerous blunder. Though we were living on a South Jersey beach from June to September, perfect ocean swimming time with a calm sea, we were not allowed even to see the beautiful ocean beach that stretches for perhaps a mile on the east side of the Coast Guard training base. I don't know whether our training officers thought we recruits might go crazy or AWOL when we saw all the girls in bikinis on the civilian beach just beyond the base's fence line into the sea. Or perhaps they thought we might get salt water up our noses, and that one of us from inland who never before swam in the sea might drown.

Let's think about the fact that we were being trained to become part of a salt-water rescue service traditionally using surf boats launched from beaches into an often raging sea, small motorboats, and oceangoing ships called Coast Guard "cutters." The Coast Guard orders its sailors, "You have to go out, but you do not have to come back!" A Coastie's duty if necessary is to die trying to rescue others. Part of our training should have been to assure that we all got plenty of salt water up our noses and that we all could swim through at least a mild surf. From living the first 18 summers of my life on the coast of Maine, I knew how to swim in a much colder sea. And I was fortunate to already have many skills that I would need to use in the Coast Guard. I arrived at the training camp experienced in reading the tides and the weather, small-boat handling including knot tying, and navigating in the fog along a rocky coast of many islands. I had taught sailing for a summer during college. But while I was already quite "salty," many of my fellow trainees from inland states were just 18 years old, had never been in the sea, and did not have a clue. I hope that no one of them panicked and drowned on duty the first time he was ordered into salt water to save a life.

It was absurd that our trainers considered it too dangerous for us to swim in the mild summer waves. The martial mind can make bad decisions, and since my military service I have come to realize the wisdom of the U.S. Constitution that places an elected President atop the military. I appreciate the related national norm that our Secretary of Defense should not be an active officer but also a civilian appointed by the President. Yes, the U.S. government makes mistakes, but the solution is not to "starve the beast" or destroy the U.S. government as so many right-wingers urge. The solution is to make government smarter to work better for all of us. And overall, my Coast Guard training was excellent. It taught me how to think autonomously for the day to come when perhaps so few as only three of us were the crew in a small boat far from shore—and far from any officer to tell us or me what to do.

In September 1963, having graduated from basic training, I reported to Groton, Connecticut, for three more months of training. By learning to tap out and receive messages in the Morse code, I would be rated as a Radioman and receive a "secret" clearance. This one-dimensional training—each day with dots and dashes, just hearing beep, beep, beeping and sending with tap, tap, tapping—was an ordeal of tedious boredom. But upon graduation from Morse code school at the end of 1963, I completed my basic training. I was promoted to "able-bodied seaman" and mustered out of active duty and into the Reserves in time for Christmas. Though ranked barely above "lower than whale shit," and as a Reservist not quite a real "Coastie," I was proud and happy that from much good food and hard training I was no longer so scrawny and had gained some muscles for the first time in my life.

In the fall of 1964, I started Harvard Law School. The law books were heavy, and the professors were tough. I was so ready for fresh salt air when the next summer finally came. Two years after joining the Coast Guard, finally it was my time to go to sea. In July 1965, I reported to the gangplank of a large cutter—165 feet long and carrying a crew of 35—docked at the Coast Guard's main North Atlantic base on Atlantic Avenue in downtown Boston. Two 18-year-old boys, "regulars" (full-time for at least a four-year commitment) fresh from Cape May's boot camp, reported at the same time, and we lined up in a row. We three saluted the officer greeting us, an ensign probably younger than I, and he asked, "Any of you three a college boy?" I was quite old at age 24, and in addition to college I had completed one year of law school. Having been trained in Cape May to say "Sir" twice in every sentence, proudly I answered "Sir, yes, Sir!" Immediately he assigned me to clean the crew's latrine (a row of several toilets called the "head" on a ship).[3] Rather than accept this as humiliation, since then I have been proud to say that I have served as a professional toilet cleaner for the largest, most powerful government in the world.

At first, I envied the two boys who reported aboard with me and were assigned to work in the fresh sea air. But my thoughts changed when I saw them working on the ship's buoy deck. I saw that like an iceberg, most of a seagoing buoy is hidden, including the enormous underwater weight to hold upright what we do see. The *Cutter Cactus*, being in the biggest class of buoy tenders, had a crane maybe 40 feet tall that could lift the biggest, 10,000-pound buoys dangling chains with links the size of your fist. Swinging from side to side as the *Cactus* rolled in the waves, somehow these enormous buoys were lowered onto the deck, there chocked and chained down to be immobile during repairs and painting, while the ship rolled and plunged ahead. A sailor could get killed on the buoy deck, or if he was lucky just knocked over the side into the sea. I realized that, if I stayed inside cleaning toilets, I would survive my time on the sea. And whatever my duties, there were always hot coffee and real donuts brought aboard each morning, the lunches were great, and the Captain always tried to return by 4:30 p.m. to Boston. From the base I would drive home, a proud commuter warrior carrying tales of my heroism at sea, ready to return by 7 a.m. the next morning.

After a week, the Captain must have heard from a junior officer that he had a Reservist on board, which was unusual, and that I was doing a great job cleaning the head. The Captain would have been told that at the daily inspection I stood proudly and smiling in command of my row of toilets, their rank straight and clean in a splendid salute with all their seats and lids up. Pleased, yet the Captain probably considered that a Reserve radioman onboard for annual training should not spend all four weeks cleaning the head, even though I seemed to enjoy it so much. The Captain may have gasped, had he looked at my file, to see that the toilet polisher on board was a privileged "preppie" who had graduated from Yale and was attending Harvard Law School! He even may have considered that perhaps my daddy could be someone important and even know a congressman or senator. (My daddy in Baltimore in fact was very friendly with both U.S. Senators in Maryland, and the personal lawyer for one of them, though he would never have complained that his son was excelling at cleaning toilets.) I like to think that the Captain valued my pride in my work no matter how low-level, and that he liked my ability to take orders with a happy smile—good skills to have in any chain of command. For whatever reason, at the start of my second week, I was ordered to report several decks up to the wheelhouse on the bridge, where I proudly confirmed that I was well trained in the Morse code and had a secret clearance.

But the junior officer on duty said that operational secrets were few on a buoy tender and that they had not used the Morse code for 20 years since the last German U-boat (*unterseeboot* or submarine) in World War II. He gave me the handset of the radiotelephone, and told me that there was an important message to transmit back to Boston. I had never handled or been trained to use a radiotelephone, and he seemed uncertain about my skills when I asked him what was the "transmit" button on the handset. Nevertheless, into the phone I spoke the given message, "*Cutter Cactus* to Base Boston, we may be in late, hold the mail, please." After I added the word "please" and then said "over" just like I had heard on TV shows, instead of a quick "Aye aye" reply from Base Boston there was stunned radio silence up and down the New England coast. At last, a stern voice in reply said, "There will be no pleasantries on military circuits." Saying "please" had exposed me as completely unable to transmit messages at sea. My officer realized that I was incompetent with a radiophone, and my first radio message also was my last. What to do with me now?

So the officer asked me if I liked to paint. I cannot truly say that this was my response, but now I like to think that that the conversation went like this: "Yes Sir, I paint landscapes, fruit bowls, and other still-lifes, and I would like to learn portraits, Sir." But this answer would have only been partially satisfactory, so with a smirk next would have come the officer's next question, "Good, and do you think you can paint Coast Guard cutters?" I might have answered, "Sir, but they are so big, Sir!" My officer actually did reply like this, "Not to worry. We have a very small project that you can do, to repaint the cutter's name in signal flags (each about one square foot) outside on either side the wheelhouse five feet above a walkway." We walked outside to look at the job site, and I saw that 11 painted nautical flags spelled "USCGC CACTUS" in a space that was only about 12 feet long and one foot high, and I said, "Yes Sir, I think I can do this, Sir."

Equipped with little cans for red, blue, yellow, white, and maybe another color or two, I worked with such great precision that the port side took a week and the starboard side another week. Being in the command center up on the bridge, there were extra donuts and a great view. I was grateful also that the ship changed my rating from Radioman to Bos'ns Mate—a "boatswain" is a lover of boats, and after growing up on the Maine coast surely I am that. For the rest of my career, I was a sailor handling ropes and boats, also cleaning "heads" and swabbing decks, and with plenty of time to paint, usually out in the fresh salt air. Later in much smaller cutters, I always asked the helmsman to dock slowly and not make a scrape that I would have to repaint in white. Since they learned that I would applaud and congratulate them when they docked slowly and carefully, they smiled and obliged.

In those long-ago days, the Coast Guard was always ready and yet at ease. To illustrate, consider that the brass engine-order telegraph standing beside the wheel helm had two handles.

Replacing the official brass ones were two very unofficial handles for tapping beer at a bar: one read "Budweiser" for direction, and one read "Schlitz" for speed. The order "Pour me a Bud and two Schlitz" meant go ahead at half speed. This breach of military appearances is unimaginable today. Only about 15 years later in the Chesapeake Bay, where my wife and I chartered a 38-foot yawl for September vacation cruises, again we encountered the Coast Guard on patrol in small boats. By then the service had entered the war against drugs, Coasties wore dark-blue uniforms like cops and packed semiautomatic pistols. I am sure that by then all the beer-pulling handles were long gone from all cutters.

On the *Cutter Cactus* in 1965, hidden somewhere on board, of course there was an armory including machine guns for which there were mounting racks welded into the rails of the upper deck. Because *Cactus* was a large, open-ocean vessel, behind the smokestack it carried as heavy artillery a three-inch naval cannon facing aft, (or "astern"; a "landlubber" would say "behind us"), presumably to cover us in a quick retreat back into Boston Harbor to hide and wait for the Navy to come to protect us from an enemy ship. A three-inch shell is about two feet long and very dangerous, as I learned when the Captain ordered a gun drill off the tip of Cape Cod. Up from the bowels of the ship came three rusty shells, probably dating from WWII. The first shot went about eight miles, so far away that we could not see where it hit and worried that we might have sunk an innocent vessel out of sight. The second shot went only about 300 yards, probably because the shell and its powder were old and defective. We in the crew all wondered if the third shot would blow up on deck or in the water three feet off our hull and send us to the bottom. Vast was our relief when the Captain said, "Stand down and secure"—this is Coast Guard–speak for "Let's stop this before we hurt ourselves." He continued, "Gun drill is suspended, they have our range, the next shot could sink us." I liked that Captain, kind and with a sense of humor too. And so I lived to tell another Coast Guard tale.

My next summer's official adventure in the service of the United States took me to the life-saving station at Southwest Harbor, Maine. Far down east near the end of the supply line from Boston, success meant self-sufficiency even through howling winters. Ready for anything, the little station had a spare part for everything. Its shop of machine tools could have made almost anything needed, and most of the Coasties were native, real "Mainers" who knew their business. Each day there were missions, some just patrols and some serious business. We had a 65-foot cutter looking rather like a tugboat, and two 40-foot cutters resembling lobster boats but with solid steel hulls in the shape of a Navy destroyer. So that a "40-footer" could tow a much larger, disabled vessel back to port, these boats packed two very powerful engines. Our station's boat dock was very close to the ferry taking families, often with pretty daughters, to their summer homes on Cranberry Island and Islesford. When our search-and-rescue alarm sounded, imagining ourselves looking strong and brave while dramatically putting on our sunglasses, we would run to our boat. While the pretty girls took our pictures, we would start the enormous diesel engines. From exhaust pipes through the stern transom, first one, then the second engine blew black smoke all over the pretty girls, just before we raced off heroically at high speed to save lives and property on the high seas. After a while, when the pretty girls on the dock saw us running to our boat, they took no pictures but ran in the opposite direction.

Gasoline-powered, inboard civilian boats have an unhappy tendency to explode and burn to the waterline. In 1967, from Boston I moved to Baltimore, and my last years of service were in Maryland's Chesapeake Bay. Here there were more county and state police boats than Coast Guard boats, and once arriving at the place of a boat explosion, upon turning off our boat's siren we could hear the fading siren of the ambulance on shore taking victims away to the hospital. What a relief, no horrible burns or dead bodies floating in sight; others had already completed the rescue. Seeing that the empty, burned-out wreckage was still smoking, with our fire hose we pumped too much water into the hulk. It sank three feet to the shallow bottom. Instead of just towing the hulk away while it still was floating, the Coast Guard created a new hazard to navigation. In the Reserves now serving one weekend a month, we were too excited and too inexperienced to do everything right like the regular Coasties would have done.

I have too many more Coast Guard stories to retell here, and I will close by urging young readers to find adventure and fulfillment for yourselves in some form of service to America. It will not be perfect, and I remain disgusted at the Coast Guard's not allowing trainees to swim in the sea off a summer beach. It was wasteful for the Coast Guard to send me through an ordeal of three months of totally useless training entirely in the Morse code. Yet after basic training, for the next three years while I was laboring in law school, the Coast Guard kindly excused me from all monthly training drills in a Boston unit of reservists, provided I did double duty (four weeks instead of two) in the summer vacations from law school. This exemption was wonderful, because for four weeks in each of three summers I would serve among regular Coasties doing the real work of the service. To finish my six-year obligation, in Maryland during my last two years I attended monthly reservists' "training" meetings that were mostly useless and repetitive "make work." The Coast Guard Reserves would do well as much as possible to minimize its separate training meetings and to integrate trained reservists more fully into the many regular, operational units.

Serving during three summers from Boston among the regular Coast Guard, I learned more that I needed to know in life than I did in any year at Yale or Harvard. On a ship or at a lifeboat station, no one cared how well a brainy individual did on a book test (and indeed I certainly kept quiet that I went to elite universities). The Coast Guard's many small units are widely dispersed and quite autonomous. Each unit and each man is trusted and expected to get done a wide variety of jobs, with self-reliant good judgment, based on local conditions and without orders if need be. When my performance was at times sparked with humor, it was with smiles and happiness all around, and I knew when to make it fun and when to be serious. The only things that really mattered were could I shut up and take orders, was I a contributing member of a harmonious crew that did well as a group, could I make or support the right decision when offshore far from supervision, and was the mission accomplished as expertly and safely as possible. I always did any serious work expected of me to the best of my ability, and the regular Coasties saw this. They were good guys and friends.

Germany, Switzerland, Israel, and some other sophisticated nations require of all young people some national service. In Austria today, the choice is six months in the military or nine months in a social service before a young person can enter a university. This strengthens the military and social services, and it builds character in young citizens of these other countries. The U.S. military today relies on volunteers to be its "regulars," but in short-term national service there are not enough opportunities for young people. Yet there is a need, and so more often today we see that many high-school graduates not ready for higher education opt take a "gap year" working or in an internship in a worthwhile program. My 11 months in uniform with the Coast Guard for me was like a gap year learning and growing, and overall it was perhaps the best time of learning and working in my life. The U.S. would be a better place were we to expand AmeriCorps and add many more programs like it.

The Coast Guard does not mostly train for Armageddon and the Apocalypse like the other services. While regular Coasties, along with the Navy, did hard duty on river boats in Vietnam, since then the Coast Guard has not been sent into unnecessary, gratuitous, and disastrous foreign wars that have wasted our national treasury and diminished the reputation of the U.S. Now focused on domestic duties and within the Department of Homeland Security, the Coast Guard is the only U.S. military arm with law-enforcement authority. It is also our seagoing fire and ambulance service, among many other roles. It is a great service for any patriotic and venturesome young person to consider, whether just for a short time while growing up in the Reserves, or as a career.

By now, it should be very clear that I was in no way a military hero, and when people ask me what I did, I joke that while I served in the Coast Guard during the Cold War not a single buoy was lost to Communism! But I am so thankful to the Coast Guard for what it did for me. Though I wore the uniform for only about 11 months on duty spread over six years in the Reserves, to this day I carry a Coast Guard spirit of pride and patriotism that is always with me. This military service provided purposeful yet joyful adventures that started me into a happy life of public service, and I wish I could do it all again.

---

1. Like President Bush's decision to invade Iraq in 2002, the decisions by Presidents Johnson and Nixon not to remove U.S. forces and these Presidents' failures quickly to end the war in Vietnam stand as two of the lowest points in U.S. history. They caused over 50,000 U.S. boys to die for political reasons, as *Personal History*, by Katharine Graham (Alfred A. Knopf, 1997), the autobiography of the courageous lady who owned *The Washington Post*, retells. The book includes the story of the Pentagon Papers and the U.S. government's Vietnam cover-up revealed by Daniel Ellsberg. *A Rumor of War*, by Philip J. Caputo (Henry Holt & Co., 1977) is an unforgettable soldier's memoir of the Vietnam War. After 16 months in Vietnam, the author returned with his idealism gone and emotionally wasted, though physically intact and able to write.

2. In 1924, the Oil Pollution Act started the Coast Guard's role of responding to spills of oil and chemicals, but I saw little response activity or capability even in the 1960s or 1970s. After the tanker *Exxon Valdez* grounded in Alaska and spilled 11 million gallons of crude, the Oil Protection Act of 1990 and its regulations required double hulls for new tankers and equipped the Coast Guard to respond effectively. Today pollution control at sea is a very important law-enforcement responsibility of the Coast Guard.

3. Toilets on vessels are called "heads" because in the days of sailing ships the toilets were in the very "bow," or front, or "head" of the ship. Here the toilets were perched out of sight and over the rushing sea that would receive and splash away the falling waste.

Chapter 3—Rachel Carson, Muse of Nature

Aɴʏ ᴘᴏʟʟᴜᴛɪᴏɴ ꜰɪɢʜᴛᴇʀ ᴡɪʟʟ sᴏᴏɴ come to know and admire one lady as patron saint above all. In 1953 Rachel Carson built a summer cottage on what she rightly called the "rugged shore" at Southport Island, below Boothbay Harbor, Maine. I did not know of her while I was a teenager in the 1950s lucky to live each summer a few miles further to the north ("down east") on the coast of Maine. Yet we were both charmed and fascinated by the beautiful, tidal coast. Here she would write and in 1962 publish *Silent* Spring, a book that changed the world. Before considering her importance both as a scientist and as a superb writer of popular books about nature, here is a relevant question: Other than in a hardware store or warehouse for chemicals, in what one place—today—can we find paint thinners, dry-cleaning fluids, wood preservatives, toilet deodorizers, cosmetic additives, gasoline byproducts, rocket fuel, termite poisons, pesticides including fungicides, stain repellents, non-stick coating, flame retardants, and hundreds of other synthetic (man-made) chemicals?

The answer is that these chemicals for decades and to this day are found in the breast milk of most human mothers of most developed or advanced countries. In 1949, a Connecticut doctor tested the milk of a mother experiencing strange, neuropsychiatric symptoms. He was first to discover in human breast milk a manufactured pesticide called DDT. In 1966, a Swedish researcher found polychlorinated biphenyls (PCBs), a synthetic oil used almost everywhere to insulate electrical transformers—in tissue of dead eagles. When he tested his wife's breast milk, he found PCBs there too. By 2009, the U.S. Centers for Disease Control (CDC), after testing the blood and urine of 2,500 Americans studied, had reported more than 200 such chemicals not found in nature. European scientists have found the human "body burden" to be as many as 300 or more of these chemicals. Also found in mothers' milk are natural elements including arsenic, cadmium, mercury, lead, copper, selenium, and chromium. At unnaturally high concentrations in mothers' milk, these "heavy metals" are there because people routinely put them into products to leach or degrade during or after human use, or during the production process discharge these pollutants directly into the environment. Then these too enter the human food chain.

All of these chemicals can be toxic if present in a sufficient concentration. But absent proximity to a special source of contamination, the level of each chemical—while measurable only with the most modern equipment—is very low in the general population. Some research indicates that the air most city dwellers breathe inside their homes is more toxic than the load of chemicals in mothers' milk. So as of this writing, I do not know that anybody advises human mothers not to breast-feed our babies. However, so many chemicals may have additive or even synergistic (catalytic and multiplying) effects, magnifying toxicity into a danger zone. But when dealing with such a "chemical soup" as human breast milk, toxicologists find it difficult or impossible to isolate and study each chemical, and of course most experiments involving dosing people are unethical. So there is reason for concern about so much that science does not yet know. What we do know we have learned because Rachel Carson taught us to look inside ourselves.

To understand how human breast milk became a chemical soup, we go back to the 1950s, when Rachel Carson's colleagues, ornithologists and naturalists, were studying magnificent raptors including eagles, falcons, and ospreys (fish hawks). Looking into their nests, they found not eggs but omelets, with the egg shells too thin and cracked open before baby birds could form. The bald eagle, found only in North America and the very symbol of the United States, was among many raptors disappearing on the road to extinction. Scientists tested their eggs and flesh, and found man-made pesticides including dichloro-diphenyl-trichloro-ethane—known by its initials, we call it DDT. During World War II, American forces used DDT successfully to control malaria and typhus among troops and civilians in war zones outside the U.S. Then DDT came home to the U.S., where it was sprayed almost indiscriminately to control mosquitoes and other unwanted insects in neighborhood and agricultural settings. When we were children, it was not unusual to run or ride a bike after the DDT sprayer truck, or just to stand happily in mist coming from the truck or falling from a spray plane. It was so much fun! And DDT was even thought to be so healthy as to prevent polio. From understandably desperate parental fear of this dread disease, sometimes children were sprayed with DDT at close range directly in the hair and on the skin. Of course, now we know that polio was only stopped by Dr. Jonas Salk's vaccine.

While the public authorities in the 1940 and 1950s proclaimed to all that DDT was harmless to humans, the authorities at the time were thoughtless and foolish not to be more careful. After the horrific chemical trench warfare of World War I, the U.S. government had encouraged the chemical companies to synthesize or create more potent chemical weapons for the next war. They developed "organochlorines" including chlorinated hydrocarbons and organo-phosphates, "families" of chemicals that do not exist in nature. Fortunately, during World War II these chemical weapons were not used, probably because their existence was known to our fascist enemies and deterred them from again using their chemical weapons against Allied forces. But from the end of WWII, the chemical companies sought a domestic market, and with the arrival of television and more effective advertising, these chemicals came home.

Cigarette companies with puffery advertised that doctors preferred a certain brand, and many of my generation's parents smoked up a storm. Back in the "good old days" in 1940s and 1950s, our parents were young and carefree, ignorant of many issues of public health, and the word "environment" was unknown. Wallpaper makers sold DDT-containing wallpaper for the bedrooms of babies and children. It was advertised and guaranteed to kill insects for a year, including flies suspected of carrying measles, diarrhea, and polio! Chemical companies advertised with the jingle "DDT Is Good for Me" on cartoon pictures showing dancing moms, children, pets, farm animals, fruits and vegetables. A U.S. Department of Agriculture poster advised mothers to spray DDT into kitchen cabinets.

The truth is that DDT is not good for growing potatoes or apples or as an ingredient entering into the human food supply. In fact, DDT was never needed in most of the U.S. or other temperate zones far north of mosquitoes carrying malaria. Today we all know that cigarettes do not make doctors or any persons healthy. Let us hope that few parents relied on DDT wallpaper to protect their children from polio or failed to get Dr. Salk's polio vaccine into their kids. Today we know that exposure to DDT and its more toxic breakdown metabolite DDE have been linked to miscarriages, other reproductive problems, and developmental problems (both mental and physical) in children—not only in eagles. For adults, DDT is linked to impaired endocrine, thyroid, liver and nervous system function, diabetes, breast cancer, and other cancers. This should be no surprise, as DDT is in that family of chemicals created as chemical weapons to kill enemy soldiers. Today we call these chemicals "persistent organic pollutants" or POPs.

Rachel Carson did not do the research on POPs. So why in 1981 did the U.S. Postal Service put her on a "Great Americans"

postage stamp? Most of us will never achieve such national honor. Here is her story: Born in 1907 to a blue-collar family in rural Pennsylvania, she excelled as a student and in 1932 earned her master's degree in zoology from Johns Hopkins University. She was only the second woman hired in a professional (non-secretarial) position at what became U.S. Fish and Wildlife Service in the Department of the Interior. There she became Editor-in-Chief of all publications for the Service. In 1953, she left the government to write popular best-sellers about the sea and nature.[1] Her final book, *The Sense of Wonder,* was published posthumously in 2011. Its photos and captions will excite your young child or grandchild's innate sense of wonder in discovering the mysterious beauty of nature.

In 1962, Rachel Carson published *Silent Spring* and the world would not be the same. It was serialized in *The New Yorker* magazine, reached heartland America as a Book-of-the-Month Club selection, and for 31 weeks was on the *New York Times* list of best-sellers. Then costing just 75 cents, it seemed that almost everyone bought *Silent Spring* to shiver in fear at revelations of the frightful poisonings by the crude first-generation pesticides. Alerted for the first time to the toxicity of pesticides man-made in factories, Americans began to ask, "In addition to poisoning the eagle, the very symbol of America, are we poisoning ourselves? Are we poisoning our children?"

Let us remember that 1962 was the height of the Cold War against Communism and that Americans feared nuclear annihilation. Not yet 20 years after WWII, American technology was tied to patriotic anti-Communism and not be questioned. Pollution was "okay," or at least tolerated as the price of progress and maintaining U.S. national power. So the chemical manufacturers freely called Rachel Carson "a hysterical woman," "a nature nun," and "a fanatic about the balance of nature." The U.S. Secretary of Agriculture called her a "communist," while his department continued to heedlessly promote overuse of pesticides. These bitter attacks from the prevailing ethos were quite the same as attacks by another threatened orthodoxy in 1859, when Charles Darwin's *The Origin of Species* described evolution that would come replace creationism. Like this book, *Silent Spring* was not half-baked or "nutty." Before publication, Carson sent it for peer review by many other scientists, and it contained 50 pages of their research footnotes.

Rachel Carson was certainly courageous intellectually to challenge the agricultural and chemical industries and the U.S. government. But far greater than anyone knew was her physical courage in 1963 when she testified before the U.S. Congress. Just 56 years old, finishing *Silent Spring* had kept her alive—she had been writing for her life. She had had a radical mastectomy, and her pelvis was so riddled with fractures that it was nearly impossible for her to walk to her seat at the microphones in the Congressional hearing room. She wore a dark brown wig to hide her baldness from many radiation treatments. She had told almost no one she was dying, and in 1964 Rachel Carson...was dead. Toward the end, she had been thinking that her next book would be about her observations—made now almost 60 years ago and very early—that perhaps the sea was rising and the climate was changing. But her prophetic and poetic voice was ended by cancer.

Yet the alarm she had raised helped to move U.S. government from promoter to regulator. In 1970, we saw creation of the U.S. Environmental Protection Agency, which is small but probably the biggest (and until dismantlement beginning in 2017 was the best) pollution-control agency or environmental ministry in the world. One of EPA's first acts was to ban—outlaw—DDT, and in the 1980s we began to see some recovery of ospreys, peregrine falcons, and other magnificent raptors. By the 1990s it was clear that they were back, and that Rachel Carson had saved from extinction the very symbol of America, the bald eagle. By the

1980s, EPA had banned or severely restricted in total about a dozen of the primitive pesticides.

By the 1980s, scientists had learned that POPs persist and can only be destroyed in very high-temperature incinerators; that POPs can kill or poison indiscriminately, meaning that their toxic effects are random and not limited to target pests; that POPs vaporize and can concentrate at the poles of the Earth (where the breast milk of Inuit mothers is the most contaminated); and that just as antibiotic overuse creates dangerous bacteria resistant even to hospital treatment, overuse of a pesticidal POP causes more resistant bugs to come into being. Most astonishing is persistence—that a synthetic POP chemical is not metabolized or biodegraded in the environment. Instead, as larger creatures eat smaller ones, a POP chemical can become 10 million times more concentrated in flesh—mainly in fat—as the chemical moves up food chain. This is the called "bio-accumulation" or "bio-concentration." At the very top of the food chain are fish and meat eaters including predatory birds—and people—with the highest concentrations and body burden of POPs.[2] This is why our mothers' milk has so many man-made, unpleasant chemicals that would not be there in a natural state. This is why the eagles by 1962 were coming to the edge of extinction.

Then in 2002 in Stockholm, Sweden, the legacy of Rachel Carson went global. An important environmental treaty, The Stockholm Convention on Persistent Organic Pollutants (at EPA during my career there in the "pollution-control business," we just called it the "POPs Convention"), completely banned—"outlawed"—by international law the "dirty dozen" of 12 POPs as too dangerous to be made, sold, or used. It is absolutely remarkable that most of these were the very same chemicals that Rachel Carson in *Silent Spring* was first—and very much alone—in identifying and naming explicitly as dangerous toxic culprits.[3] It took the world 40 years to catch up to this woman whom the chemical companies had called a "hysterical female," though in fact she was clear-headed, learned, of a calm demeanor, and the rare scientist who could write for the popular market.

Today, with so many other man-made chemicals now in mothers' milk, we know that humans—like eagles—are vulnerable to bio-concentration from POPs. And we never imagined such a shocking thing until *Silent Spring* opened our eyes and caused the mentality of America to shift to a new and better paradigm. We have come a long way since 1947 when U.S. Dept. of Agriculture urged the moms of America to spray DDT into cabinets where dishes are kept.

But the use of pesticides is enormous today—in the U.S. over one billion pounds, and worldwide a total estimated at 5.6 billion pounds, are applied to crops annually. Synthetic chemicals will always be with us, and many are suspected or known to be toxic.[4] The U.S. government estimates that more than 20,000 children and workers in American farmland are poisoned each year by pesticides. All Americans are exposed to other chemicals used in food processing and packaging, and traces of some of these other chemicals along with pesticides are now showing up in the American food supply. Many of these chemicals are variously linked to dangers including human reproductive or developmental harm such as brain damage in children, cancers, and to impairment of functions including those of the liver, thyroid, endocrine, immune, and neurological systems.

Pollinating insects also work in the farm fields, and today a great many varieties of insects—many beneficial—are diminishing and becoming extinct.[5] The number of all bees in all the world has been cut in half in the last 20 years. In May 2018, following what Europeans call the "precautionary principle," the European Union banned three modern pesticides called "neonicotinoids" because of evidence these pesticides may damage nervous systems of human children and in the same way be causing the deaths of bees. Of course, both European and U.S chemical manufacturers dispute this evidence. There has been no significant regulatory action in the U.S., where the precautionary principle is seen as a curiosity of a foreign culture.[6]

Chlorpyrifos is a pesticide almost as deadly to pollinators. And it has been linked to many forms of brain damage in children, including IQ and memory loss, ADHD, autism, and slow development. Most at risk are children living near farm fields, but there is evidence that all American children consume much too much chlorpyrifos in our food. EPA finally banned it at the end of the Administration of President Obama, but the next President removed that ban and now is defying the order of a federal appellate court to maintain the ban.

The "land of the free and the home of the brave" typically does not regulate before there is a "dead-body count" and near absolute certainty as to the cause. Indeed, it does seem a perverse American cultural characteristic that as food lovers we tolerate agricultural chemicals that the EU says both directly threaten us and kill bees and other beings essential to pollinate our foods. Or maybe this transatlantic difference is not so strange, considering that Americans eat so many things that Western Europeans do not and would never buy or allow sold in their street markets, where stalls sell vegetables and fruits that are farm-fresh, organic, and delicious.

And consider butterflies, said by many indigenous people to carry the spirits of our departed human family members and of our new babies waiting to be born. My soul or spirit needs to see butterflies like the monarch butterfly, a lovely and harmless creature living only in North America. But in last few years, maybe 90 percent of monarchs are dead of starvation. U.S. factory farms apply enormous volumes of the herbicide called glyphosate (its trade name is Roundup). Its spray drifts out of farm fields into buffer strips and along roadsides where it kills a wildflower called milkweed that is the monarch's favorite and almost only food. This herbicide kills many other wildflowers that bees and hummingbirds need too. Only in Western Europe is there stiff regulation of glyphosate.

Today's scientists not funded by special interests tell us that poorly regulated tinkering with nature has speeded up the process of evolution. As Charles Darwin might have predicted, because of "survival of the fittest," for both traditional and genetically modified crops, herbicide spraying causes the evolution of new weeds that are bigger, stronger, and harder to kill because they are herbicide-resistant. As if in an arms race, chemical companies synthesize ever more potent "super-chemicals" to kill superweeds. These herbicides drift out of the fields to destroy wildflowers, food sources needed by bees, butterflies, and hummingbirds. (In the same way, new pesticides must be made ever more potent to deal with the flourishing of harmful insects resistant to the old pesticides. These new pesticides readily also poison the beneficial pollinators.)

So now in the U.S. with agricultural chemicals, we are both poisoning and starving our food-crop pollinators. It seems that to feed ourselves we Americans readily sacrifice other species that are not only helpless and harmless but even vital to maintain the human food supply. Such a twisted state of affairs in the United States could only occur because it is profitable to special interests in the agriculture and chemical industries. These dominate the Congress, and their political appointees to the Executive Branch who capture and pervert agencies such as the U.S. Department of Agriculture and the Office of Pesticides and Toxic Substances within the Environmental Protection Agency.

A new public-health risk comes from the widespread overuse of antibiotics fed to fatten healthy farm animals. Even a minor scrape on the playing field or in the garden, or mishandling of food in a kitchen, can be fatal. Many thousands of hospitalized people—too often children—each year in the U.S. die from untreatable bacteria that have become resistant to the same antibiotics fed to the animals we eat. Independent scientists today also are seeking to find environmental causes of Parkinson's, Alzheimer's, and ALS (called Lou Gehrig's disease). While little is proven, here too they are seeing suspicious coincidences and possible links to agricultural and other chemicals. On the defense, chemical companies point out correctly that correlation does not prove causation, and that the Food and Drug Administration recently has attempted to ban the use of antibiotics in healthy animals. However, where conditions—stress, overcrowding, and filth—put animals merely at risk of illness, the animal-feeding "factories" still can and do put antibiotics into their healthy animals. Sales of over-the-counter antibiotics are increasing in farm country, and veterinarians (paid by the animal producers to write prescriptions) are not under effective FDA oversight.

Beyond pesticides and antibiotics, chemicals intended to kill, there are many other ways that industrialized agriculture impacts the environment—the land, fresh water, and even the seas receiving agricultural runoff. Here it is impossible to address these many issues, or many questions attending genetic modification of our foods. One impact upon the public health does deserve special mention—the additives that food manufacturers intentionally put straight into what we eat in the U.S., including bakery products, soft drinks, and other processed foods.[7] They do so even after some food additives have been proven to cause cancer in animals, are suspected human carcinogens, or are linked other human health impacts including to possible loss of activity and attention span of children, memory loss, nerve damage, and skin problems including itching and hives. The U.S. Food and Drug Administration either does not know, or knowingly allows without testing for safety, that food manufacturers often secretly put over 1,000 strange chemicals into our food.[8] Here again we see a cultural difference, in that the International Agency for Research on Cancer will often do the first research, and the European Food Safety Authority or

51

individual EU nations are more likely to recommend and take action to protect their people against such additives. And clever U.S. food processors wanting European market access will sometimes "game" the system by removing dicey additives from processed food made in America and exported to be sold only in Europe. Meanwhile, back in the USA, richer still is the blend in the chemical soup that is mothers' milk.

For chemicals, U.S. regulation has been weak and federal funding for independent science has been declining for years. It crashed in 2017, and today the USEPA protects the environment about as poorly as the FDA well protects the U.S. food industry. From this chapter's *smorgasbord* of issues of chemicals found or placed in our U.S. food supply, we have only been able to taste a sampling. But there is yet so much more to study and learn about chemical safety. My hope is that some younger readers find this to be as interesting, intellectually challenging, and alarming as it is— more than enough reason to consider a career in biochemistry, medicine, or environmental science. And consider also food science. While beyond the scope of this chapter, it is questionable whether our human food supply will be sufficient in quantity (quite aside from its cleanliness and the environmental impact of big agriculture) to feed the growing population on our planet as its climate deteriorates.[9] Depending on who signs your paychecks, in such careers, you could join the fight for enough and better food.

To end this chapter, let us remember that Rachel Carson said we should "bear witness." In words familiar today when terrorist bombs may be left in public places, this means "If you see something—say something." Rachel Carson made that choice when she published her scientific insights in *Silent Spring*, the book that said so much. Today, beyond nuclear war, we know that the biggest, man-made threat facing humanity is climate change caused by an excess of conventional air pollutants. The amazing Rachel Carson suspected early that the climate might be changing, and she would have known that the toxic chemical hydrogen sulfide could be deadly. I do not suppose that she foresaw what we now know—that by continuing on a "smooth and easy road" emitting fossil-fueled air pollution as usual, in about 200 or 300 years humanity will have so polluted the air and the sea that hydrogen sulfide emitted by the sea is likely to cause our extinction on land.

For chemicals, for climate change, and for all serious environmental and public-health threats, we all have to make a choice like she did. After seeing and saying, then we must act by taking the better path forward. Here are Ms. Carson's poetic words taken after Robert Frost:

> We stand where two roads diverge,
> one—a smooth and easy road—leads to disaster.
> The other fork in the road, though less traveled,
> offers our last, our only chance to reach a destination
> that assures—the preservation—of the earth.

---

1. To understand the life of the lady behind her books, well worth reading is *Rachel Carson—Witness for Nature*, by biographer and historian Linda Lear (republished by Houghton Mifflin Harcourt in 2009). Its reading leaves one feeling sad that Rachel Carson's family and personal life were filled with difficulty and little happiness, and wondering whether this could be why her love for nature became so intense. Professor Lear also edited *Lost Woods: The Discovered Writing of Rachel Carson* (Beacon Press, 1998) that collects the writings—so surprisingly almost poetic—of a woman who was trained as an ocean biologist.

2. Updating *Silent Spring* is the book *Our Stolen Future: Are We Threatening Our Fertility, Intelligence, and Survival? A Scientific Detective Story* (Dutton, 1996). Theo Colburn and two colleagues found

more recent evidence linking synthetic contaminants including POPs to damaging health effects. Especially alarming is how prenatal hormonal or endocrine disruption in pregnant mothers—both human and wildlife—also impairs their young. The damages include developmental, neurological, immune-system, and reproductive impairment. In the decades since 1996, the fears and the damage have grown.

3. Chemicals named in *Silent Spring* and banned globally by the Stockholm Convention are aldrin, chlordane, dieldrin, eldrin, heptachlor, toxaphene, and hexachlorobenzene. DDT is severely restricted and may only be used in public health emergencies such as to suppress outbreaks of malaria.

4. From a much longer list, here are some chemicals in wide use that today are problematic for people or our environment: atrazine; bisphenol A (BPA); chlorpyrifos; dicamba; per- and poly-fluoroalkyl substances or PFAS, including PFOA and PFOS, used in non-stick food wrappers and cookware and a wide range of stain-resistant consumer products; phthalates, used in food packaging and plasticizers; flame retardants, including TDCP (Tris) and TCEP; and trichloroethylene (TCE).

5. Edward Osborne "E. O." Wilson is a retired Harvard professor of entomology considered to be the intellectual father of biodiversity. He has published best-sellers and twice won the Pulitzer Prize. In his book *The Future of Life* (Abacus, 2002), he predicts that half of all species on Earth, most of which are insects including beneficial ones, will be extinct in 100 years if present trends continue. Since 2002, the use of chemicals killing food pollinators has expanded enormously.

6. *The Politics of Precaution: Regulating Health, Safety, and Environmental Risks in Europe and in the United States,* by David Vogel (Princeton University Press, 2012). The Maastricht Treaty in 1992 among EU nations specifically allows government to regulate where resulting damage could be great but there is not yet scientific certainty as to the cause and effect. Across many fields, Europeans have shown themselves unwilling to wait for unacceptable harm before constraining risks created by corporate profit-making.

7. Food additives known or suspected of carrying serious human health concerns include potassium bromate, azodicarbonamide (ADA), BHA, BHT, brominated vegetable oil (BMO), bovine growth hormones, ractopamine, and certain yellow and red food dyes, especially Red 3.

8. The source for this fact and others in this chapter—a good source of independent information on food safety—is the nonprofit Center for Science in the Public Interest (CSPI), publisher of the *Nutrition Action Healthletter*. It tells us that it accepts no advertising or donations from either corporations or the government, and that its positions are based only on science and considerations in the best interest of the public.

9. *The Fate of Food: What We'll Eat in a Bigger, Hotter, Smarter World*, by Amanda Little (Harmony Books, 2019).

Chapter 4—Waking Up to Toxic Waste

DURING THE MID- AND LATE 1970s, the U.S. was waking up appalled to find many communities throughout our country afflicted by toxic-waste dumping. To energize the pollution fighters of tomorrow who I hope are reading this, to get some details of the toxic-waste horror that was discovered in the 1970s, I suggest that you google "Love Canal." Buried chemicals were oozing into a school built atop a toxic-waste dump and into homes close by, where there were high rates of miscarriages, birth defects, and cancers.

While this example in Niagara Falls, New York, may be the most notorious case of toxic-waste disposal, around the nation were thousands of cases more. Irresponsible businesses—too often well-known, major corporations, some even household names—asked no questions as they hired shady "midnight truckers" to make their industrial waste disappear. Until the end of the 1970s, there were no federal laws, and weak laws from medieval times in too many states only prohibited open dumping and burning of trash. But modern, industrial-scale waste is comprised of a huge array of many tens of thousands of man-made, synthetic chemicals that do not exist in nature. If their disposal is mishandled, these are poisons that cause horrific injuries, often as smoke if burned and by leaching into ground water that is pumped up through wells to become drinking water. That the managers of so many corporate enterprises, lacking even basic morality and knowing there were no laws, would cut costs by dumping their toxic waste on America, shocked and energized me to undertake my life's work as a pollution fighter.

After being elected to the Maryland state legislature and serving the years of 1975–78 as a lawmaker, I had obtained both an overview of state government and a good reputation that was publicly visible. In 1979, Stephen Sachs, the Attorney General of Maryland, appointed me to be an Assistant Attorney General assigned to the Department of Natural Resources (DNR) in Annapolis, where I would represent the Department's Water Resources Administration. After exploring for more than 10 years among the various fields of the law for my calling, I had finally matched my trade (the law) with my passion (environmental protection), and as the saying goes, "If you really love what you are doing, you will be very, very busy but never work a day in your life."

Almost immediately, I encountered frightful cases of toxic-waste dumping. Consider what was facing a Maryland State Highways crew called to clean up many plastic bags dumped along the roadside. Swelling in the sun, the bags were filled with dead rats from the cancer laboratories of the U.S. National Institutes of Health. Even the U.S. government's primary health research lab had hired a "midnight dumper" to make its toxic waste disappear. How awful for that road crew, hardworking men without chemical "moon suits" to protect them during a cleanup. It seemed like the little state of Maryland was alone and under siege even from the sleeping "feds," and it was about to get much worse.

The next year and a half of my legal career would be "hands-on" and provide a solid foundation of on-the-ground experience in anti-pollution enforcement that I would soon bring to the U.S. Environmental Protection Agency. To the new problem of toxic-waste dumping, the State assigned its staff of water-pollution fighters that included four or five uniformed DNR police officers and more than a dozen civil inspectors having basic scientific training. For the violations they found and brought to my desk, I was empowered to file misdemeanor criminal charges on my own signature, and of course DNR operated statewide. With the officers or inspectors as witnesses to the crimes they had investigated, eventually I would go to every county courthouse in the state. In addition to waste dumping, most of the cases involved violations of the laws protecting waters of the State from direct discharges, and a few cases protected wetlands from illegal development. During my short time all defendants whom I prosecuted were convicted, and my team won every case for the State.

I could tell many stories of my exciting pollution cases just in Maryland, but there is room here for just three. A very ordinary and common case involved a gasoline-truck driver who failed to stand close by while pumping gasoline from his tanker truck into the underground tanks of a gas station. In a low-lying town on the flat Eastern Shore of the Chesapeake Bay, every street had drainage ditches containing water. Here a driver took a long break and walked away from his truck, which kept pumping after the station's tank was filled. Many hundreds of gallons of highly flammable fuel overflowed into these ditches and spreading atop the water surface was carried through some of the town, with gasoline coming even to the doors of the town's volunteer fire department. As in this case, for a truck driver to leave his active pump to go to the bathroom, have a smoke, or even go to lunch, was a criminal misdemeanor when found and charged. At least this driver did not throw a smoking cigarette butt into the ditch and perhaps burn up part of the town.

A bigger case involved a foreign freighter discharging filthy, oily bilgewater while sitting in the anchorage off Annapolis just south of the Chesapeake Bay Bridge. DNR's efforts to contact the ship and its representatives in New York were telephone calls not returned. To my amazement, one of my colleagues, a more experienced Assistant Attorney General whom I had known since the days he had been an Assistant State's Attorney prosecuting murder cases in Baltimore, ordered a DNR Marine Police boat out to the ship. The State's police boat passed through the ring of

Coast Guard boats that were only watching the "spill" and going around in circles, probably because this was months before they were ordered up to full speed in water-pollution enforcement. DNR officers boarded the ship, took its foreign captain off in handcuffs, motored again out through the circling Coast Guard boats, and put the captain in the Annapolis jail!

Suddenly "suits" from a New York law firm were calling us to complain that the State had illegally arrested the foreign captain of a foreign ship and had no authority to create this international incident. After arriving off the Amtrak train from New York, the "suits" met with my more knowledgeable colleague who had ordered out the DNR police. This Assistant Attorney General told the ship's highly paid, Manhattan lawyers what—despite their bluster—they surely already knew, that each State has concurrent jurisdiction for its own waters even extending to three miles seaward off a beach facing the open ocean. My colleague said that further, "waters of the State" clearly include every drop of water in the entire, almost landlocked Chesapeake Bay where the ship was within the Annapolis anchorage. While the ship's counsel feigned surprise, without research they pleaded "no contest," and the DNR won again! And I learned a legal lesson regarding the sometimes surprising reach of governmental jurisdiction that would serve me well later in both national and international work at EPA.

My biggest case with DNR involved toxic-waste dumping. It began with a call from the fire department in Sharptown, a large village remote in what we call "the Eastern Shore" of Maryland in the center of the "Delmarva" peninsula. In town at the edge of the Nanticoke River sat a large cluster of empty, unused, and rusting former storage tanks that once were filled from oil barges. DNR investigators talking to town residents learned that at night for many months big, unmarked tanker trucks had been seen rolling through town. Sampling and testing found that the old tanks had been filled mysteriously with a witch's brew of toxic (flammable and carcinogenic) pesticides, solvents, PCBs, and unusable residues that would be found in the bottoms of the tanks at an oil refinery. The suspected culprit, William Grigsby, an interstate transport trucker, lived just across the line in Delaware, but again the feds were missing in action. EPA was still without staff and legal authority, and the Coast Guard initially did not seem interested.

So the State of Maryland began an interstate investigation that should have been (and today would be) federal. We sent DNR officers to New Jersey where they found the refinery, and then to North Carolina to see another dump site believed to contain a similar mix dumped by the same man. With the approval of Maryland's Attorney General as required for felony charges, we charged Mr. Grigsby. With the cooperation of the Attorney General of Delaware, we had him arrested by the Delaware State Police and extradited to the county jail in Salisbury, Maryland.

With another Assistant AG from the Felonies Division, for DNR I co-prosecuted this case. Because these chemicals posed a serious danger to the town, the water in the river, and the Chesapeake Bay fisheries, a key witness was J. William Kime, the U.S. Coast Guard's Captain of the Port of Baltimore. He arrived in his summer "dress-white" uniform, and to establish rapport, I told him that I was very proud to have been ten years before a second-class petty officer in the Coast Guard Reserves. I said that I had never earned the rank to wear such a handsome hat as his with gold braid and "scrambled eggs" on its brim. He smiled, knowing that—despite my low rank and being only a reserve bosun's mate —still I was fellow "Coastie" who must have done well to become an Assistant Attorney General prosecuting for the State. I asked him when he testified could he put his hat on the rail of the witness box, with its "screaming eagle" and all the gold facing the jury. Without more words, he understood that I wanted the jury to realize the full authority and importance of his high rank and the honor of his presence in our little country courthouse. He nodded and smiled again, he did keep his hat before the eyes of the jury, and yes—the jury was impressed by his appearance and his testimony. The next time I heard of him, he was Admiral Kime, and many years later he retired as the four-star Commandant of the U.S. Coast Guard.

From the trial that took eight days, of the more than forty witnesses here I will recall the testimony of just two, Mr. Grigsby's drivers, each charged with filling, driving, and after midnight emptying his trucks into the riverside tanks. One driver was so befuddled and wasted that he could hardly talk and walk, and with questioning he mumbled enough to reveal that before he began working around chemicals for Mr. Grigsby he had been very healthy and indeed athletic. The jury got our intended implication that he had been poisoned in his work, though we did not have direct medical evidence of this. The other driver could talk normally, and based on pre-trial interviews we were able in front of the jury to question him something like this:

Q. When you worked for Mr. Grigsby, what shoes did you wear?

A. I wore a different pair each night. First, I had old boots, but then I had to buy cheap sneakers.

Q. Why a different pair each night?

A. Because after walking in chemical puddles on the ground my shoes would always get soft and then melt by the next day.

Q. Did you ask Mr. Grigsby for proper safety boots to wear around his chemicals?

A. Yes, but he never gave me any.

Our jury of farmers and townsmen had no difficulty quickly convicting Mr. Grigsby. Unfortunately, for reasons I have never understood (perhaps he had never seen a toxic-waste crime before), much to his discredit the county trial judge imposed a ridiculously low penalty, just a fine, on a man who should have been put in a state prison. But who would clean out the decrepit tanks tottering at the edge of a big river leading to an important Bay fishery? With Captain Kime now on our team, suddenly the U.S. Coast Guard found that it had some extra money in its Clean Water Fund, and it made arrangements to empty the tanks at federal expense. The waste would be going into safely guarded storage by the federal General Services Administration (GSA) in its military ordnance depot at Curtis Creek in north Anne Arundel County.

The factual part of the matter was proven and over, but little did we know that this case was about to explode legally.[1] Just on the west side of the Chesapeake Bay Bridge, the volatile Anne Arundel County Executive claimed that the toxic waste was too dangerous to pass through his county and be stored there in a very well-guarded federal ammunition depot. For a while it appeared that his county police would attempt to block the western end of the Bay Bridge to keep out the federal-state convoy of toxic-waste trucks to be led by the U.S. Coast Guard and the State's police! DNR sued Anne Arundel County to stop this ridiculous political stunt by the County Executive, a man who probably wanted to be elected Governor of the State. The State did defeat the County in the Court of Special Appeals, and the Attorney General was very pleased as the turmoil subsided. Without a physical confrontation, the waste went into national control and was disposed of safely. And I—a formerly elected State legislator myself—saw again how outrageous could be the behavior of politicians in front of TV cameras, another lesson that would serve me well soon enough at EPA.

The Sharptown case of toxic-waste danger was one of several that I saw or handled for the DNR in 1979 and 1980. In another case near Elkton, Maryland, a small chemical plant persisted in discharging toxic chemicals into the ground and surface water, and when confronted they said that if the State of Maryland did not like it they would just move a few miles north to Pennsylvania. This attitude was highly offensive to me. Fortunately, the national government had passed powerful new laws to address the rampant and dreadful toxic-chemical waste dumping and force responsible parties everywhere to clean up their messes. Suddenly having this nationwide legal authority, on an emergency basis the EPA in Washington D.C., was forming a new Hazardous Waste Enforcement Task Force. Its Director asked each State to send to EPA cases that a State found difficult to handle, particularly cases where there was a threat to move a dirty plant out of state or where there was a flow or plume of actual interstate pollution. In response to EPA's invitation, I had the pleasure of handing off to the federal government the case of this small chemical plant, which soon found itself a defendant in federal court.

The more I saw, the more angry I became at the callous disregard of profitable corporations ready and willing to dump toxic waste almost anywhere to poison water, wildlife, and people. My emotions were reinforcing my intellectual fascination with the new and expanding field of science-based environmental law, where I continued my hands-on legal education into new legal maneuvers. The Sharptown PCB case had involved an interstate investigation, an extradition, an inter-jurisdictional dispute, and state-federal cooperation. And I believe that the case may have been the first such toxic-waste-dumping felony tried anywhere in America. During the six days of trial, the proceedings were reported in the Washington newspapers as of national interest given first the involvement of both the Coast Guard and the GSA's ordnance depot near Baltimore, and then the outrageous shenanigans of the County Executive trying to obstruct a cleanup funded by the national government. So it happened that the Sharptown PCB case would be the highlight of my brief career prosecuting criminals as an in-court trial lawyer, and the case would propel me out into another orbit.

Because I had the good fortune to be one of the first experienced attorneys in America already visibly and successfully combating toxic-waste dumping, in late 1980 EPA hired me into the new Hazardous Waste Enforcement Task Force. I was appointed to be a Branch Chief with civil enforcement responsibility for about one-third of the country or about 17 states stretching from the Midwest through the Mid-Atlantic to New England and happily including my beloved State of Maine. My new job would be to supervise the development of hundreds of civil suits against many corporations to force them to clean up their toxic-waste dumps. Starting in 1980, they were liable for cleanup costs under a new federal statute that we called the "Superfund" law. I felt badly to be so soon leaving the historic county courtrooms across Maryland, my new friends in the DNR police force and inspection teams, and the Office of Attorney General. But Steven Sachs generously congratulated me, and in November 1980 I began commuting on the train from Baltimore to Washington to my new job in EPA Headquarters. I was 39 years old, already quite ancient to begin a federal career.

By 1979 when I began working at DNR, my 12 years of meandering through the fields of the law—searching for a "white-hat" role where I could find satisfaction with the results of my life's work —had ended with maturity in the profession and finding environmental law to be my specialty. At this point, I want to offer some reflections to any young person who may be thinking about the law as a career, perhaps also to become a pollution fighter. Obviously, I think that to uphold the rule of law is a great calling in life, and to be empowered to be a statewide prosecutor is an honor of high achievement. To bring these skills to fighting pollution to me seems best of all. But in this path were many dangerous pitfalls into which I have come close to falling—indeed, "the law is a jealous mistress." Why in the world would anyone want to have such a life of intentionally throwing oneself into endless conflicts? I often hear this question from friends who throw themselves into playing tennis or card games. And who could possibly want to be a lawyer? I will try to answer these questions.

People most likely to pass a state bar exam come to it with intelligent and often complicated minds—a good thing, because the rules and complexities of the law are endless. After all, the law addresses every aspect of human experience, and people will do and say almost anything to get what they want. Any lawyer in any case is caught in the center of a triangle. One on lower corner is one's client, who may not pay you and can sue you if you commit malpractice in a civil case; as a prosecutor your client is a state or nation and your boss is an attorney general who had best not be displeased by your performance. On the other lower corner of the triangle is the opposing counsel, representing his client, and trying to destroy your client's case and make you lose completely. At the top of the triangle is the judge whose duty it is to bring the hammer down on one side or the other—there has to be a decision. Accountability is unavoidable and instantaneous; a courtroom is not a bureaucracy where issues may linger undecided indefinitely amid unending debate. The average lawyer will lose as often as he wins, and the stress of trying to always win can be overwhelming. If as a lawyer you lose a case, there may be an appeal, but the grounds are limited and usually you don't get to correct your mistakes or do it over with a retrial from the beginning.

As a person, after some bad habits in my twenties, by my thirties I realized that my workday lunch could only be a healthy salad with some protein, and never even one beer. I learned that lifting law books, typing, or standing up when a bailiff announces "Order in the Court, All Rise, the Honorable Judge Whomever presiding," is not enough daily exercise. And in the evening, I learned that one glass of alcohol should be enough to relax, and never, ever to pour more than two glasses of booze. But to get to this new beginning had been a voyage through shoals. If my reader is or wants to become a young lawyer, I hope you can navigate with prudence to a great career sustained by good habits—and also by pride. The law is a "learned profession" and every lawyer is an "officer of the court." Yes, some lawyers do deserve derision as members of the "Chickenshit Club" (to be described in an upcoming chapter) or even "the second oldest profession."[2] But if lawyers (and the lawyers who become judges) did not exist, most disputes would be resolved by the knife, the gun, or the firebomb of private vengeance. Your first role will be good planning with your client, explaining what is right and what is wrong, and to help your client proceed without creating a dispute. If a dispute comes to you to handle, you must learn the facts of every case as a mystery that you can solve, and you will never be bored. You will help people, who may be in great distress, to make their lives as right again as is possible in the circumstances.

Many times in recent decades I have been asked by law clerks working for me at the EPA, and by young lawyers who find it very difficult to gain employment—how can one find a job as a lawyer in the public service or in a good law firm? My answer is always the same—network and start where you can at any (city, county, or state) level in any job handling cases that may take you (or you may take) to any court. Before any court appearance you will need to do your homework, which can mean essentially writing a script of your questions and anticipated answers for a "play" that the next day may roll out, diverge, or explode in any number of directions for which you must have prepared multiple scripts—no easy task. The "real-world" trial experience that you gain will make your *curriculum vitae* stand out to lawyers both in trial-law firms and in public agencies reviewing applications for employment.

At the national level, while a few lawyers with the very highest academics may find employment immediately after law-school graduation, for lawyers with a few years of demonstrated "hands-on" experience there are many more openings obtainable. And as a basis for working in private practice, where usually the goal is not to go to trial but to prevent or settle a dispute, still it is so valuable to have some experience in trial work. This will enable you to identify the evidence necessary to prove or defend your client's case, and you will know the likely legal consequences of those facts. Only with trial experience will you be able to reliably predict the likely future outcome, and to advise your client as to what to expect if he does not settle the case but proceeds to trial. This knowledge is essential even if you do not continue to try cases yourself, because as you get older it becomes clear that arduous trial work is mostly a younger person's game.

To conclude this chapter, may I reprise my career to 1980 when I began my federal service. From law school graduation in 1967, I had worked one year in the judicial branch of government (I was law clerk to the Chief Judge of Maryland), four years reading and writing in the library of a big law firm, and then out on my own struggling yet learning the ways of a courthouse and helping the few clients of my own. During the remainder of the 1970s, I served in Maryland's legislative branch and then prosecuted cases for the executive branch as a member of the Office of the Attorney General of Maryland. By 1980, having worked in all three branches of a state government was an unusual credential that would help me to navigate at the far more complex national level, yet also a domain where the three branches of government rule. I was ready to move upward and onward into the big-league fight against pollution.

1. *Anne Arundel County v. Governor*, 45 Md. App. 435, 413 A.2d 281 (Court of Special Appeals of Maryland, 1980).

2. Prostitution is said to be the oldest profession, and lawyers too have always served mostly in the halls of the rich and powerful. I will address this subject fully and soon in the chapter about lackey lawyers in the "Chickenshit Club" who bend the law to shield the rich and powerful from the justice they deserve for their evil misdeeds.

Dear reader, should you become a lawyer, rather than a member of Chickenshit Club, I do hope that you will choose to be a shield against injustice while upholding the rule of law. Although the appellation "Esquire" may not exist today in England and is perhaps going out of style in the U.S., some American lawyers still use "Esq." after their name. A thousand years ago in England, the term "squire" described the young nobleman who carried a knight's shield, and the word also may refer to or derive from the knight's shield itself, called an "escutcheon." Along with the shield, like a knight you will carry a sword, but it will consist only of your words. And as your goal, you should always keep in mind another symbol, which is the balancing scales of justice in the hands of a blindfolded maiden.

Chapter 5—Headquarters, U.S. Environmental Protection Agency

By joining the Office of Enforcement in the Headquarters of the United States Environmental Protection Agency (USEPA, or EPA) in late 1980, moving from a state orbit to a national orbit, I had finally married my useful skills or "trade" (the law) and my passion (environmental protection). Perhaps for a second time, to each of my young readers I express the hope that you can discover both your useful skills in any constructive line of work, and also your passion—and then link or combine them, ideally doing so at much a much younger age than I did. I would be very, very busy at EPA for the next 31 years while doing work that suited me, and even in the worst of times never did it feel like a chore. Such a fulfillment can be the same for you.

During the tumultuous 1960s, the U.S. woke up to many wrongs and needs to reform. In 1962, Rachel Carson wrote *Silent Spring,* one of the most consequential books of the 20th century. It awakened the national mindset to the need for environmental action, and a major result was the creation of the USEPA. As I wrote in an earlier chapter, today she is considered by many to be the mother of modern ecology or environmentalism. She was the very rare scientist who could write for the popular market with prose that was gripping and almost poetic. In no particular order, here are three more examples:

> Only within the moment of time represented by the present century has one species—man—acquired significant power to alter the nature of the world.

> The more clearly we can focus our attention on the wonders and realities of the universe about us, the less taste we shall have for its destruction.

As crude a weapon as the caveman's club, the chemical barrage has been hurled against the fabric of life.

Let us remember again that 1962 was at the height of the Cold War against Communism. In those years, pollution was "okay" or at least tolerated as the price of progress and national power. The U.S. government heedlessly promoted overuse of pesticides, and technology was tied to patriotic anti-Communism and not questioned. Rachel Carson alone courageously challenged the companies and the government. Tragically, she died of cancer too soon in 1964. But the alarm she had raised helped to move the government from promoter to regulator of chemicals, and in a national paradigm shift, in 1970 President Nixon created the USEPA. In the 1970s, the Congress enacted some of the strongest anti-pollution laws in the world, the new EPA quickly banned DDT and other similar pesticides, and by the 1980s Americans began to see the recovery of raptors including the American eagle. Today we know that technology is not always benign, and that pollution is to be prevented, limited, or banned—not ignored and suffered.[1]

By the early 1970s in the absence of laws, it was clear that a combination of greed, irresponsibility, and ignorance of science had caused too many American corporations to dump their toxic waste across America. My last chapter told how this problem impacted Maryland, which until 1980 did not have a federal partner also chasing after polluters. Though Congress passed laws in 1976 and 1980 to address toxic-waste dumping, too many reckless businesses continued this now illegal practice, and there were many dangerous "legacy" toxic-waste dumps needing remediation.

From 1981 to 1994, I was involved with Headquarters' oversight of civil enforcement by the ten EPA offices across the nation, and I worked often with EPA's national forensics laboratory in Denver. Later in the 1980s, I moved gradually into providing legal advice to criminal investigations and some involvement with training at the Federal Law Enforcement Training Center (FLETC) in Brunswick, Georgia. To coordinate such a large effort, from the mid-1980s we usually held an annual, national conference for the ten EPA Special Agents in Charge (SACs), the law-enforcement supervisors of all pollution-control criminal investigations throughout the nation. One national meeting took me up to Maine, the state of my boyhood summers where I had not lived for at least 25 years, and after work there was a boat ride in Portland Harbor to an island picnic dinner. The smell of Maine's tidal seashore so overwhelmed me with long-ago memories as to bring tears to my eyes, tears that I had to hide by taking a short walk away from my dinner with EPA's tough federal cops and prosecutors from the Department of Justice (DOJ). I later came to understand the emotion when I found these words by Rachel Carson, who also loved above all to walk by the edge of the sea: "For the sense of smell, almost more than any other, has the power to recall memories and it is a pity to use it so little."

By the end of 1980, EPA's fleet of vehicles had prototypes of some of the first electric cars, and President Jimmy Carter had installed 32 solar panels on the White House roof. He left office in January 1981, replaced by President Ronald Reagan. The first smell I encountered at EPA Headquarters was the stink of political stunts driven by scientific ignorance. When President Ronald Reagan took office, though he certainly was likeable and charming, he said that government was the problem, not the solution. EPA's electric cars were replaced by gas guzzlers, and he ordered the solar panels removed from the White House, supposedly saying that they were "just a joke."

The ever-amazing Rachel Carson, 25 years earlier in the late 1950s, had planned a book on climate change, writing, "We live in an age of rising seas. In our own lifetime we are witnessing a startling alteration of the climate." And President Lyndon Johnson's science advisors had warned him that by 2000 climate change could be veering beyond human control. In 1965, Johnson was the first President to inform Congress that "This generation has altered the composition of the atmosphere on a global scale through . . . a steady increase in carbon dioxide from the burning of fossil fuels." At least from 1979, among government scientists and thoughtful policymakers in Washington there was growing awareness of climate change. During the next 10 years, action was considered even at the highest levels, until incoming President George H. W. Bush (who called himself "The Environmental President") put an end to proposals for effective legislation and a treaty. This blundering cost us 40 years as humanity has been racing closer to the climate cliff. Since 1979, the rise in atmospheric CO_2 has accelerated by a factor of five, to a point higher than the entire increase above natural levels in the previous 200 years.[2] Today, after too many wasted decades, climate chaos has come very clearly into view, and with business as usual the future looks very dire indeed.

The second smell I encountered was different, not of scientific ignorance but a stink of political scandal. From early 1981, President Reagan had tried to give EPA a "sleeping pill" by installing contemptuous political appointees to throw the entire EPA into turmoil, quite like what happened again starting in 2017. It is impossible here to retell it all, and I will just recall the scandal in the cleanup of toxic-waste sites, the very activity into which in late 1980 I was hired to enforce the law as one of three supervising national Branch Chiefs in the Hazardous Waste Enforcement Task Force. Staff attorneys handling particular cases first alerted my two colleagues, Branch Chiefs Richard Mays and Anne Allen, and me. Then I was among supervisors to carry staff concerns to EPA's General Counsel, Gerald Yamada, who became alarmed and took appropriate action.

So I was very pleased one day to walk out of my office to find FBI investigators to my left, and the EPA Inspector General's investigators to my right. They were interviewing our staff attorneys in adjacent offices who had become convinced that politics, not the relative need for relief from danger posed by each toxic-waste site, were causing cleanup funds to go first or mainly to the districts of Republican Congressmen. My staff attorneys had the direct knowledge of each case, they were witnesses, and I was not interviewed. As a consequence, in 1984 the EPA Assistant Administrator for Waste, President Reagan's political appointee Rita Lavelle, was fired and then convicted on federal charges of perjury related to an investigation into misuse of the "Superfund" of federal money used to clean up abandoned toxic-waste sites.[3] This unhappy episode alerted me to keep my eyes wide open, and it was a precursor to another EPA scandal in which I would be the victim ten years later.

Lavelle's boss at the time was EPA's first Administrator under President Reagan, Anne Gorsuch from Denver, Colorado, an intelligent, conservative, and colorful woman of the West. During only 22 months in office, she chopped EPA's budget by 22 percent, deregulated, and hired top assistants coming from the polluting corporations. When she refused to turn over for Congressional oversight documents revealing mismanagement of the "cleanup" of toxic-waste sites, she became the first agency director in U.S. history to be cited for contempt of Congress. Amid her self-created media firestorm, in 1983 she "resigned," and the tumult ended.

Though my 31 years at EPA was a roller-coaster ride, not until 36 years later would EPA ever again be brought so low. In 2017, the President appointed EPA Administrator Scott Pruitt, who came to a shameful end probably worse than that of Administrator Gorsuch. Not incidentally, our President in 2019 also appointed for life to the Supreme Court of the United States the son of Administrator Gorsuch, a man who may share his mother's distaste for clean water and clean air. Time will tell whether Justice Neil Gorsuch by his decisions uses this opportunity to undermine environmental protection for decades.

EPA rebounded in 1983 when President Reagan replaced Anne Gorsuch in "the second coming," not of Jesus Christ, but of William Ruckelshaus. This savior had been EPA's first Administrator from 1970 to 1973, the man responsible for creating the science-based, yet powerful new regulatory agency. In the spirit of Rachel Carson, to save the American eagle from extinction, it was Ruckelshaus who in 1972 decided that DDT was a potential human carcinogen and banned its production and use in the USA. In 1973, he moved on to become Acting Director of the FBI and then Deputy Attorney General of the United States. Famously, in an episode known to history as "The Saturday Night Massacre," on a Saturday night in October 1973, Attorney General Elliot Richardson and his Deputy Ruckelshaus both resigned rather than obey President Nixon's order to fire Archibald Cox. This Special Prosecutor was on the trail of Nixon, whose henchmen burglarized the offices of the Democratic Party in the Watergate building. Facing impeachment, Nixon soon resigned in complete disgrace because of the "Watergate affair."

How lucky we EPA employees were from 1983 to 1985 to be led again by Bill Ruckelshaus, a man of great wisdom and integrity who wanted EPA to get back to work protecting the environment from pollution. Among his many memorable instructions to staff is this: "Don't do anything you would not want to see on the front page of the *New York Times*, because you easily could be reading about yourself there!" He also told us to do our jobs as if we were fish in a glass fishbowl. Today we call this "transparency," and his point is that eventually the most important EPA matters—good and bad—vital to the public interest will always become known, and should be so that there can be knowledge-based political accountability in a democracy.

He left us too soon in 1985, yet with EPA's integrity and reputation restored.

Many years later, when Ruckelshaus was back in the private sector, he wrote this sentiment, with which I am in complete agreement:

> I've had an awful lot of jobs in my lifetime, and in moving from one to another, have had the opportunity to think about what makes them worthwhile. I've concluded there are four important criteria: interest, excitement, challenge, and fulfillment. I've never worked anywhere where I could find all four to quite the same extent as at EPA. I can find interest, challenge, and excitement as [board chair of a company]. I do have an interesting job. But it is tough to find the same degree of fulfillment I found in the government. At EPA, you work for a cause that is beyond self-interest and larger than the goals people normally pursue. You're not there for the money, you're there for something beyond yourself.

Although USEPA is roughly one-tenth the size of any big American corporation, such as an automaker, airline, or oil company, other than the Federal Reserve System, EPA is the regulatory agency with the largest impact on the U.S. economy that is driven by corporations. Despite EPA's many mistakes and periodic subjection to political manipulations, after working there for about 20 years, by 2000 I had come to realize two things: (1) our EPA is the biggest and best environmental protection agency in the world; and (2) together with the proliferation of nuclear weapons, because climate change is taking us all down a spiral toward human extinction in about the 23rd century, the very future of life on our planet will depend on the future of our EPA. I will address this existential threat, climate change, in a coming chapter.

Fortunately, for most of the 1980s the Congress remained in the hands of the Democratic Party which favored the protection of the environment. Congress provided new legal authority, oversight of EPA's behavior when it strayed into politics, and additional funding despite the President's constant requests to cut EPA's budget. From 1981 to 1993 at all times EPA itself was in the hands of political appointees of the Republican Party. We civil-service employees in the Office of Enforcement and our political appointees never talked politics or even mentioned the names of the political parties. We were too few and too busy, and from 1983 it was considered to be—and it is—in very bad taste to do so unless one worked in an obviously political office like the Office of Congressional Affairs. The politically appointed Republican lawyers who came in to lead the Office of Enforcement mostly believed in the rule of law. They might not see the need for or fully appreciate an environmental law, but because it was a law it was to be applied fairly and effectively like any other. Non-partisanship generally prevailed inside EPA's enforcement effort during the 1980s.

I left the Hazardous Waste Enforcement Task Force for broader responsibilities after 1983. I gained familiarity with all of EPA's science-based pollution-control laws and helped build the new and growing corps of EPA's criminal investigators who are law-enforcement officers (LEOs). Called "Special Agents," they are fully the equivalent of FBI agents, but employed by EPA and trained in the scientific and legal intricacies of crimes of pollution. When I had arrived at EPA in 1980, EPA had just two. Because we wanted to buy experience, EPA began staffing up by hiring young or mid-career Special Agents from other federal agencies. We also hired some experienced environmental law-enforcement officers from states, including one of my former colleagues from Maryland's DNR Police. After a while, we recruited some outstanding EPA civil inspectors to become criminal investigators after police training at the Federal Law Enforcement Center. My work gravitated more and more into providing legal advice for EPA's growing corps of Special Agents handling only the most serious cases and deserving the imprisonment of the persons responsible. Because all federal criminal cases are referred to and prosecuted by the Department of Justice (DOJ), I was not myself prosecuting cases in court.

By 1988, after eight years in the "ivory tower" of EPA Headquarters, though my career was advancing, my batteries were running down. From near the top of this tower of bureaucracy, I wanted to return to the action in the field, but not like attorneys in "Main Justice" (DOJ Headquarters), half their time having to spend weeks living in hotels and working in remote federal courthouses across America. So I sought a temporary assignment "on detail" back to the State of Maryland's new Department of the Environment that was created in the mid-1980s to handle the State's pollution cases formerly handled by the Department of Natural Resources. The rationale, a good one, was that I would strengthen the federal-state partnership and bring some federal expertise to Maryland's new department. Maryland Attorney General Joseph Curran appointed me as a Special Assistant Attorney General.

From 1988 to 1990, I did not have to commute 17 or 18 hours a week between Baltimore and Washington, and I had more time with my family. I felt more like a "real lawyer" again, not supervising junior lawyers, but directly in charge of my own cases. I was dealing hands-on with investigators (both pollution inspectors and State Police), victims, witnesses, grand juries, trial juries, opposing counsel, and judges assigned to bring the hammer down with a decision right or wrong. Back again trying cases in the courtrooms of Maryland, handling administrative, civil, and criminal cases, I relearned which process was appropriate for any particular case. I recharged my batteries, always intending to come back to EPA a better lawyer.

It seemed to have worked, because from Maryland refreshed when I returned to EPA in 1990, I was appointed the nationwide legal advisor—my title was Acting Director of the Criminal Enforcement Counsel Division—for all EPA criminal investigations. My work ranged from helping to design and sometimes conduct training, to reviewing performance of our Special Agents in Charge working within the ten EPA regional offices around the nation, advising on matters of criminal-enforcement policy at the Headquarters political level, and reviewing draft regulations and statutes. Trying always to be sure that a case was neither undercharged (handled administratively or civilly when it should be criminal) or overcharged criminally (when it was not that serious but the complaint just happened to come first to a Special Agent), my main function was to carefully review and sign off on every case referred for criminal prosecution to the Department of Justice.

But while I had been working as an Assistant Attorney General again in Maryland from 1988 to 1990, EPA's criminal-enforcement program had begun slipping. Little did I know that upon my return to Washington I would be stepping into an abyss. Beginning in about 1991, slowly I would realize that federal anti-pollution enforcement was being led astray by new political leaders and their compliant top civil servants. Criminal enforcement fell into a pit of cronyism and injustice reminiscent of what toxic-waste cleanups suffered under Gorsuch and Lavelle, and this is the subject of the following chapter.

Before relating how EPA and DOJ had slipped, here by contrast is a good example of how during most of the 1980s the growing criminal program ran very well. Of all the good people I might remember and "war stories" I might tell, here is just one. It begins with one of the Special Agents in Charge whom many of his colleagues and I too most admired: Dixon McClary, who worked out of the EPA regional office in Seattle, was EPA's top criminal investigator responsible for the Northwestern states including Alaska. If I recall correctly, Dixon came to EPA from the Drug Enforcement Administration, and central casting for a western movie would have set him as a lean yet rugged sheriff. He was afraid of nothing, had a thousand-yard stare, and was a man of few words except the right words. While looking every inch the Westerner, Dixon was no swaggering cowboy. He was prudent, measured, and smooth. Instead of breaking down a door to make an arrest, he would watch the house for a few mornings until he saw the pattern, then cleanly—with no fuss—arrest the culprit when he came sleepily out his front door to get the morning paper or walk his dog. He told me that to send people to prison was not his job; it was only to gather evidence and to be a witness to the truth, then let the juries and judges decide. "Witness to the truth" is a memorable phrase that has stayed with me, and I have rarely met a better lawman. The following case under his direction from 1986 will show you why.

Do you like Nabisco cookies? There is a river in the State of Washington where dead fish were appearing far, far downstream from a Nabisco plant. A water pollutant does not have to be a "methyl-chloride-ethyl-awful," unnaturally synthetic and obviously toxic. A conventional pollutant is excessive biological oxygen demand; even waste cookie ingredients can suck all the oxygen out of the water by a natural process called "BOD" or eutrophication. One of the many difficulties of environmental cases is that just as cancer in humans may not appear until 20 years after the impact of a carcinogenic pollutant, the dead bodies of fish killed by water pollution may not appear before floating miles downstream in a river with multiple possible sources of pollution. For reasons of both time and place, it can be very hard to connect the corpses to the crime. Water inspectors sometimes have to work their way upstream (and often then up storm drains by popping off manhole covers), sampling each site all the way back to the source. Like detectives seeking a murderer, this work is high-stakes, because having a dead-body count (whether fish, birds, humans, whatever) makes an ordinary pollution case more rightfully and likely to be charged as a crime rather than as an administrative or civil case.

So, after plenty of careful work to identify the likely source of the fish kills, in woods across the river behind the back of the Nabisco plant, a Special Agent working for Dixon McClary hid in the foliage and set up a night-time camera. From the back of the cookie plant, a big discharge pipe extended to the river, and the camera operator was about to become a "witness to the truth." Each day in the afternoon or dark of evening, a Nabisco worker would come out and open the valve on the big pipe. After many, many gallons of cookie-making waste were discharged into the river, he would return to close the valve. For several nights it was the same, and all was recorded into a very nice EPA movie.

The best scenes were filmed in the final night of the action. Soon after the Special Agent in the woods across the river radioed that the big pipe was open and spewing waste, about ten EPA Special Agents and biological inspectors suddenly roared up to the plant gate with flashing lights and badges visible. They presented a search warrant, and the flustered gate guard, not knowing what to do, called the plant-management office—just as EPA knows they always do—and the predictable result followed. From the woods and trying not to laugh, the EPA movie-maker soon recorded the same worker returning, now running around back frantically to close the valve. As EPA expects in such cases, investigation would reveal that he was sent by the culpable plant management after the gate guard had telephoned to tell that federal lawmen were at the gate. The movie-maker radioed the EPA force now coming through the gate, and a few moments later EPA officers arrived around back to see the pipe, arrest the worker, and wave to the hidden camera across the river!

To my readers who may want to be pollution fighters too, I say, does this sound like fun or what! To be a lawman can be a great career, or if you are science-minded perhaps to be a government inspector who is also a biologist or chemist. In this case, these technicians were essential in sampling the concentrated cookie waste at the pipe and, back in the EPA lab, matching this to residues of cookie waste taken from the stomachs of live fish and (diluted in the water) far down the river where the fish were found dead from the resulting insufficient oxygen. In almost any pollution case, science-minded experts are indispensable to prove cause and effect in this way. Here "criminal intent" also was clear—this means of disposal was far in excess of what was allowable under waste-water discharge regulations, and this illegality had to be known, approved, or ordered at least to the level of the plant manager. There was no possible defense. The company, plant manager, and production supervisor all pleaded guilty.[4]

In those early days, the Department of Justice handled EPA cases properly. Culpability was assessed against both the responsible corporate officers and the corporation. No low-level, laboring employee was charged or scapegoated just for following orders, even for working the valve on the pipe, because this pollution could only have been directed from the plant's office. The corporation and its top two managers at this plant were charged with water-pollution-related offenses. Because of his routine false reports to EPA of "no pollution," the plant manager was charged also with mail fraud and making false statements to the government. The latter charge is for a violation of 18 U.S. Criminal Code section 1001, a statute that I will quote to you in the next chapter and that has been much in the news in 2019.

Do consider the justice and wisdom in the sentence that the judge imposed in this case:

- Nabisco the corporation paid a fine of $300,000, contributed $150,000 to a river fisheries enhancement fund, and was placed on three years of probation.

- Nationwide at the corporate management level, Nabisco agreed that any criminal water-pollution violation at any Nabisco plant anywhere in the U.S. (of perhaps about a dozen plants) during the next three years would be a violation of probation in this case.

- The production supervisor, who took orders from above, paid a $2,500 fine, and was ordered to 250 hours of community service and three years of probation.

- The plant manager paid a $5,000 fine and went to federal prison for a year and a day as a felon.

I was not in the courtroom at the time of sentencing, but I was told that the plant manager was crying in tears. One can feel sorry for him and his family, and I do not know whether he could have been turned or "flipped" to testify that he was just following orders from a higher corporate officer in national corporate headquarters. In any case, the important point is that DOJ in those days did not let the lawyers representing a powerful, national corporation shield from guilt at least its on-site and clearly responsible higher-level corporate officers. Furthermore, EPA and DOJ leveraged the case to national significance and impact by putting the entire company on notice that any serious Nabisco water pollution anywhere in the USA within three years would bring the hammer down on the corporation. Even after the end of the three-year period of probation, were Nabisco to lie or pollute again, as a second offender Nabisco by EPA law would be exposed to more serious penalties. This case and others like it before the end of the 1980s were a high point of EPA enforcement, and—given the integrity then of the top leadership at DOJ and EPA's enforcement office—there were other high points then and also with changes of Administrations after 1992.[5] But EPA rides a roller-coaster up and down, and as of this writing in 2019, I do not like to imagine what the policy may be or how far EPA has fallen.

When I returned from Maryland in 1990 to head EPA's Criminal Enforcement Counsel Division, little did I know that since I had left Washington in 1988 the program had been plummeting down from the excellent Nabisco model. To both DOJ and EPA, the first Bush Administration starting in 1989 had brought in new political appointees, operatives and manipulators including some disguised as top civil servants. Slowly it became clear to me that some of these operatives just above me and in the most key positions were "get-along, go-along" types. Inside that EPA Headquarters tower former administrator Ruckelshaus had called a "glass fishbowl," in 1991 and 1992 we were all swimming in circles unseen, and the newcomers were looking away. But from around the nation, the Special Agents in Charge from the field were seeing and regularly were reporting to me and asking for my help. I was becoming more sure that soon a time would come at both DOJ and EPA when a public spotlight would be shining into the fishbowl to reveal the mismanagement of EPA's criminal cases across America. Also, because my *curriculum vitae (CV)* in government personnel records showed the Republicans in power that long ago I had been an elected Democrat in the 1970s, I wondered if I was being set up to be silently complicit, using as *kompromat* my assumed desire to be promoted by going along to get along. Or perhaps, were I to complain, there was a plan to scapegoat me. Living the ups and downs of environmental enforcement policy, and now riding on the downward track, I did not want to be blamed or even seen as complicit in the political miscarriages of criminal justice that the Special Agents were to bring to my attention.

Trouble was brewing, and the next chapter is the story of how it happened that by early 1993 I would be forced to file a whistleblower suit against EPA because of the behavior of its managers above me. Before an administrative court within the U.S. Department of Labor, a matter of public record, is Case No. 93-SDW-4, captioned "In the Matter of: RICHARD W. EMORY, JR., Complainant, v. U.S. ENVIRONMENTAL PROTECTION AGENCY, Respondent. [6] My case is hardly unique, and many non-partisan civil servants have had to fight it out with political operatives. A true pollution fighter is by definition exactly that—you have to combat the pollution where you find it. But it is not to be undertaken lightly that one little person would to sue the United States of America. What in the world had gone so terribly wrong?

---

1. In a future chapter is the story of how in 1994 I would move from domestic criminal enforcement to foreign assistance—from a national to an international orbit—working with environmental treaties and assisting foreign countries wanting to create effective pollution-control inspectorates on the U.S. model. Here it was amazing in 2002 to see the legacy of Rachel Carson go global. As I have previously related, the Stockholm Convention on Persistent Organic Pollutants—we in the business call it the "POPs Convention"—completely banned or outlawed by international law the "dirty dozen" of 12 man-made chemicals that were too horrible to be allowed to exist on this planet. Most of these 12 chemicals were the very same pesticides that Rachel Carson in *Silent Spring* was first to call out by name as deadly culprits.

2. Throughout the 1980s, the top leaders of the American government knew from scientists all they needed to know, and they came close to acting. But they failed to address climate change, they allowed the danger to more than double, and the governments of Presidents Reagan and the first Bush are the first to be responsible for what is about to befall us all. This sad story is well told in *Losing Earth: A Recent History*, by Nathaniel Rich (Farrar, Straus and Giroux, 2019).

3. Amazingly, in 2004, Lavelle was convicted again on federal charges, one count of wire fraud and two counts of making false statements to the FBI. She committed these crimes in her private business as an environmental consultant. Some people never learn.

4. These three criminal cases are numbered 86-00041, -42, and -43 in the Western District (federal court) in the State of Washington, with the defendants being Nabisco Brands, Willard Kaser (plant manager), and Wm. Parks (production supervisor).

5. See the Addendum "Combining Legal Mandates with Economics in the Application of Environmental Law." It describes the 2003 criminal case of a responsible corporate officer who violated EPA legal requirements, new with the 1990 revisions to the Clean Air Act, to implement an international law called the "Montreal Protocol." I was

not working in criminal enforcement after 1993, but from about that time EPA's Special Agents, often working with U.S. Customs officers in joint "Operation Cool Breeze," made many successful criminal cases against smugglers of illegal refrigerants. These chemicals, mostly used in our air conditioners, were destroying the stratospheric ozone layer that shields us from the sun's harmful rays.

6. In the words of the opinion of the Administrative Law Judge ruling that my case against EPA stated a good claim and could go to trial, this case is a "...whistleblower action brought under the employee protection provisions of seven federal environmental protection statutes: the Clean Water Act ("CWA"), also known as the Water Pollution Control Act, 33 U.S.C. §1367; the Energy Reorganization Act ("ERA"), 42 U.S.C. §5851; the Clean Air Act ("CAA"), 42 U.S.C. §7622; the Safe Drinking Water Act, 42 U.S.C. 300j-9(i)("SWA"); the Solid Waste Disposal Act ("SWDA""), as amended by the Resource Conservation and Recovery Act ("RCRA"), 42 U.S.C. §6971; the Toxic Substances Control Act ("TSCA"), 15 U.S.C. §2601; and the Comprehensive Environmental Response, Compensation and Liability Act ("CERCLA"), 42 U.S.C. §9610. Complainant, Richard Emory, is a former acting director of the Criminal Enforcement Counsel Division ("CECD") of the Office of Criminal Enforcement of the respondent, the United States Environmental Protection Agency ("EPA".). He asserts that he has suffered retaliation in his employment because of his work in documenting alleged mishandling by the United States Department of Justice of criminal cases involving enforcement of the federal environmental laws under EPA's jurisdiction."

Chapter 6—Speaking Truth to Power

At the close of the Constitutional Convention of 1787, Benjamin Franklin was asked, "Well, Doctor, what have we wrought—a Republic or a Monarchy?" He answered, "A Republic, Sir, if you can keep it." In 2019 when I write this, democracy is under attack by Russians hacking elections in Europe and in the USA. On top of this threat, Americans are undermining our own democracy. We have the ongoing tradition of "gerrymandering" voting districts to favor one political party over the other. There are concerted and official efforts to discourage unwanted persons from voting, spreading to many states because the Supreme Court in 2013 tore in half the federal Voting Rights Act. Using "dark money," hidden, wealthy "persons" including corporations can buy elections.[1] Today whether we can keep our democracy intact is an open question. And beyond that, our justice system is also under threat of debasement at the hands of wealthy corporations, plutocrats, and their lawyers.

My suit against the government, though EPA was the named Respondent defending the case, was really a complaint about the Department of Justice and their minions appointed to very high positions in EPA's Office of Enforcement. As historical context, prostitution is said to the oldest profession, and—as I have noted before, only half-jokingly—lawyering is said to be the second oldest profession. Indeed the legal profession first and since has always served in the halls of the rich and powerful. First were chieftains or warlords who expanded their grasp to become rich and powerful kings, supported by an armed nobility holding the lands that they ruled. Kings needed educated persons, often churchmen invoking the rules of the local religion, to help maintain social stability. In early medieval England, the King's top lawyer was a churchman called the "Chancellor," and his role was to apply the rules to keep the nobility from usurping the king. A top priest speaking Latin, he was the most important member of the second oldest profession serving the rich and the powerful. Over time, these churchmen and educated noblemen and knights evolved into lawyers.

For modern context, do read Jesse Eisinger's book *The Chickenshit Club*[2] about the perversion of too many lawyers in the Department of Justice. Until the late 1980s, federal prosecutors routinely charged individual corporate officers and rarely charged corporations. This began to change from about 1990, and over the next decade the focus switched. While a "little person" would still be charged individually, if the wrongdoer was a big business it would get away with a slap-on-the wrist, admit-no-guilt, deferred (or even dismissed) prosecution agreement with the corporation. While on usually temporary duty at DOJ, federal prosecutors found this the path of least resistance in dealing with former DOJ attorneys, now in the private defense bar, whom they do not want to offend. Too many DOJ attorneys, after they have learned from inside DOJ how to work the justice system, then seek to join private law firms to get rich. While working within the government, many DOJ lawyers avoid the hard, and future-career-damaging, work of bringing corporate officers to justice, especially within the field of financial crime. Eisinger's book documents their "clubbiness"—friendliness to defense counsel who are members of the profession that outside of DOJ is like a private club they want to join—and the resulting spread of injustice that was just beginning in about 1990 and which I was facing upon my return to EPA.

Since then, DOJ has greatly expanded its complicity in allowing the role of the corporation, historically created only to limit civil liability, to morph into also becoming a *de facto* shield to criminal culpability for the guilty human persons. The corporation is a legal fiction with the status of a "person" who can be charged in court. Irresponsible and criminal corporate officers today can usually blame their business crimes on the imaginary corporate "person," and then hide behind this new shield against any human accountability. Their private lawyers (often "graduates" coming out of DOJ) in the Chickenshit Club are very well paid for hiding corporate officers behind the fictional person called a "corporation." Federal Judge Jed Rakoff has written and spoken extensively of why this is so wrong, and at a conference on corporate crime in 2015 he said this:

> I am a big fan of individual prosecutions. I don't get terribly upset if I see the individuals responsible for committing the crimes being prosecuted if there is also some ancillary prosecution of the company. Even then I would not add that ancillary prosecution [of the corporation itself] in most cases, although there are some cases where you can make a case for it.
>
> What I fear most is not going after [by charging criminally] the people [corporate managers responsible] who [have] done it [committed the crime]. That's important for deterrence purposes. It's important for accountability purposes. It avoids all of the difficult questions when you just go after the corporation—are you hurting the shareholders, who are, in most cases, totally innocent? How much are you really achieving? What is the deterrent effect? How much can you change corporate culture? All of those questions seem to me to be quite secondary to the approach of prosecuting the people who actually committed the crime.

By early 1991, soon after I returned from Maryland to receive a "top secret" security clearance and to become chief legal advisor to all EPA criminal investigators, many of the ten EPA Special Agents in Charge (SACs) around the nation were telling me recent concerns that were affecting staff morale. They saw that the top attorneys in the Environmental Crimes Unit of DOJ had begun "giving away" EPA's good criminal cases while not charging responsible persons who were actually humans. And the top enforcement officials at EPA were silently allowing EPA's criminal investigations in DOJ's hands to produce little or nothing more than a monetary penalty paid by a corporation, the same result that could be obtained in a civil case that is cheaper to investigate and much easier to prove. I was not the only supervising EPA enforcement official to think that to misapply our few and high-cost Special Agents to prove criminal acts with intent and to a level of proof beyond a reasonable doubt—just to get a civil result—looked to like gross mismanagement causing the misallocation of scarce and valuable resources and the waste of taxpayers' money. After all, a corporation exists legally as just a piece of paper—a corporate charter, often filed in Delaware—and even if convicted in court the judge cannot put a piece of paper in a federal prison. Not only was this most serious punishment not available, but a very weak, dismissed (or even a deferred) prosecution agreement with a corporation would provide little or no real deterrence to future wrongdoing.

Records of such early misconduct by DOJ in pollution-control cases developed by EPA's Office of Criminal Investigations have been preserved in at least three reports: one prepared by George Washington University's National Law Center for then New York Congressman (now Senator) Charles Schumer who released it October 29, 1992; another report (102nd Cong., 2nd Sess. 12 [1993]) by Congressman Howard Wolpe of Michigan; and the most significant by the great Michigan Congressman John Dingell who was Chairman of the Subcommittee on Oversight and Investigations. Dingell issued his report (102nd Cong., 2nd Sess. 9-55, September 10, 1992), and what follows are short extracts and summaries from it. The Subcommittee in more than twenty cases found these repeating problems:

1. failure to pursue aggressively a number of significant environmental cases. A pattern seemed to emerge in which prosecution is strongly supported by the EPA and local Assistant U.S. Attorneys...but is rejected, or

undermined, at the senior management level of [DOJ Headquarters, "Main Justice"]...;

2. a serious lack of environmental law expertise at [the top of Main Justice]...;

3. an extremely ineffective use of limited EPA investigative resources;

4. serious morale problems within the EPA criminal investigative units and within [the ranks of the staff attorneys at Main Justice]...;

5. failure to inform the EPA of the reasons why [DOJ] management has declined to prosecute the cases, notwithstanding official requests from the EPA...; and

6. a lack of creativity and aggressiveness among some of the attorneys at the [staff level in DOJ]....

To judge for yourself, here are abbreviated summaries of the EPA six cases that are exemplary in Dingell's report:

1. In 1987, the PureGro company dumped about 3,500 gallons of pesticides (insecticides and herbicides) and fertilizers in the corner of a field in the State of Washington. Toxic fumes caused more than 21 persons living nearby to become ill. EPA investigated and DOJ indicted the company and several employees for illegally storing, transporting, and disposing hazardous waste, for misapplication of toxic pesticides, and for knowingly endangering human life. The man living closest to the dump site died within 14 months. Main Justice dropped all the charges against the responsible PureGro employees, and allowed the company to plead to a misdemeanor and pay a small fine of $15,000.

2. For more than a decade since at least the late 1970s, a Weyerhaeuser Forest Products Company mill in the State of Washington without a permit dumped a hazardous waste and a lesser pollutant into a storm drain leading to a river. A 1989

search warrant jointly executed by EPA's Special Agents and investigators the Washington State Department of Ecology (WSDE) revealed a written internal report showing beyond all doubt that for at least two years management had known of these gross violations but intentionally did not stop them. Main Justice refused to charge any individuals and ended the case with a plea by only the corporation to five misdemeanor charges of criminal negligence (despite the written proof of intent), a fine of only $125,000, and a contribution to the Clean Water Fund. The WSDE was so disgusted that it refused to be associated with the case and even refused an invitation to sit on the board to manage the cleanup fund.

3. In 1988, EPA and state investigators found that the Thermex company in 1985 had abandoned its former facility in Wyoming, leaving 27 drums of toxic chemicals and 13,000 gallons more of toxic wastewater used in the manufacturing of blasting explosives. All was left in an unsecured condition and with no permits to store or dispose it. Interviews with employees revealed that management knew of these facts and their illegality, and yet did nothing. Several managerial-level officials were ready to testify that the company's president in Texas told them to dump the stuff in a stream and said "f—k the EPA." Thermex went bankrupt, the human managers lived on, and Main Justice refused to file any charges.

4. An interstate case against Chemical Waste Management involved false statements and a cover-up of the illegal transportation from Louisiana to Alabama and storage there of exceptionally hazardous waste. The first trial in Louisiana in 1991 did result in felony convictions of several individuals. But the second trial in Alabama, where the transported waste came to rest, was more important to environmental protection, and the facts involved higher-level officials of this national company supposed to be in the business of proper waste disposal. From Main Justice, the Chief of the Environmental Crimes Section

talked the Alabama grand jurors out of any indictment, over the objection of EPA and all other enforcement officials involved, and never provided the written explanation that they requested.

5. In 1986, the Hawaiian Department of Health discovered that the Hawaiian Western Steel Company had been dumping toxic metal dust and also storing it illegally on its grounds. There had also been repeated spills of toxic waste and emissions of dangerous levels of lead through the holes in the roof of the almost derelict steel mill. The local U.S. Attorney wanted to file criminal charges. But from Main Justice the Chief of the Environmental Crimes Section and a large entourage flew to Hawaii where it is so sunny and scenic and a great place for a good time. There Main Justice dropped all charges.

6. In 1989, EPA and FBI agents observed a Mr. Van Leuzen directing dump trucks to fill the lot under his house built sitting atop poles in a federally protected wetland on the Bolivar Peninsula in Texas. He absolutely refused repeated warnings by the Corps of Engineers to stop, and he continued dumping with criminal knowledge and intent. He called in the local press and a conservative legal defense group, the Washington Legal Defense Foundation, which all opposed wetlands protection. An Assistant Attorney General in Main Justice killed the criminal case. When EPA insisted that enforcement proceed at least with a civil case, DOJ did nothing but announce a press conference to trumpet its strong support for federal wetlands protection.

Dear reader, is this the way that you want your Justice Department to handle pollution cases? These Congressional case summaries should be sufficient to allow you, my reader, to generate some of the same emotional revulsion as I did. We can draw the rational conclusion that justice is not achieved and the environment is not protected when no culpable corporate officer or employee acting with criminal intent is held responsible, punished, and deterred from doing it again. A year before Congressman Dingell's exposure of DOJ's misfeasance, in the fall of 1991 reports of dissatisfaction inside EPA with DOJ's apparently botched prosecutions were even floating to the top, reaching EPA's Presidentially appointed Assistant Administrator for Enforcement. A lawyer himself, he then asked me, as EPA's top criminal lawyer in his staff, to survey and interview the nation's ten SACs and to write a full report and legal assessment. I did so; my report covered between 20 and 30 cases (including the six related by Dingell), and I passed it up through my manager to the Presidential appointee. But presidentially appointed lawyers seldom stay long before they are gone through the revolving door to private practice. I was not surprised when this Presidential appointee suddenly resigned, perhaps to get out before getting hit by the train that was about to hit me. It was early 1992, President "Poppy" Bush was running for re-election, sometimes calling himself "the Environmental President," and the still-hidden potential for political embarrassment was obvious and extreme.

So my nationwide survey report of the SAC's discontent with DOJ came into the hands of two other persons. One was a former DOJ lawyer assigned to fill in for the just-departed Presidential appointee, and the other was a former, very high-ranking Secret Service Agent who had come to EPA rumored to have been Dan Quayle's top bodyguard in the 1988 national election campaign. Now I was to report directly to this top cop. He was very new to EPA, and he had not heard Ruckelshaus admonish us that to work inside EPA was to be in a glass fishbowl where one must assume that anything wrong will eventually become known to the public. He was always talking about following a "new paradigm," though it was never clear what he thought was wrong or missing or needed changing to improve EPA's work, while the problem at DOJ was so obvious. Yet it was clear that in the investigation of crimes of pollution, the specialized work of EPA in which he had no experience, he seemed determined to make his mark. And so he did.

Unexpectedly, this gold-badge-carrying—and for all I know even pistol-packing—lawman one day came into my office. As he was in the Senior Executive Service (SES), he carried a civil-service rank at the level of a general in the Army, while I was surely his subordinate with my rank equivalent to colonel. When he closed the door, I was instantly on edge. I knew this meant that he wanted there to be no witnesses, and I thought that I was about to get information or orders that might be sensitive or even unpleasant. But he was a clever player slow to reveal his strong cards, and instead I got some interrogation. As his first question, he asked me if I thought that my report on the many troubled cases would or could somehow avoid becoming public. I cannot say that he asked me if my report could disappear, and I cannot say that he was giving me an implicit order. He may have been asking for my legal advice, and I would like to give him the benefit of the doubt. I was silent for moment, thinking fast, but I knew instinctively that either answer could be unwelcome and might put me in jeopardy. On the one hand, I did not want to be involved in the disappearance or destruction of an important government document. On the other hand, were the document to become publicly known, I knew that as the author of this document I could be seen as causing political trouble for the top of the Office of Enforcement, now so cozy with its clubby criminal trial lawyers at DOJ who were undermining EPA cases. In the worst-case scenario for the Chickenshit Club, my report could even make trouble for the so-called "Environmental President" Bush now running in his 1992 campaign for re-election (who fortunately for me would lose to Clinton).

I answered "no," and I told him that the document was known to and existed in too many hands—including his and mine and the hands of all ten of his SACs—and our computers. It should have been obvious to him that the document or knowledge of it was dispersed already to so many other of his "direct-reports" (supervisees), above all the SACs. These supervising environmental lawmen around the nation had complained to me and sought my help as their in-house lawyer to improve the behavior of the lawyers at DOJ. The SACs had identified the mishandled cases, reviewed my report's drafts, and helped me to produce the document at the request of the just-departed Presidential appointee. None of these officers could be expected to destroy or deny the document, and too many of their staff—people among the very best of EPA's employees—also were too upset by what DOJ was doing to their cases. Yet I can understand my new supervisor's uncertainty navigating in EPA's culture that was unfamiliar to him. It is well known that Secret Service agents, being "palace guards," sometimes (and I hope not too often) look the other way when the President or other protected or politically powerful persons stray from a path of integrity.[3]

At my refusal—indeed, my complete inability—to guarantee that my report would never appear, the top cop seemed confused. He harrumphed, then said that he would have to talk with the former DOJ lawyer (who from DOJ had come to EPA supposedly "to help us") assigned to fill in for the just-departed, former Presidential appointee. I had committed myself by an irreversible "no," and I would have to bear the consequences for assembling information embarrassing to DOJ and its buddies at EPA. The top cop left my room to report to the top DOJ buddy now placed in power at EPA, and henceforth I was to be *persona non grata*. At personal risk, I had spoken truth to power. I believe that only once did I speak again directly with my supervisor. I do recall speaking with him for the last time about ten months later in November 1992, a few days after President Clinton was elected. In a closed-door meeting of just the three of us, I told him and DOJ's top lawyer buddy placed in EPA that for reasons soon to become clear, I would be filing suit against EPA.

Through a combination of circumstances and perhaps from multiple sources, in early 1992 the report that I had compiled must have come into the hands of the staff of Congressman John Dingell. They scheduled investigative interviews with me and all EPA attorneys supporting criminal investigations in Headquarters who were under my supervision. Now for the benefit of my descendants who may ever become part of a federal investigation, I hope your mama told you that "honesty is the best policy." If you are not sure about this, then please contemplate section 1001 of the U.S. Criminal Code:

> (a) ...whoever, in any matter within the jurisdiction of the executive, legislative, or judicial branch of the Government of the United States, knowingly and willfully—
>
>> (1) falsifies, conceals, or covers up by any trick, scheme, or device a material fact; (2) makes any materially false, fictitious, or fraudulent statement or representation; or (3) makes or uses any false writing or document knowing the same to contain any materially false, fictitious, or fraudulent statement or entry;
>>
>> shall be fined under this title, imprisoned not more than 5 years, or both....
>
> (c) With respect to any matter within the jurisdiction of the legislative branch, subsection (a) shall apply only to—
>
>> ... (2) any investigation or review, conducted pursuant to the authority of any committee, subcommittee, commission or office of the Congress, consistent with applicable rules of the House or Senate.

To make this perfectly clear, one's federal interrogator does not have to be a law-enforcement officer, no warning need be given that it is a crime to lie, and even if one is not talking under oath or if one is just filling out a federal paper form, this statute applies. One's interrogator can be any known or self-identified federal employee, perhaps a harmless-looking EPA biologist walking and poking around a site while asking questions and even taking a few samples. Many unlawful polluters in the field or their offices would lie to our technical inspectors without badges or guns just asking questions, and as a result many EPA criminal cases would also include a section-1001 charge as one more felony. And other statutes prohibit destroying government-required documents except on a schedule and in a prescribed manner.

The last part of the quoted law says explicitly that one's federal interrogator may include an authorized Congressional investigator. Soon enough, the day in March 1992 came when Chairman Dingell's authorized Congressional investigators were in my office sitting in front of my desk. They directly asked first whether there was a report of EPA criminal cases suspected of manipulation by DOJ, and then whether I had prepared it. To both questions, I answered honestly "yes," that at the direction of the President's former Assistant Administrator I had surveyed the nation and compiled the report. I was surprised that the Chairman Dingell's investigators did not ask me for a copy (presumably because they already had it), and I was pleased that they were investigating apparent misconduct at DOJ in EPA's pollution-control cases.

That very same day that I told the truth to Congressional investigators was my last day as Acting Legal Director for Criminal Enforcement, because my top management without explanation removed me and ordered me out on that day and into a remote, windowless office down the hall that was the size of a large closet, a bureaucratic "doghouse." At the time, I felt like EPA wanted to make me the scapegoat for being in office as EPA's top criminal lawyer when DOJ was going off the rails, even though I could scarcely have prevented or controlled DOJ's misbehavior. Obviously the truth in my report was unwanted and potentially very embarrassing to the top U.S. officials responsible for federal cases of criminal pollution. The synchronous timing of my removal from office would haunt EPA management, because it belied their later claims that the timing was just coincidentally on the day I also spoke the truth to Congressional investigators. Nevertheless, the Agency would brazenly defend and to the end deny retaliating against or scapegoating me for assembling the information as I had been ordered and for reporting accurately as I must.

Lawyers, usually prosecutors, always supervise policemen and law-enforcement officers. The previous Director of the Office of Criminal Investigations had been a former United States Attorney of great integrity, yet he was replaced not by another lawyer but by this new top cop who had last worked for elected politicians. I was perhaps the first lawyer that this top cop—as mentioned, a former Secret Service agent—had ever supervised, and perhaps he was confused about how to behave. When he removed me, EPA's top criminal lawyer, on the day I told the truth to Congress, I like to think he was just taking orders from DOJ or the former DOJ lawyer now at EPA above him and to whom he reported, but I do not know.

As fate would have it, this top cop left EPA after a few years to become Inspector General of another important part of the U.S. government. I was pleased that there were news reports that he performed there with integrity in ferreting out serious wrongdoing by powerful outside special interests and their cronies implanted within the government. All in all, it appears that before and after bouncing in and out of EPA he had an outstanding career and came down on the right side of the rule of law. I regret that he was still learning about EPA and the rule of law when he came up against me, and it is a sadness that he could not have worked well with me as so many colleagues have done. It is good to see that taken as a whole his service was good for our country, and I wish him well now in retirement too or wherever he is.

In my little doghouse on the hall across from the janitor's closet, at first I was given no duties. I could not survive without a paycheck, and I was afraid that under some pretense they might altogether fire me from the federal service. But they did not blame or fire me. I surmised correctly that they just wanted me to keep quiet, and over the spring and summer I was given some real work and I did it well, always keeping a big smile on my face. While as a kid I had often complained and talked too much, it was a good thing that by age 51 I had learned when to say nothing. Toward the close of the federal fiscal year (September 30, 1992), I expected no positive recognition. So I was astonished—and thrilled—in early September to receive two cash bonuses and three certificates of outstanding annual achievement bearing the undeniable signatures of the Acting Assistant Administrator and the Chief of Criminal Enforcement who had put me in the doghouse! Never in any previous year had I—or would any civil servant typically—received more than one annual cash bonus and one commendation certificate. With an astonishing pile of *five* awards in the same year, and doing good work in my doghouse, I might have seemed to be the best EPA employee of the year!

This cornucopia of five commendations came when everyone knew that Congressman Dingell had called a hearing on September 22, 1992, based on my report. The witnesses included EPA Special Agents and lawyers (some of whom I had supervised until I was removed) who handled the troubled cases directly. I was not on the witness list, and so I considered these multiple awards as "hush-money" for me having seemed a scared little mouse with continued silence and a low profile. After November, when I sued the government, so many awards and their signatures were my valuable armor. They shielded me by blocking any possible assertion that I was removed from my office because I was not capable. Of course, a common practice is for management to "black-ball" a whistleblower as an incompetent malcontent, whether he is so or not.

After I followed orders to write an honest report and it did not disappear, what the superiors who had trashed me did not know was that the scared and trashed mouse was also furious. Ever since they removed me from office I had been taking secret measures. During the summer, I had slipped over to Capitol Hill to meet with Congressman Dingell's staffers who had obtained my report and wanted to meet me. Already they were preparing for the September oversight hearing as to the misdeeds of DOJ. Much more time I spent secretly preparing my own case to sue alleging retaliation, abuse, gross mismanagement, and waste of expensive criminal resources investigating good cases that DOJ would crush. To do this without detection, I could not be seen having lunch downstairs with friendly colleagues who were my corroborating witnesses. So instead we would take morning and afternoon breaks, meeting in good weather outside a block away in a park hidden behind a branch of the D.C. library. Sometimes we would talk without using a government phone.

At home in Baltimore, my dear wife was afraid that our phones were tapped—and even that a parabolic antenna placed hidden in the back alley could be recording my conversations from the vibrations of our rear window panes! While I had to acknowledge that the Secret Service certainly had their tools and ways, I also knew that my wife enjoyed sci-fi and space-exploration shows on TV that were so high-tech, like the familiar workings of the hospital that employed her as an R.N. Later, in 1998 with the release of the movie *Enemy of the State*, she was ever more alarmed by the tools that could be brought to bear by a corrupt government. Indeed, the years 1992–93 were frightful and legitimately very stressful to both of us. It did not help that my father—who as a young lawyer served several years as the former Deputy Attorney General of the State of Maryland and then left to private practice—did not seem to really understand why I enjoyed and stayed working in a career for the government, and the importance to me of EPA's mission to fight pollution. Based on his long experience as a top lawyer in Maryland, my father did well know how political the all-powerful DOJ could be. I felt the weight of my father's reasonable doubts about his son preparing to take on the United States of America.

Nevertheless, before the November 1992 election I was secretly and well represented by Joanne Royce, Mick Harrison, and Richard Condit, high-minded young lawyers at a Washington foundation called the Government Accountability Project (GAP), charging a low hourly rate that I could afford. Working then at GAP as part of my legal team was Jeff Ruch, who left in 1996 to establish Public Employees for Environmental Responsibility (PEER), another nonprofit, organized to handle only whistleblower cases also coming out of the many natural-resource agencies as well as EPA cases involving pollution control. I can never say enough good about GAP and PEER, and they continue today to help many civil servants threatened or in peril like I was. Today PEER is headed by another very good man, Tim Whitehouse, who was my close colleague at EPA during some years in the early 2000s.

As GAP's co-counsel on my case was my truly wonderful friend, Richard H. Mays, an accomplished attorney from Arkansas who once had run for Congress. He had been with me one of the three Branch Chiefs in the Hazardous Waste Enforcement Task Force from 1980 to 1983. Then he rose to become the best Deputy Assistant Administrator for Enforcement that I ever saw at EPA, before he left us too soon in 1987 for private practice in Washington. I will forever be grateful to him for helping me *pro bono publico* (meaning without a fee, as being for the public good). I will remember forever his wisdom embellished with folksy charm, reminiscent of North Carolina's Senator Sam Ervin of the Watergate investigation that brought down President Nixon. For example, Richard Mays would say, "He's as smart as a tree full of owls" after a person who had said something stupid had left the room. Or if another lawyer said something that was in fact smart and persuasive, he might have said, "You are a lawyer who could talk a dog off a meat truck."[4] I advise my descendants to never underestimate a person who says, "I'm just a simple country lawyer." A lawyer coming from the heart of America in fact may be as smart as a fox and the next Abraham Lincoln, in no way dense like a block of wood attractive to owls.

Just after the country lawyer Bill Clinton (also from Arkansas) was elected President in November 1992, I finally felt safe enough to go on the offense. I knew that there was an increased risk that I would be fired from federal service when I broke cover to sue the government, but "Poppy Bush" was on the way out of the White House. Yes, it is good, "down-home" advice to wait and "don't taunt the alligator until you have crossed the creek."[5] But were I to be fired during the transition to the new Administration, I felt quite sure that, both to the lawyers from Arkansas and to the public, I would become a *cause célèbre.* Surely the new Administration would rescue and restore me right after Inauguration Day, and my case was ready to start now. So with GAP and EPA's former Deputy Assistant Administrator for Enforcement as my co-counsel, we filed my case suing EPA, charging waste, abuse, gross mismanagement, and retaliatory discrimination, and I emerged from the shadows.

Soon GAP was asking me if I wanted to appear on some national TV shows (*60 Minutes, Primetime Live, Inside Edition*). I think that GAP for itself would have liked the publicity of national exposure, but much to their credit they never pressured me to go on TV. From hard experience as a former politician (in the 1970s, when elected to the Maryland legislature), I knew that reporters would often either misquote or quote someone accurately but out of context, giving the public an erroneous impression. I had no goal to become a public figure, I just wanted to restore my reputation, shine a light on a problem within the justice system, and in the future see DOJ better support the hard work of EPA's criminal investigators. I had been a state prosecutor for a few years but never been a federal prosecutor, and I wondered if I had "the creds" (cop talk for credibility) in the media to take on the United States Department of Justice.

My decision to keep a low profile may have been a mistake, because there was no public pressure on EPA and helping GAP during the year that my case was litigated. Nevertheless, GAP first defeated the government's motion to dismiss my case, and then GAP took depositions of EPA officials both implicated and as witnesses. We came to a point in late 1993 when a trial was imminent, and the pressure was on the government more than me. GAP was ready to go to trial by the fall of 1993, but I realized that I could craft a settlement better tailored for me than the judge would likely or even could order for me. Often a judge will restore a wronged *plaintiff* to the *status quo ante*. But I did want to return to the position of being the legal advisor under the supervisors who disrespected me and had not yet moved on. Equally distasteful would be to return to being responsible for approving all criminal case referrals to DOJ without clear indications yet at DOJ of reform that would end its sabotaging EPA's good work. Often a judge will restore pay or benefits, but mine had continued—I had lost no pay or benefits needing to be restored. And a judge could not or might not order for me some very much wanted and novel relief to which EPA might agree were I to settle and the court need only ratify the settlement.

In addition to reimbursement of about $10,000 that I had paid in heavily discounted legal fees (for legal work worth much more than $100,000 in the dollars even of those days), specifically I knew that I wanted EPA to agree to:

- a transfer from criminal investigations into international work for EPA,
- a year of "sabbatical" time working and residing in a foreign capital or a foreign university, where I could pick up skills and languages useful to EPA in foreign assistance work,
- a fast track into the Senior Executive Service, and
- an EPA plaque for my wall featuring an honorary, gold EPA Special Agent badge numbered 2 and reading "for outstanding service as Acting Director of the EPA Criminal Enforcement Counsel Division of the Office of Criminal Enforcement, from October 1990 through March 1992, by providing sound legal advice and national management to achieve a fair and effective program of environmental criminal enforcement."

While the trial of my case perhaps could have become national news, and GAP might have liked to take my case through a trial, again much to their credit my counsel there and the management of GAP never pressured me. If I had been independently wealthy and did not need a job, with such a strong case I might have gone through with the trial so as to achieve with the impact of a judicial order that would have become public news and could have helped reform the system. But I could not afford to risk a loss, and I did not want to win without receiving some desired remedies available only by settling. Meanwhile, President Clinton's new Attorney General Janet Reno seemed to be talking about perhaps taking at least some vague steps to clean up the Justice Department.[6] In 1993, I could not know that Attorney General Janet Reno and the new Congress would fail to remove the corporation as a shield to personal culpability, and that the future DOJ's failure to prosecute corporate executives would grow to the point that today the Chickenshit Club rules the roost.

So I settled my case, and to cover up the cost of its misdeeds, the government required me to sign a non-disclosure agreement (NDA).[7]

On December 8, 1993, GAP issued a press release titled "Whistleblower Settlement for EPA Enforcement Chief—EPA Lawyer Revealed Interference in Major Prosecutions." In part the press release reads:

> This settlement vindicates Mr. Emory's concerns regarding the failure to effectively prosecute environmental crimes during the Bush Administration. Although the substance of the agreement is confidential, Mr. Emory agreed to dismiss his complaints in return for what he describes as 'very favorable' terms....
>
> On March 20, 1992, in response to questions by subcommittee investigators, Mr. Emory identified the existence of a list of problem cases. That same day, he was removed from his position as Acting Director of the Criminal Enforcement Counsel Division....
>
> The list of problem cases was subsequently turned over to Congressman Dingell by the EPA. Cases on this list which later became the subject of Congressional hearings included the Rocky Flats, PureGro, Thermex, ChemWaste, Hawaiian Western Steel, and Weyerhaeuser cases....
>
> Unfortunately, we have yet to see evidence that DOJ and EPA enforcement policies and personnel have changed significantly, and the enforcement problems identified by Mr. Emory appear to be unresolved.

Yes, it was done and over. I had risen from the depths of despair on March 20, 1992, the day when I was both removed as national legal advisor and answered honestly to the Congressional investigators about the existence of my report. Yet the system was not reformed—to this day the "corporation" is a cunning legal device and corporations still shield criminally responsible corporate officers. I no longer wanted to be a part of this charade of justice. Going forward, for many years my most admired friends and now former colleagues, the Special Agents, would greet me in the halls of EPA Headquarters, where I was considered to be a minor yet brave hero who by supporting them had to pay the price of no longer working with them. Because I had faced down some very powerful people, I was considered to be somewhat of a "sacred cow"[8] for most of the next 17 years working in the same building.

So by my choice I left the criminal investigators to move to a desk in the International Compliance Assistance Division in the Office of Federal Activities, from which I would work with colleagues in EPA's Office of International Activities. Let us recall that I had studied international relations at Yale, but (for reasons I cannot now recall or understand) upon graduation in 1963 I had neglected to stand for the State Department examination that could have opened an alternative path to the law. Now 30 years later at age 52, I was so excited that a new, outer orbit beyond U.S. borders was about to become my life! I would address pollution anywhere and everywhere, using law (national environmental law created since 1970 and even newer international environmental law[9]) that had not even existed in the 1960s when I was in college. For the next 17 years, international missions would take me to many places in the world, and I would address many foreign delegations visiting Washington to study USEPA. Christmastime 1993 was the best one of my life; my wife and I were so relieved and happy, and in my elation I imagined that I was off to save the world! In fact, starting in 1996 we would be packing our suitcases when EPA would send me to live and work in Paris.

But while I had saved my career, I could not save the world. I know today that, with business as usual, the world remains in dire peril from climate change.

I hope that none of you readers ever face such an ordeal—but if you do, you must either get (or embody within yourself) good legal advice. Though at the time I suffered great anxieties, today I realize that I came through intact because I had become a mature lawyer. I was age 51, and I had gained unusually broad experience, having worked (1) at the national and state (sub-national) levels, (2) in all three branches of government and also in the private sector, (3) in criminal, civil, and administrative law, and (4) as a manager and supervisor for 11 years, mostly of other lawyers. My position was at a high level of trust and national importance in which I would not have been serving if not able.

GAP and I realized that I had a strong case because I was removed from my position on *the very same day* that I spoke honestly to Congressional investigators in my office, an otherwise inexplicable fact flashing red indicating retaliation. Also, I saw and avoided the pitfall that I could destroy my case should I reveal any secrets. Although I held a "top secret" security clearance, I did not possess any classified or national-security information, so this was not a problem. But I did have access to plenty of confidential information in criminal cases under investigation, and I recognized an obvious danger should I improperly reveal them. Without identifying any confidential informants, other sources, methods, or spin-off investigations contemplated or ongoing, my report that eventually went to Congress only covered what already had been or could properly be made public about cases entirely and forever closed.

If you, my reader, are ever facing such a pickle, if compliance even with a lawful order would violate your deep and rightful principles, your first thought should be to quietly get another job, taking a good recommendation from your wayward boss. Your experiencing routine mismanagement and serious though ordinary policy differences are not enough to allow you to claim the protections afforded a whistleblower, and you had best put a smile on your face and move on. Doing what I did is only a last resort to be taken in extraordinary and propitious circumstances where you have firm and corroborating evidence and outside support for your allegations of fraud, waste, abuse, or gross mismanagement. And if you are not a mature lawyer like I was, or even if you are, you had better get one. Even the kings of old knew when they had to call for help from the world's second oldest profession. I hope that you too can find a litigating foundation like the wonderful Government Accountability Program or PEER. What could be better than a respected nonprofit organization actually wanting to take your case to advance its mission of integrity as well as your mission of survival. If you have a good lawyer-friend like Richard Mays who will take your case without charge, you too will be fortunate indeed.

After about a year probably questioning my sanity to sue the U.S. government, even my father—surely a "big-bucks" private lawyer himself yet also with many good works done *pro bono publico*—was quite impressed when he read GAP's press release and realized that I would still have a job, and a very good new one too. I felt that in his eyes I had finally proved myself and become a man. To end this part of my story, here is a favorite poem[10] that—despite Rudyard Kipling's overtones of 19th-century British imperialism—may well guide a person, female or male, as badgered and beset as I was:

> If you can keep your head when all about you
>   Are losing theirs and blaming it on you,
> If you can trust yourself when all men doubt you,
>   But make allowance for their doubting too;
> If you can wait and not be tired by waiting,
>   Or being lied about, don't deal in lies,
> Or being hated, don't give way to hating,
>   And yet don't look too good, nor talk too wise:

If you can dream—and not make dreams your master;
    If you can think—and not make thoughts your aim;
If you can meet with Triumph and Disaster
    And treat those two impostors just the same;
If you can bear to hear the truth you've spoken
    Twisted by knaves to make a trap for fools,
Or watch the things you gave your life to, broken,
    And stoop and build 'em up with worn-out tools:

... If you can talk with crowds and keep your virtue,
    Or walk with Kings—nor lose the common touch,
If neither foes nor loving friends can hurt you,
    If all men count with you, but none too much;
If you can fill the unforgiving minute
    With sixty seconds' worth of distance run,
Yours is the Earth and everything that's in it,
    And—which is more—you'll be a Man, my son!

---

1. This work to expand corporate impunity to damage our country was done by the same kind of lawyers who brought us the Supreme Court case *Citizens United v. Federal Election Commission*, 558 U.S. 310 (2010). This opinion held that corporations are like natural people having First Amendment protections to spend big money that is "dark" (from secret sources) to support or defeat political candidates. Three-quarters of the funding for the biggest political action committees now comes from just 100 American plutocrats, and often unidentifiable special interests steadily undermine our elected representatives. Instead of making good laws, Congressional representatives often spend half their time daily "dialing for dollars" to win re-election. And it was lawyers—*lawyers*—appointed to be Justices on the Supreme Court who approved this decision that is devastating to our democracy!

2. *The Chickenshit Club: Why the Justice Department Fails to Prosecute Executives*, especially p. 93 *et seq.*, by Jesse Eisinger (Simon and Schuster, 2017). I cannot say whether today's Attorney General, William P. Barr, who was also Attorney General for the first President

Bush during 1991–93, is responsible for the degradation of justice that I am describing. It may or may not be a coincidence that during Barr's first tenure as AG the formerly valiant DOJ began to morph into the Chickenshit Club. To determine the cause for this would require research beyond the scope of my book, and Eisinger does not cover those earlier years.

3. A member of a "palace guard" who does not know when to look away will soon be sent back to the rank and file of the regular force in uniform. Let us recall the behavior of Secret Service agents who assisted President Kennedy, who was constantly whisking members of the first oldest profession in and out of the White House. One memorable lady friend was Judith Campbell Exner, reputedly sleeping also at the same time with Sam Giancana, the head of the Chicago mafia. Perhaps she carried messages between the two men, and there are reasons to believe that the CIA hired Giancana in failed attempts to assassinate Cuba's Fidel Castro. Another former Secret Service agent, who had guarded the home of the widow of President Johnson, and after he too retired came to work at EPA, told me that if Lady Bird Johnson had asked him to bring in the morning paper in his teeth and crawling on all fours like a dog, he would have done it! He was a nice guy, and I do hope he was mostly joking with me.

4. In fairness, I think that this saying is attributed to the former TV news anchor, Dan Rather from nearby Texas.

5. Actually this also probably was said by Dan Rather, and I cannot remember what Richard Mays said—but it would have had no less down-home charm and deep wisdom.

6. In fact, even in the Obama Administration from 2009 to 2017, the Chickenshit Club was hard at work, and it is so today. As we know from the words of Judge Rakoff that began this chapter, after the "Great Recession" in 2008 caused by federal deregulation allowing Wall Street and the banks to become casinos with paltry reserves, no banks considered too big to fail or their responsible corporate officers were ever brought to justice by the Obama Administration. Instead, the taxpayers "bailed out" the banks, which then handed out bonuses and "golden parachutes" to many of the highest and most responsible bank officers. This sad deterioration of federal justice stands in sharp contrast to how in the 1980s many state attorneys general did jail

many hundreds of corporate officers of state-chartered savings banks that had also operated recklessly.

7. Today we are seeing called into question NDAs that the current President requires of White House staff. In an ideal public service, there would be more transparency. Government managers should not be able to cover up their misbehavior and its costs, and within the government a NDA usually should be against public policy.

8. The Hindus venerate cows as sacred, and they roam the streets with impunity. Nobody can hurt them or try to carve off a chunk of meat. For the next 17 years, within the halls of EPA most enforcement staff and top officials knew that I was somebody to be respected and not to be the object of political pressure or any prohibited personnel practice. I never expected or ever had any more trouble.

9. Any person wanting to be an international environmental lawyer may well obtain the textbook *International Environmental Law and Policy*, by David Hunter, James E. Salzman, and Durwood J. Zaelke (Foundation Press 5th ed., 2015). An earlier edition of this would be my "Bible" in my international work from 1994 to 2011.

10. "If," poem by Rudyard Kipling, first published in *Rewards and Fairies* (Doubleday, 1910).

Chapter 7—Saving the Earth

To INCREASE THE RISK FOR INTENTIONAL POLLUTERS, and to deter more of them, I had worked almost ten years from 1983 to 1992 helping to build EPA's Office of Criminal Investigations, happily until 1993, after which I transferred to work in EPA's foreign-assistance effort. From today and going forward with much greater support from the U.S. Department of State (State), to save the climate the U.S. will need to restore and greatly expand the work of its small group of international pollution fighters of which from 1994 to 2011 I was so fortunate to be one.

My readers today surely want to stop the air pollution, mostly from burning fossil fuels, that is killing our climate, and to do this we need to understand, appreciate, and plan to replicate or expand the reach of the Montreal Protocol. To begin this chapter, here is the story of this amazing scientific and political success. The 1987 Montreal Protocol was and is targeted at another set of man-made air pollutants creating hidden stratospheric ozone holes. Thirty years ago, these holes in the sky were another problem in the air about to cause global death and destruction, but not the same problem as the greenhouse gases bringing on the coming climate chaos.

The science of ozone holes can be quickly summarized. Synthetic ozone-destroying chemicals, mostly refrigerants and propellants, were manufactured to contain chlorine. The first such refrigerant, chlorofluorocarbon (CFC, also called R-12), starting in the 1930s was installed—eventually globally—in refrigeration and then air-conditioning. Sooner or later from any closed system a chemical will leak, and before 1990 it was not illegal for technicians to vent refrigerants directly into the air when repairing or replacing equipment. From the Earth's surface, CFCs slowly rise into the stratosphere, where relatively scarce natural ozone serves as a sun screen or filter. (While ozone at the Earth's surface contributes to air pollution, problematic low-level ozone is not to be confused with stratospheric ozone that is beneficial.) Just one molecule of highly reactive chlorine can catalytically destroy over 100,000 molecules of stratospheric ozone, and the damage is measurable as chlorine monoxide. As natural ozone diminishes, excessive solar ultraviolet radiation comes through and down to the Earth's surface, damaging and eventually killing many forms of life.

By the 1980s, in the late winter of the Antarctic, the seasonal loss of ozone was almost complete and was expanding into some remote yet populated areas of the southern hemisphere. Humanity's continued ignorance about the effects of man-made chemicals had taken us far down a path toward the destruction of nature's stratospheric ozone layer that shields us from the UV radiation of unfiltered sunlight. While my limited admiration of President Ronald Reagan includes his sunny disposition, we are so fortunate that this conservative leader was not entirely blind to science. With Margaret Thatcher, the "Iron Lady of Toryism" and Prime Minister of the U.K., President Reagan would actually listen to scientists. Even though no injury at the Earth's surface was yet measurable to a scientific certainty, the Antarctic ozone hole would become a proven fact, as would the effects of too much UV radiation. You would not think that skin cancer is a good thing, but perhaps we all are lucky that by 1987 Reagan had just had two skin cancers removed. Reagan and Thatcher would agree to a treaty that would save life on Earth from the ozone-depleting family of man-made air pollutants. And the rest of the world would follow their lead.

During the mid-1980s, only a few years after 1974 when scientists in California and the Netherlands first merely theorized the horrific danger ahead, British and U.S. scientists were able to measure and prove beyond doubt that there was a large hole, an almost complete loss of stratospheric ozone seasonally over

Antarctica. The 1985 Vienna Convention for the Protection of the Ozone Layer had called for more research, and the World Meteorological Organization and the United Nations Environment Programme (UNEP)[1] in 1986 published a report of more than 1,100 pages that alarmed leaders around the world. As a result, in 1987 many nations signed the Montreal Protocol on Substances That Deplete the Ozone Layer. Reagan was no pollution fighter, yet he signed the Montreal Protocol and sent it to the U.S. Senate, which ratified it unanimously. It entered into force in 1989, since then has been signed by 197 parties including the European Union (EU), and is the first treaty to have been ratified by all members of the U.N.[2]

We owe our health, and our grandchildren their lives, to the many politicians around the world who did not deny the science or declare it all to be a hoax. Had Reagan and Thatcher not led the way, the National Aeronautics and Space Administration (NASA) recently stated that by end of this 21st century many of our grandchildren and many forms of non-human life would have been harmed and eventually fried, killed by ultraviolet solar radiation—through deadly mutations, skin cancer, cataracts of the eyes, suppression of the immune system—not to mention also radiation damage to building materials, plastic, crops, and marine organisms. Popular opinion considers the big success of Reagan's presidency to be his pressure on Communism which led to the dissolution of the Soviet Union. But in the 1990s the U.S. mishandled foreign-assistance efforts to reform Russia, which since has slipped back into Tzarist Putinism.[3] Reagan's big success that continues today is his key role in saving the stratospheric ozone layer.

We must remember the scientists responsible for their work, whether done theoretically, in laboratories, in the field, or in the halls of power. Mario Molina and Sherwood Rowland of the University of California and Paul Crutzen of the Netherlands were awarded the Nobel Prize in 1995 for first theorizing this danger in 1974. British scientist Joseph Farman was named by the Queen a Commander of the Most Excellent Order of the British Empire for his work in the 1980s using research balloons to collect the first physical evidence of an ozone hole over the Antarctic. Harvard scientist James Anderson was honored by the United Nations and received Harvard University's Benson medal for the most valuable contribution to science by a member of the faculty. Amazingly, he convinced the U.S. National Aeronautics and Space Administration (NASA) to convert two U-2 spy planes to science. They collected conclusive evidence, and then Dr. Anderson effectively helped to forge broad international awareness of the danger.

International law is not self-implementing but relies almost entirely on national laws and enforcement. So in 1990 a Democratic Congress amended the 1970 Clean Air Act[4] to authorize the U.S. to meet our obligations under the Montreal Protocol, and EPA within its Office of Air created a new unit, the Stratospheric Protection Division. But after a new law redefines formerly innocent old behavior to be illegal, if the behavior continues it becomes criminal, and so it was with ozone-depleting chemicals. The old and damaging chemicals were taxed to speed their phase-out, and tax evasion is always an enticement to some miscreants. And as we saw with smuggled wildlife, the U.S. is a vast black market for so many things.

It was no surprise that EPA's criminal investigators immediately began catching smugglers of tax-evading chemicals regulated by the new federal law. In the 1990s in sunny and hot Miami, illegally smuggled refrigerants for air conditioners were second in street value only to smuggled crack cocaine. Working closely with the U.S. Customs Service, EPA's Special Agents caught and charged smugglers individually and personally. Unlike many pollution cases involving big companies, usually there was no supposedly "reputable" corporation that DOJ's "Chickenshit" lawyers would allow to block personal culpability and protect persons operating just like *narcotrafficantes.* Convicted smugglers usually received stiff prison sentences and forfeited to the government their vehicles, real estate, bank accounts, and other fruits and tools of their criminal enterprise. And the new U.S. law prohibits even residential technicians from intentionally venting refrigerants when home equipment is repaired or replaced. The Clean Air Act has teeth that are taking a bite out of those taking a bite of the ozone shield.

The genius of the Montreal Protocol had many aspects, one being that it allowed time for existing air-conditioning equipment to wear out and need to be replaced anyway. Over a 20-year period, chlorofluorocarbons were phased out globally and finally banned in 2010, and new chemicals were required in new, replacement equipment. Because of the gradual approach, there has been no damage to the booming business of air conditioning or to the overall economy, and while the required replacement equipment may be somewhat more expensive, it uses less electricity. This treaty has been very successful at minimal cost and with enormous benefits.

During the 1990s, scientists were disheartened to learn that refrigerants also were "greenhouse gases" and that one molecule of CFC can be as much as 7,000 times more climate-damaging than one molecule of carbon dioxide (CO_2). While we self-centered humans party on enjoying our air conditioning and refrigerated food, how ironic it is that our refrigerant chemicals escaping into the air have been warming the planet and melting the Arctic ice. Now polar bears without ice cannot catch seals, they are starving—and drowning if they try to swim too far in the now ice-free, open sea. Yet a surprise benefit of the Montreal Protocol is that it has also been able to slightly slow climate change. Banning CFCs in 2010 certainly helped both the ozone layer and the climate.

Taking action to gradually ban and replace CFC illustrates how wisely and well the Montreal Protocol is implemented by an international process of continuous reevaluation, research, and revision to find and allow only the right chemical(s). But CFCs' replacement refrigerant, hydrochlorofluorocarbon (HCFC, also called R-22), while not as bad as CFCs' rating (7,000 times more climate-killing than one molecule of CO_2), was still 1,900 times worse than a molecule of carbon dioxide. So HCFC is just a transitional chemical, now also being phased out and to be banned by 2030. New equipment installed today must have the third-generation chemical, hydrofluorocarbon (HFC, also called R-410a), but it too has a per-molecule rating that is too high. Being about 1,500 times worse for the climate than one molecule of CO_2, HFC too is likely to be phased out and banned in the future.

So within the framework of the Montreal Protocol, the world's search continues for the right refrigerant, both climate-friendly and ozone-friendly, that will be phased in and then required to protect the ozone while at the same time protecting the climate. It may be surprising that the ultimate ozone-and-climate-friendly refrigerant could be CO_2, with the lowest and baseline per-molecule climate-killing rating of just 1 (one)! When being emitted from smokestacks and exhausts in enormous volumes, CO_2 certainly does destroy our climate. But when confined in very small volumes sealed in refrigeration equipment, cheap and readily available CO_2 will not threaten the climate. This is a very encouraging possibility now getting a close look and pilot applications.

Since the 1980s, during the late winter of the northern hemisphere, scientists have documented ozone thinning over the Arctic and extending down over well-populated northern latitudes. And there are places of very short-term ozone loss localized above tall thunderstorms that rise to pierce the stratosphere over the United States. Ozone holes have not been eliminated, and the work of this treaty must continue for generations if not forever. Yet as knowledge expands, the Montreal Protocol has been revised many times, and with global cooperation, its controls will be upgraded many times again. These ongoing revisions also will be effective, as almost all nations are continuing to fulfill the Montreal Protocol's evolving legal obligations.

Today it is clear that the treaty is slowing stratospheric ozone loss and stabilizing the diminished ozone layer. Considering that the treaty has also reduced the emission of these same chemicals that are powerfully damaging to the climate, the Montreal Protocol is the world's best story of success linking environmental science and policy. Perhaps the only treaty with a planetary, life-saving effect that compares is the 1963 ban on nuclear weapons testing in the air, space, and sea. Today of all environmental treaties the Montreal Protocol stands as the most important and effective, and it is the model for taking effective global action on climate change. There is still time to hope that humanity will act decisively to control greenhouse-gas air pollution that also is man-made and globally dispersed.

From ozone-hole theory in 1974 to proof of danger, followed quickly by the Montreal Protocol in 1987, this breakthrough took about 13 years. This stands in stark contrast to the tragic situation for climate change—first correctly theorized in 1896, conclusively proved by 1979 well before the end of the 20th century, and yet with no effective treaty more than 120 years later to the day of this writing. In the decades since the 1980s until now, the problem has accelerated to the point that the weather is becoming abnormal and more damaging—some people would say "weird." During this time, we have lost decades that would have allowed a gradual phase-out of climate-changing "greenhouse gases." A climate treaty effective to save life on Earth now may not have time to allow all fossil-fuel-burning equipment to wear out to scrap or salvage value when it would need to be replaced anyway, as does the Montreal Protocol. The longer we continue our human blundering and dithering, the more we will need a tough climate treaty requiring disruptive implementation on an emergency timetable. This will not be like visiting the dentist for a scheduled appointment, it will be like an ambulance ride to the emergency room. And we will not have an international emergency vehicle, unless UNEP is greatly expanded and empowered.

From 1994 until retiring in 2011, as part of the undersized and under-supported EPA effort, my international work was under the controlling umbrella of the State Department. State did invite and bring to the U.S. a steady stream of foreign environmental officials, academics, and leaders in civil society interested in learning about many of the effective programs of our government that in my day were much admired. Thoughtful foreign visitors coming by invitation of the State Department realized that the U.S. is the world's third most populous country, made up of diverse people arriving from everywhere. These visitors saw that our 50 states are in many fields sovereign and independent, almost like separate countries. They saw that in these ways, the U.S. is a microcosm of the world, yet our economy was so strong even though capitalism was regulated. Twenty years ago, our visitors often remarked how clean were the water and air in the world's then biggest economy, and they knew that if EPA had not been created in 1970, the air and water of the U.S. would have been as dirty as India, China, or anywhere in the world since then and today. They saw that because the U.S. had controlled pollution without impairing the booming U.S. economy, it would be reasonable to think their nations could do so too. In the years 1994–2011 when I was doing international work, most of EPA was not captured by U.S. special interests that favor pollution and in 2017 would begin to dismantle EPA. Many visiting delegations wanted their own countries to have an EPA on the U.S. model.

These good people coming from around the world needed our help, and today they still do. Many of our distinguished visitors came from nations that in recent decades had to a greater or lesser extent democratized, developed, and grown a middle class less tolerant of pollution. Their nations usually had some environmental laws, but not the ability to put them into effect, and how to enforce environmental law was a topic often requested by visiting foreign delegations. Perhaps every other month for 17 years, I would be called to EPA's Office of International Activities to present the topic. To experience the interaction with foreigners visiting Washington, usually I would invite one or two of the law-student "clerks" or interns in the Office of Enforcement to come along. My students and my audiences seemed to enjoy and to be encouraged by my overview of what the biggest and best EPA in the world was doing to enact and enforce pollution controls. After meeting people coming from everywhere wanting to effectively fight pollution in their countries, my students and I always came away feeling uplifted and energized. And we could sense our visitors' yearning for more U.S. leadership to solve global pollution problems. The world knows that U.S. leadership can be highly effective, and that without U.S. leadership a global success is unlikely.

I would provide an overview or survey talk for an hour, and upon requests to focus upon specific subtopics of enforcement I would bring in specialized experts. To give you a glimpse, here is a list of ten features that I would describe as key to making EPA enforcement so effective:

- a pollution-control enforcement capacity that is national and operates in parallel or concurrently with subnational units of government (we call them "states") and acts whenever a state fails to take timely and effective action to control pollution;

- a national environmental enforcement training institute available to national, state, local, and tribal officials;
- a national pollution-control police capability (like the Office of Criminal Enforcement, from which I had just come);
- a system of national, administrative pollution-control courts to handle most (for EPA, about 85 percent) of all violations not considered deserving of the most serious punishments in the national courts of general jurisdiction (we call them "U.S. District Courts");
- a dedicated unit within the justice ministry (we call it our "Department of Justice") that provides expert representation in the national courts of general jurisdiction, on both the criminal and civil-enforcement sides;
- legal requirements that holders of permits to pollute must conduct extensive self-monitoring, self-recordkeeping, and self-reporting to EPA (as well as allow official inspections);
- a principled and economics-based methodology for penalty-assessment calculation, applied with a process having anti-fraud controls;
- even-handed and stern control of federal facilities (meaning all installations of the U.S. government, including military bases) that are held to the same standards as private enterprise;
- encouragement for marginal violators to self-audit and reform their operations to come into and stay in compliance, applying incentives that are principled, monitored, and not amnesty or a substitute for enforcement; and
- transparency, meaning systems to assure that the details of concluded cases are public information, and that enforcement statistics and results are available on the Internet.

EPA's rationale for foreign assistance to improve global pollution control was sound—to create a fair and level global economic playing field. If world-wide there were elevated and equivalent environmental standards and enforcement, fewer U.S. jobs would be lost by moving production offshore. But this very good economic argument rarely seems to win over too many Congresses where corporate-globalist special interests can rule supreme. Too many so-called "American" corporations roam the world seeking the cheapest labor costs and the dirtiest (most polluting), lowest-cost production facilities in countries with governments that look away. An "American" corporation moving a factory to a foreign land really does not want to find there an effective foreign government that will force it to meet high foreign standards modeled on the EPA standards with which that the corporation must comply for any factory it might leave behind in the U.S. As "special interests," these corporations make big-money political contributions on Capitol Hill. Starting in about 1997 just after I began my international work, more and more of the elected Congressional representatives seemed not to like EPA in general, did not like EPA enforcement in particular, and above all could not see any reason why EPA should be allowed to teach its highly effective enforcement techniques in foreign countries. While EPA was not absolutely confined to a small, domestic box, we were denied Congressional funding sufficient to meet many foreign requests for our assistance.

This is not the only reason that, in my years, sadly the size of EPA's international effort was puny, falling far below the worldwide need. Just as disappointing was the passivity and poor support from our powerful State Department, which operating globally controls any international activity by any part of the U.S. government. State was sometimes working at cross-purposes, environmental concerns being only one folder of its full portfolio of matters in the national interest. While State often needed EPA technical expertise to advise foreign nations, State also regarded EPA's Office of International Activities (OIA) as something of a competitor. Indeed, at the times when it was not under weak leadership, OIA could get competitive and "squeak up" when State was lackadaisical about environmental protection while promoting liberated international commerce. And how could EPA not push hard for more global cooperation to control pollution, seeing how State was distracted by so many problems abroad including the unplanned consequences of gratuitous U.S. adventurism into foreign wars? I expect that State's distracted obliviousness may be worse than ever today, even while the planetary impacts of environmental degradation are becoming more obvious every year.

With spotty and unreliable support from the State Department, and extremely limited funding from Congress to EPA for foreign assistance, my opportunities to help were too few. But when an outside requestor invited me to help, I would help from my desk in Washington. When offered outside funds for my travel, I did go to lecture, consult, or assess environmental ministries within other nations and to collaborate with public international organizations. These foreign missions included work in Chile, China (for the Asian Development Bank), the Czech Republic (for the USIA/USIS), three times in El Salvador (for USAID and in cooperation with the UNEP), the Dominican Republic (for the UNEP), the Republic of Georgia (for UNEP), Morocco (for USAID), Canada and Russia (both for the OECD), twice in the Kingdom of Saudi Arabia upon its invitation, twice in the U.K. (for the Royal Institute for International Affairs), and Venezuela (for the World Bank).

I am very pleased and proud to have been the only expert from EPA and among just 30 experts from the world invited in 2006 by UNEP to come at U.N. expense to Nairobi, Kenya. But I did not take this or every possible trip just because I was invited and the inviter's money was available. I also declined the U.N.'s second invitation at its expense to continue this work in Sri Lanka (formerly Ceylon), even farther away to travel for two days of work. Instead, I wrote and sent my expert's paper[5] for the meeting, and so I am listed as a contributor to the "Manual on Compliance with and Enforcement of Multilateral Environmental Agreements," issued by UNEP's Division of Environmental Law and Conventions (Nairobi, 2006). When the world decides to save itself from the coming climate catastrophe, it will need to have an effective climate treaty and to know how to apply it. This manual[6] and similar documents published by the OECD will stand as essential guidance to governments, too long overlooked, but available for rediscovery to be dusted off and used before it is too late.

As the basis for an effective climate treaty that includes decisive enforcement, the world may need to dig much deeper. Consider from 530 A.D. these words:

> By the law of nature these things are common to mankind—the air, running water, the sea, and consequently the shores of the sea. No one, therefore, is forbidden to approach the seashore, provided that he respects habitations, monuments, and buildings which are not, like the sea, subject only to the law of nations.

It is time to reactivate an ancient and fundamental principle antedating capitalism—the principle that some natural resources are held in public trust that sovereign governments must and will at all cost protect from devastation by private interests. These resources are said to be owned by all humanity and by no one person, within the "public-trust doctrine." It stems from the Code of the Byzantine Emperor Justinian of the sixth century, who held that the air, navigable waters, and intertidal zone are open to all and cannot be appropriated or impaired by private ownership or use.[7] It may be that Emperor Justinian in 530 A.D. only intended to include air subjected to bothersome local pollution, as he could not have imagined that man could pollute the entire global atmosphere and thus threaten most living things. Yet the *Magna Carta* in 1215 declared that the King must protect forms of wildlife (not only fish). In modern times, strong U.S. laws have been enacted. The Lacey Act of 1900 was expanded in 1969 to become the Endangered Species Act, protecting both plants and animals. We also have the Migratory Bird Act of 1913, the Marine Mammal Protection Act of 1972, and more that give teeth to the protection of natural species. The potential expansion of the public-trust doctrine to include both the now-endangered human species and the climate—and far more extensively the nature of the air and sea that support both—could save humanity on our planet.

A concept from modern international law (traditionally called "the law of nations") is the "global commons," defined to include shared natural places or realms that cannot be owned or even normally inhabited (except temporarily in a vessel, life-support capsule, or high-tech survival structure). The global commons include the "high seas" (oceans beyond territorial waters), international straits where there must be freedom for all peaceful navigation, space, the atmosphere, and Antarctica— places where no one nation rules so all must share and rule cooperatively without allowing overexploitation.

International law is essential to give meaning to the inclusion the atmosphere in the concept of the "global commons," and a number of treaties do address the atmosphere. But the Montreal Protocol explicitly addresses only ozone-destroying chemicals in the stratosphere (not in the troposphere where different greenhouse gases cause climate change). The Convention on Long-Range Transboundary Air Pollution (LRTAP, 1979) does not address key climate-killing air pollutants including CO_2 and methane. The several climate-change treaties (beginning in 1992 with the U.N. Framework Convention on Climate Change, UNFCC) have been too weak to bring the sub-stratospheric air and atmosphere squarely within the public trust and under strong, sovereign protection.

A federal civil lawsuit by Our Children's Trust, filed with a diverse cross-section of American youth as attractive plaintiffs, now seeks to revive the public-trust doctrine. Winning this case would add humanity to the list of natural species to be protected by the sovereign (our national government that replaced the King) in America. To this end, the lawsuit would stop activities of the U.S. government that subsidize or otherwise cause damage to the air and the climate. Winning would define these as natural resources essential for there to be livable habitat for the plaintiffs as land mammals not covered by the Marine Mammal Protection Act. The young American plaintiffs in this case, who will suffer the terrible effects of climate change, also seek "intergenerational equity" with my generation that since at least 1979 has knowingly refused to effectively protect the climate. In play is the 14th Amendment to the U.S. Constitution that requires "equal protection," arguably now between human generations.

This is no ordinary lawsuit, and NGO partners are taking similar actions abroad in countries including Norway, the Netherlands, and even Pakistan. Pushing this case for the planet and our grandchildren are Oregon attorney Julia Olson and more of the best members of the American natural-resource and public-interest bar, good and gutsy lawyers. Sadly, they are resisted at every step by the soon-to-go-through-the-revolving-door "Chickenshit" lawyers in the Department of Justice. Yet presiding federal Judge Ann Aiken has approved the case for trial, sensibly stating that "...exercising my 'reasoned judgment,' I have no doubt that the right to a climate system capable of sustaining human life is fundamental to a free and ordered society."[8]

To receive such opportunities as I have described, the pollution fighters who follow me will be well-advised to take up writing. Invitations come if one develops a platform or profile as an "expert"[9] whose abilities can be known from papers presented and published works that can be cited. Having long been a scrappy bureaucratic lawyer, realizing in 1999 that I needed to build some recognition as a thinker and writer, with the permission of my EPA management I began to write.[10] The fruits of this work would support my successful applications to teach at a German university, and to consult again in Paris at the OECD in 2002.

My writing also created opportunities to collaborate with three units within the U.N.—all places where some demonstration of academic or professional writing is a well-regarded credential. As a result, in 2004 I became a Special Fellow of the United Nations Institute for Training and Research (UNITAR), with a week in Geneva, Switzerland, learning about the U.N. while conferencing with their environmental law program. During 2005–06, working in Washington I was detailed part-time as consultant to UNEP's Division of Technology, Industry and Economics in Paris, and several times after that in their missions abroad I worked closely with them. In a preceding paragraph, I have described my work in 2006 with UNEP's Division of Environmental Law and Conventions (DELC).

While elements of the United Nations too often may be justly criticized, I worked with and saw first-hand that UNEP, DELC, UNITAR are staffed by knowledgeable, caring, and dedicated people. But in those years, and I assume today, UNEP lacked adequate numbers of staffing and funding. To do what must be done to save our planet now losing its life, many more pollution fighters like my former U.N. colleagues are needed. Surely someday many more international positions will become available for well-trained young people who want to join the fight. They will also need much more legal authority, including the ability to take effective inspections and even enforcement action, a topic to be addressed in the upcoming chapter on climate solutions.

You may recall that a year of "sabbatical" time—residing in a foreign capital or a foreign university (where I could pick up needed skills and languages)—was one element I wanted to see included in an EPA settlement agreement that would take me out of domestic criminal investigations and into the international orbit. I have mentioned that EPA imposed a clause to prohibit me from discussing or revealing here the contents of the signed agreement; the government does this when it does not want the public or other employees to know what the government has done. Yet this agreement—legally binding EPA to make things right—sitting in my personnel file open to management, necessarily would come into the hands of two gentlemen who would be my new EPA manager and supervisor—Richard Sanderson, Director of the Office of Federal Activities, and Michael Alushin, Director of International Compliance Assistance Division, located within OFA.

While the OFA led by Dick Sanderson oversaw EPA's international compliance work, in a second division he oversaw also all U.S.-government compliance with the National Environmental Policy Act (NEPA). A controversy around the spotted owl, a species facing extinction threatened by logging in the northwest U.S., resulted in his making high-stakes decisions invoking NEPA. Despite political pressure, he bravely supported a case referral to the President's Council on Environmental Quality, and in the ensuing litigation a federal court ruled in favor of NEPA. This little owl received protection under the Endangered Species Act, and it can be said that Dick Sanderson famously saved the spotted owl.

At about the same time, I too was fluttering about, looking to settle down in a roost that would not blow away in a political storm. Dick had just hired EPA's top enforcement lawyer for air pollution, Mike Alushin, to head OFA's International Compliance Assistance Division, and then he quickly hired me coming from heading EPA's Criminal Enforcement Counsel Division. I was thrilled to be on this new team led by the best managers. They were happy to fulfill the legal obligations that my settlement placed upon EPA management following my mishap in the Office of Criminal Enforcement. Both Dick and Mike routinely shared with me their deep wisdom, always acted with integrity, and made sure that EPA fully complied with its settlement obligations.

So it would come to pass with their help that on several occasions between 1996 and 2002, my wife and I would live and for USEPA I would work in Europe. My collaborative relationships with the OECD and the U.N. would develop and be useful spreading EPA's effective methods to parts of the world. While employees of the U.S. military, FBI, Customs, and other federal agencies quite often work and reside abroad on foreign assignment, even for an experienced and capable EPA employee a foreign assignment is very rare. Sadly, EPA seldom provides such opportunities, and only because of my extraordinary personnel file would I be able to build needed foreign-language and operational skills. These would to become very useful in my work offshore in a world of nations needing many more effective EPAs like ours was in those years.

Financially, my wife and I were supposed to be treated like any officer of the U.S. military or other U.S. government employee assigned abroad with his family. But during my 17 years of international work, the State Department only provided two very short-term government apartments in Paris, and State paid for just one two-day mission when they sent me to give a speech in the Czech Republic. So at EPA expense, it was for me to find and rent two longer-term apartments in Paris. To rummage for money for our other travel and living expenses, the scramble expanded. Amazingly, the nation of Japan paid to EPA $10,000 because it so valued my OECD work in Paris in 1996. The Fulbright program in 2000 paid our travel and living expenses for me to teach in Germany, where the university provided an apartment. When such outside support was not offered and EPA money was needed, Dick Sanderson for me would go directly to the highest officials in the Office of Enforcement, which was headed by a Presidential appointee. Administrative staff would be ordered to scour the Office's budget for money from somewhere. This was pathetic. Plenty of time was wasted, and not just for me were opportunities lost. EPA could not fund all requests from the waiting world asking for EPA's help in general, and often mine in particular, to improve environmental protection in countries really needing our help.

You may recall also that "a fast track into the Senior Executive Service" was another element I wanted to see in my settlement agreement. Lest you think that as a pollution fighter I lacked ambition, it deserves explaining why I never sought entry into the SES. By now I was near the top of the civil service (with a GS-15 rank equivalent to a full Army colonel or captain in the Coast Guard). Next above me at "flag rank" (equivalent to a general or admiral in the military) in the non-military, civil service was the SES. But their pay was capped at the level of the pay of a Member of Congress, not much more than I was earning. The SES positions are almost entirely managerial, most being Office Directors with the authority to hire and fire scores of people working under them. As some underlings might say, the SES must know how to "kiss up" (please the political appointees above to whom they directly report), "kick down" (rate the performance of staff and determine their careers), and "push and pull" sideways among all powerful SES Office Directors all fighting for limited funds and staff. Yes, there is also inter-office cooperation, certainly when ordered from above to stop bickering—or better yet when both offices can voluntarily agree to cooperate.

By about 2000, I was thoroughly absorbed in my new work, hands-on and sometimes in the field overseas with foreign assignments. I was enjoying exposure to foreign cultures in on-the-job training essential to make a person a more capable international pollution fighter. I came to realize that as a senior staffer I would be far happier doing the tasks and projects inherent to this work and interacting directly with the wide world. My appointment to the SES almost certainly would have immediately brought me home and taken me out of international work, where SES positions were so few. By staying out of the SES, I would avoid spending most of my time fighting turf, budget, and personnel battles within the EPA bureaucracy. And I would avoid most duties of supervision. Since my first day EPA in 1980 until 1992, I had also had my fill in 12 years of supervising other attorneys, a task that some say is like "herding cats," meaning it cannot be done!

Furthermore, as I have already implied, over the years I had observed that scum as well as cream may rise to the top of the civil service. Too many members of the SES were there as charming and clever sycophants who had ingratiated themselves to, and been overly promoted by, too many political appointees. Most political appointees would in a few years be gone out though the revolving door to multiply their paychecks in big corporations or law firms. In their turbulent wakes, the worst political appointees behind them would leave a floating residue of the most obsequious and obliging staffers as their appointees to the SES. Of course, good political appointees would appoint good staffers who did merit promotion to the SES, such as most of my SES supervisors in the Office of Federal Activities. The first two, Alushin and Sanderson, and during my time in OFA all but one of their successors, were good managers who treated me like a partner and as much as they could put foremost the success of our international environmental mission. After 1993 I was happy to stay as a staffer in a happy place, working for "the cream of the crop," whom I gladly supported and helped to meet the demands of the political appointees above them.

Over the years, I have found that one of the joys of being a pollution fighter at EPA is the generally high quality of the non-managerial staff. They come from an interesting, wide variety of scientific and professional fields, and most share a deep commitment to a clean environment and good public health. While EPA at an intellectual level is like a university, the diverse capabilities of the well-educated colleagues are not applied to educate students, though there are often student interns. The Agency wields tremendous power to reshape the huge U.S. economy so that it does not poison itself with pollution. And my staff-level colleagues also doing EPA's international work, though numbering too few, with very few exceptions were all excellent.

To conclude the story of my travail at EPA, I have tried to show how good people thinking of joining a government, a business corporation, or even a nonprofit organization, need to be watchful and ready for mismanagement followed by mistreatment. But if you can keep your head clear, the good times will prevail and can be wonderful. To encourage you who are considering the U.S. civil service, it is time to tell you about what my wife and I regard as the best times of our lives. These were the three happy occasions when EPA sent me to work and we lived in Paris, and the one occasion when I taught law and we lived in Germany. I was proud to take to Europe what they were looking for—my knowledge of environmental law, and my expertise in how to reduce pollution—and to fight polluting lawbreakers using effective enforcement.

In Europe I would learn much and gain perspective on the United States. Gradually I realized that many European nations achieve much higher levels of energy efficiency and recycling. I saw much better conservation of farms, often in greenbelts near cities preserved from American-style suburban sprawl. I saw cleaner and more efficient transport by trains, bicycles, and not just cars, and much quicker uptake of climate-friendly energy sources. For many activities beyond direct pollution fighting, to protect the environment the U.S. is backward and a poor model for the world. To find so the many of the reforms needed in the U.S., it is essential to look instead to Europe, and we will begin to do so in the next chapter of adventure abroad.

---

1. The United Nations Environment Programme (UNEP), or *Le Programme des Nations Unies pour l'Environnement* (*PNUE*), comprises about 500 international civil servants. It is the part of the United Nations focused only on the environment, with small offices in Nairobi, Kenya; Paris, France; and elsewhere. Among too many duties for such a tiny secretariat, UNEP provides the administration for most environmental treaties that are global, of which there is a large and growing number.

2. A "protocol" is a supplement to an existing treaty or convention. *Ozone Diplomacy*, by Richard Elliot Benedick (Harvard University Press, 2nd ed. 1998), written by the chief U.S. negotiator for the Montreal Protocol, well describes the melding of economics, science, politics, and diplomacy that lead to such a planet-saving success. The last chapter covers lessons learned that must be applied to climate change before it is too late. For the role of NASA, see *NASA and the Environment: The Case of Ozone Depletion*, by W. Henry Lambright, No. 38 in the series "Monographs in Aerospace History" (NASA SP-2005-4538; May 2005), online at https://history.nasa.gov/monograph38.pdf. Robert Watson, director of the unit of NASA responsible for U.S. research into the stratospheric ozone problem, and other involved scientists deserve far more credit for doing the full-time hard work needed to reach the right result than does Ronald Reagan, though he did at least apply the final, top-level political decision to support sound science.

3. Also in 1987 in his speech in West Berlin, using his best Hollywood skills as the "Great Communicator," this actor pronounced, "Mr. Gorbachev, tear down this wall!" Thereupon, the leader of the Soviet Union, Mikhail Gorbachev, opened the Iron Curtain across Europe, of

which the Berlin Wall was just a small part. Eastern Europe peacefully threw off the yoke of Russian occupation or domination. But unlike the Montreal Protocol, this accomplishment of Reagan's was temporary, not lasting. The U.S. in the 1990s botched its efforts to bring Russia into the fold of civilized nations, and by the 2000s it was becoming clear that Vladimir Putin would become a neo-Tzar, crush progress inside Russia, create a kleptocracy of oligarchs serving him, and more than ever try to flood the world with climate-destroying oil and gas.

4. The Clean Air Act Amendments of 1990, 42 U.S. Code sections 7671 and following sections comprising Subchapter VI "Stratospheric Ozone Protection," are U.S. national laws fully implementing the Montreal Protocol.

5. My paper entitled "Improving National Enforcement for Better Governance Implementing Multilateral Environmental Agreements" contains my recommendations requested by and submitted to the "Meeting of Experts Called by the Division of Environmental Conventions of the United Nations Environment Programme, Sri Lanka, January 21–22, 2006." This paper is attached in an addendum at the end of this book.

6. "Manual on Compliance with and Enforcement of Multilateral Environmental Agreements," UNEP Division of Environmental Law and Conventions (Nairobi, 2006; ISBN 93-807-2703-6).

7. For the recent rediscovery of the public-trust doctrine, an ancient legal concept that has the potential to save the planet, we should thank a professor of environmental law at the University of Oregon. Her book is *Nature's Trust: Environmental Law for a New Ecological Age*, by Mary Christina Wood (Cambridge University Press, 2014).

8. This case to watch is *Juliana, et al., v. The United States of America, et al.,* case no. 6:15-cv-01517-AA in the Eugene Division of the U.S. District Court for Oregon.

9. An amusing definition of "expert" is "someone who knows more and more about less and less until eventually he knows everything about nothing." To be an expert as I was in international environmental compliance is indeed a narrow field, but I never reached a point that I knew everything about nothing! During my EPA years, non-governmental expertise in this just-emerging field was built steadily by

the International Network for Environmental Compliance and Enforcement (www.inece.org), with its office in Washington, D.C., led by Durwood J. Zaelke. Any person wanting to be an international pollution fighter may well obtain the textbook that he co-authored, *International Environmental Law and Policy* (Foundation Press 5th ed. 2015).

10. An incomplete list of significant professional publications of which I am the author, an author, "ghost writer," or a substantial contributor is published as an addendum at the end of this volume.

Chapter 8—Missions to Paris

IN MY NEW TASK OF "SAVING THE WORLD," from 1994 on I would not be doing U.S. law enforcement or dealing with violators. While there are exceptions, the rule is that the U.S. usually cannot enforce our laws in places beyond U.S. territorial limits. From chasing down polluting criminals in America, it would be a big jump to working in France with pleasant and cooperative international civil servants coming together from many nations to work in a public international organization, the Organisation for Economic Co-operation and Development (OECD, as spelled in British English). I would also be collaborating with officials of national governments, academics, and progressive leaders of civil society in their countries. Such people must be regarded as colleagues who should not be approached with suspicion (though there may be official corruption), and as partners who in any event cannot be compelled by U.S. law to do anything. Some international partners would be corporations. After in the U.S. only seeing polluting corporations fully deserving criminal investigations, I fully appreciated coming to know some good corporations that are not deceptive or recalcitrant. Yes, many corporations will do the right thing, especially when they can make money at it or at least avoid a bad reputation with retail consumers.

I was and still am nostalgic about the thrill of my 14 years of pollution-crime busting, starting in Maryland in 1979 and ending in Washington in 1992. To all who love the Earth, I do recommend hands-on detective work, pollution fighting in the field, and prosecutions in court. Having done this myself, I was much more effective—while experiencing vicarious fun—working from Headquarters as legal advisor far from crime scenes and courtrooms. But after 14 years as a pollution-crime fighter working in the world of victims, perpetrators, witnesses, pollution inspectors, and law-enforcement officers, I had come to see the world like a cop. This is natural when every day you only see the worst, the criminal cases. And any good lawyer is a "professional skeptic." On top of this, I was irritated by how I had been treated, even though I had emerged intact from my ordeal of litigating with EPA. I needed to process my anger and accomplish a total attitude adjustment. I achieved this because my new managers in the Office of Federal Activities were so welcoming and forthright when I began there in 1994. And with their support, learning international environmental work was so fascinating. By 1996, I had processed my anger, my attitude changed to one of trust, and my expression became the smile of a happy pollution fighter.

By 1996, with regular home study I had reactivated what I had learned 30 years earlier in college studying one year of the French language. To my ear, it is a most beautiful language, like *les chansons des oiseaux*, the singing of the birds, elided and lilting. To know the language would be useful living in Paris where EPA had plans to send me. I would be a temporary international civil servant loaned from the U.S. to the OECD (*en français, l'Organisation de Coopération et de Développement Économique, OCDE*), an international think tank with treaty-making powers. I was to bring my USEPA expertise to the OECD's Environment Directorate, which would control and supervise my work. This Directorate was led by an Englishman, and within the OECD the official language is English properly spoken and written in the British way. I would have to eliminate American colloquialisms and acronyms, and when writing to spell like an Englishman. In presentations I would learn to talk using what I call generic English "international speak," which is useful almost anywhere abroad when one is trying to be understood while speaking English.

Finally, in early spring of 1996 at age 55, with travel orders from the U.S. government, I arrived with my wife Donna in Paris.

A big American smile was stamped firmly on my face. But immediately we noticed that in Paris almost nobody smiles unless you have been introduced. A person walking in the street with a constant smile may be seen as having lost his mind. My hard-won smile soon faded to expressionless neutrality. I would have much to learn about a culture of great sophistication that would endlessly fascinate and astonish. During almost each of the next nine years, from time to time I would work in Paris and on holiday visit somewhere in France, and Donna and I came to believe an old saying: "Everyone has two countries, his or her own—and France." What follows in this chapter will mix pollution-fighting business with some pleasure in describing the customs, traditions, and sights that we, like anyone, would encounter while residing on official assignment abroad—and the joy a pollution fighter may find there while working hard to save the world.

I arrived for my first day at work, just west of Porte d'Auteuil with my desk four floors up in a modern, satellite office building located a mile or two from the OECD's main building (that is a former royal *chateau*). My small, windowed office looked northwest to the Bois de Boulogne. All was in the 16[1] *arrondissement*[1] and not far from the center of Paris. Looking out my office window, I could see parked down at the curb of the Boulevard de l'Amiral Bruix (along Boulevard Périphérique) two white vans. From the side door a man emerged buckling his belt, and in the front passenger seat a woman appeared. After counting some money, she rolled down the window and began to greet and wave to any likely man walking by on the wide sidewalk. With a proper permit, it was all perfectly legal. I was hypnotized watching, then mildly disgusted, then bored by it all. So I sat down at my desk to start work, thinking—exactly what I was supposed to do in the think tank that is the OECD.

Founded in 1961, the OECD is sometimes considered to be the civilian counterpart to NATO, and it remains a key part of the international "architecture" that the U.S. government helped to create following World War II. Its original role was to aid the restoration of western civilization by helping to reconstruct and then to maintain effective civilian governments, economic progress, and free trade—all preconditions to a peace in Europe that, after two ghastly world wars, this time must be lasting. Early members included Japan, Australia, and New Zealand. Thirty years on, after the collapse of the USSR, the OECD expanded to include many Eastern European countries. To help its member nations make good decisions, the OECD collects the economic, social, and environmental statistics for the world, and researches and publishes guidance documents describing good-government policies and programs. Being treaty-based, it can bind its members—an outstanding example is the OECD convention (treaty) establishing the illegality of bribing foreign government officials.

Later that morning I took a break, walking out the front door of the building and a short way to the west. I was attracted there by the open-sided, temporary tents on the wide sidewalk that had just been set up by the city. Vendors were arriving to sell the most beautiful and delicious assortment of fresh fruits, vegetables, flowers, fish, meat, and of course—chocolates! At mid-day, out from their apartments came well-dressed older ladies, some with hats and gloves, and all with recyclable cloth shopping bags (no throw-away, blow-away bags here). Scarcely noticing the parked white vans nearby where business also was thriving, the proper ladies had come to buy their evening meals and *parler* with their neighbors. I was glad to see the elegance among the tawdriness, and amused that neither seemed to notice the other so nearby. I could see that Paris was truly the beating heart of French commerce.

Economists may be the dominant profession within the OECD, which generally opposes government ownership of productive assets and would discourage or time-limit government subsidies. The OECD encourages capitalism, provided it is regulated to control its destructive social and environmental excesses, above all being market fraud, market collapse, monopoly, and intolerable pollution. Consequently, the OECD promotes open, free, and fair markets. My task in 1996 and 1997 was to study the details of the then very new German approach to recycling. Germany in 1994 had taken the household waste-management function out of the hands of local governments, and placed the responsibility on "producers," meaning manufacturers and retailers. Such innovative privatization was of great interest to the OECD's economists, and this new policy needed serious study.

My main colleague in this work was Claudia Busch, known then as Claudia Fenerol. She had formerly been at EPA Headquarters and was now living and working in France, where she became and remains a close friend to Donna and me. We would research, write, and the OECD would eventually publish the fruit of our work as "Extended and Shared Producer Responsibility—Phase 2 Framework Report," OECD, Paris, 1998.[2] With our friend Claudia, I am proud to share principal authorship of a significant guidance-to-governments document.

German-style recycling is the most effective in the world, and consistent with the OECD's economic views, the role of government has been minimized—no socialism here. After Germany in 1994 privatized management of such ordinary trash and garbage (not to include hazardous waste that must be specially managed) and as at the OECD we documented this program's free-market virtues, soon most of the EU followed Germany's lead. The essence of Extended Producer Responsibility (EPR) is that by law the manufacturers and retailers own the materials in their containers, packagings, and even some products. They own them forever, with responsibility extending through endless recyclings, recoveries, and reuses. Among themselves, they sell and buy the recycled materials in a new, free market that would not exist without government regulation as invented by modern Germany.

The wisdom and fairness in shifting this burden is that manufacturers and retailers should bear responsibility for all that they set loose into commerce. Valuable secondary materials should not and need not become waste and a heavy burden upon local governments able to deal with the mess only by building ugly landfills and incinerators making air pollution. While manufacturers and retailers by law also are required to achieve high recycling rates, also they are incentivized to do so. They save money because they do not have to buy large quantities of expensive virgin materials, often coming from far away, to make their new containers and packagings. Because of the greater efficiency of the private sector, many European countries recycle at about twice the rate in the U.S.

To my knowledge, in most places in the U.S., residential waste management remains a function of the local governments, which looks like socialism (although we Americans could never admit it!). There has been little or no interest in privatizing all management of ordinary trash and garbage as does EPR. But another OECD member was serious about learning how to improve household recycling. In Paris I had a meeting with a diplomat of the government of Japan who handed me a check for $10,000 made payable to the U.S. government. It was Japan (not our State Department) that to support my work reimbursed EPA for most of my travel expenses. And a few years later, in 2000 my wife and I would experience EPR personally in our lives when I would reside in Germany to teach law there. In an upcoming chapter about *Deutschland*, I will describe the satisfaction of living with the best recycling in perhaps the best-managed large nation of the world. The flip side of every problem is an opportunity, and we will see how the producers would turn their new burden into a profit center by keeping for themselves all the valuable materials that were no longer wasted, buried or burned by local governments.

From my first day at work in environmental protection, I knew that without proper regulation in a completely free market the corporations will offload dirty waste and intolerable pollution upon the people and the planet. And I knew that some misbehavior can be tolerated and mitigated with proper regulation. But at the end of my first workday in the think tank in Paris, all big thoughts almost ended. Two women outside in the street were loudly contesting who would be first with exclusivity to engage men standing waiting for a rush-hour bus along the Boulevard Périphérique. These women had dressed themselves in the belief surely shared by the OECD's economists—that in a free market, a good, profit-making enterprise would foster and reveal the display of an attractive product. But each woman sought to drive out her competitor and to monopolize the bus-stop marketplace, a shameless and blatant practice of which no OECD economist would approve. In this way, they exceeded the bounds of benevolent capitalism, and they were not friendly business competitors.

Personally, as a member myself of the second oldest profession, I was impressed to see that members of the first oldest profession could be as scrappy as any defense counsel I might have met opposing me in a courtroom.[3] After watching this working marketplace for a while, I closed my computer, gathered my belongings, and walked out from the think-tank building to board a bus toward home. By then, the bus stop was calm—both women had gone elsewhere, I suppose to deliver or perform contracted services, so I escaped any aggressive merchandizing.

In the calm before my bus arrived, I continued to think. OECD economists would generally approve of the *bona fide* delivery of goods and services as advertised. This is essential to maintain the integrity of a free market in a regulated product that is tolerable with required permits and frequent public health inspections of the delivery mechanisms. This French regulatory approach is not unlike the environmental permits and inspections, officially required by environmental protection agencies, to achieve the accepted social goal—to keep factories operating with pollution controlled down to scientifically acceptable levels.

After riding a first bus about two miles west, I transferred to a smaller bus that would take me past Roland Garros Stadium, the site of the French Open, a springtime tennis grand slam. Then walking, I passed a small building, wondering why it was surrounded by concrete crash barriers and watched by police from their car. Looking closely, I realized it was a neighborhood synagogue that must have been threatened, and I knew that Paris was experiencing Algerian terrorism. I walked on, finally reaching the Seine River in a remote residential neighborhood with no stores or street activity. I came to a nondescript, completely unmarked, three- or four-story apartment building. Behind an unusually strong fence, with a locked, solid metal gate, all at least eight feet tall, it looked like a small prison. But I was home.

Punching in my secret code to open the gate, I entered, threw my best Coast Guard military salute and a smile to the young man watching the lobby, and passed through and then back out again to an almost separate, one-story little building standing in the garden in the rear. Amazingly, it looked like a modern design straight from America, with glass walls on three sides looking out in three directions at a walled garden, and it contained just one spacious, complete apartment. Inside I found a most beautiful sight—waiting for me with two wine glasses and looking very French was my adorable wife, Donna! Since in the civil service I held the rank of a full colonel, as guests of the State Department we were living temporarily in the guest quarters reserved for any high-ranking U.S. Marine Corps officer who might arrive. The young men in the apartment building were Marine guards not on duty at the time at the American Embassy.

In 1983, a suicide bomber had driven a truck packed with explosives into the U.S. Marine barracks in Beirut, Lebanon, killing 241 U.S. military personnel.[4] In a separate suicide terrorist attack that same morning, 58 French soldiers also had been killed in their barracks two miles away. So for the U.S. Marine guards in Paris, their residence was this remote outpost, intended to be unidentifiable. To be always inconspicuous, our Marines traveled to and from the Embassy in unmarked cars and civilian clothes. Never in our lives had Donna and I been so safely hidden away from the world. We would not be so hidden away again until 2002 when, for another 15 weeks working in Paris, we lived behind another watched gate in a sometime safe house belonging to a former CIA officer.

Isolated with the U.S. Marines on the far edge of the 16th *arrondissement* in Boulogne-Billancourt, we were not where we wanted to be downtown, *au centre-ville*. We were waiting for our lease to begin in the 5th *arrondissement*, for an apartment I had rented in Georgetown from a State Department retiree before we left the U.S. After about ten days we left the Marines' residence, piled our belongings into a taxi, and about 25 minutes later arrived in the Quartier Latin (Latin Quarter). One floor up on the southeast side of Place de l'Estrapade, our rental was in the former home of Denis Diderot, who with Voltaire and Rousseau had been an outstanding writer-philosopher of the 18th-century French Enlightenment.

Through the building was a driveway leading to the stables in back. Its massive carriage doors at the street contained a smaller, pedestrian door, and we entered to meet *Madame la Concierge* who lived on the ground floor. She walked us up the grand staircase to the *premier étage,* and she opened the door to our two-bedroom apartment. It was one block from the Pantheon (a massive, 18th-century, neoclassical church converted to a burial place for French heroes), the Mayor of Paris lived around the corner with police guarding his door, and 75 feet from our front door was a *patisserie* selling *pain aux raisins, baguettes,* and *croissants.* Best of all, surrounded by elements of the Université de Paris (everywhere known as the Sorbonne), students filled the streets of the Latin Quarter. It was like our Bolton Hill neighborhood where we lived for forty years in Baltimore yet far more fascinating, and for the next three months it would be our home.

My government daily expense account was far less than that of a corporate employee; it did not cover dining out for every meal. Consequently, Donna and I went looking for food stores. To shop for the first time in an *épicerie* would be a cross-cultural exploration. A French grocery store uses the metric system, a foreign language, French francs (in 1996), a then-unusual weigh-it-yourself process for many fruits and vegetables that then had not yet come to the U.S., and many of the foods not only are different but have unrecognizable names. Computing so many variables at once made me dizzy. Seeing about 500 varieties of cheese and not knowing how to buy one slice of it, we lurked near the cheese counter, watching as several French customers dealt with the cheese man. After ten minutes, we were brave enough to try.

We pointed to the wheel of cheese from which we wanted a small wedge. The *fromagier* placed the wheel on the top of the counter, put his knife over a usual-sized wedge, looked at us expectantly, and said *"plus ou moins?"* Wanting *plus du fromage,* we made a slightly wider motion with our hands, he moved the knife a bit to make a larger slice, and asked, *"Ça va?"* I like to think we answered affirmatively, *"Ça va,"* but we may have said "Okay." He sliced our wedge, wrapped it, and gave it to us with a smile. Probably we said "*Merci, Monsieur,*" and he said *en anglais,* "Great! Enjoy the cheese and come back again." Realizing that he (like many of the other shopkeepers we would meet) was playing us by not wanting to reveal too soon that he spoke English, we smiled, and he became a regular friend. The *poissonnier* did not speak English, but fortunately "salmon" sounds like *saumon,* so from the fishmonger it was not a problem for Donna to buy that fish—or any type to which she would point while nodding her head "yes!"

For U.S. government employees going to live and work in France, on a list of recommended reading were the helpful books *Culture Shock—France* and *French or Foe.* While a large grocery or department store is not so personal, the first rule of good manners upon entering a street-front *patisserie* or any small shop is simple: introduce your presence with *"Bonjour, Madame* (or *Monsieur).*" And the only polite way to leave is with *"Au revoir, Madame,"* thus to suspend the relationship properly. Upon your second visit, you may be rewarded with a first smile from the shopkeeper. Entering or departing in silence is *gaucherie* and marks one as an American. And there was so much more to learn—such as do not take your monetary change from the hand of *la caissière.* To avoid human touch, the cashier will place it for you in a small tray atop the counter, from which the customer scoops it up before saying *"Merci, et au revoir, Madame."*

The Latin Quarter provides endless fascination. Where we lived in the center of it all, Place de l'Estrapade, is a short walk from Place de la Contrescarpe, which may be the most authentic and colorful little plaza in Paris; it is always lively and sometimes a movie set. Just around the corner behind the northeast side of Place de la Contrescarpe, you may discover on a wall the sign quoting Ernest Hemingway, *"Tel était le Paris de notre jeunesse, au temps où nous étions très pauvres et très heureux"* ("Such was the Paris of our youth, at a time where we were very poor and very happy"). If this does not bring tears to your eyes, then see on the corners of buildings and walls many permanent little signs, each with the name and date in August 1944, marking where the Germans shot dead the named resistance fighter[5] during liberation of the city.[6]

Place de la Contrescarpe sits at the top of the former Roman road leading south, today called Rue Mouffetard, bustling with cafés, charm, and local commerce. At the bottom of Rue Mouffetard, you will find a church where, some centuries ago, the priest became so famous for miraculous cures that the King became jealous. As an historic sign tells us, the King decreed that a parchment be nailed to the church door reading, "By order of the King, from today God is forbidden to work miracles in this place." In both 1981 and 2017, American Presidents (the present one openly aping a king) imposed a somewhat similar edict upon the USEPA when they attempted to shut down its miracles of pollution prevention, mitigation, and crime busting.

What I have described is just a taste of what is to be found throughout Paris; everywhere the enchantment, melancholy, and amusement abound and overwhelm. As Hemingway also wrote, "There is never an ending to Paris." Though Donna and I would never be natives, as residents we became more than tourists. Immediately we obtained our Metro ID cards, bought our unlimited monthly Metro passes (that also worked on the buses), and began to explore, leaving the expensive taxis to the tourists and wealthy businessmen with unlimited expense accounts. If for more than three days (and not on official business in a dangerous city) you find yourself visiting any civilized city, do make the small effort to learn to use the mass transportation. You will be well rewarded with complete freedom to go quickly anywhere at low cost, and you will not be worsening the air pollution that you will be breathing caused by cars. The Paris Metro when not on strike was always efficient and mostly beautiful. So were the French ladies who on the Metro carried shoulder bags containing their tiny poodles, their little heads peeking out and snuggled warmly next to cozy *poitrines.*

Such sights soon become unremarkable. While mingling among the real people of the city, you feel the unfamiliar becoming normal, and you can relax in growing satisfaction. Venturing out into quiet, good neighborhoods, you discover excellent and less-expensive little restaurants. Here family dogs are always welcome, each dog well behaved and quieter than an average American tourist might be. You may encounter a unisex bathroom with no urinal, two separate stalls, and just one sink to share with an unknown lady. French ladies are completely free and equal, living life on their own terms, and men had best behave in any place and at all times unless invited not to behave. You may come to realize that the French have achieved a higher level of civilized conduct. You may imagine yourself living comfortably in France for a long time or in your next life.

Of course, I am talking only of Central Paris, beyond which the suburbs can be dingy and dangerous. Europeans generally value their old buildings, and often their cities are the opposite configuration from Baltimore (one of many American cities where the wealth is in the suburbs and much of the urban core is abandoned to rot). But on the beautiful main Metro number-one line in downtown Paris, it could be rough—once on a train I saw a rider end the fight with a pickpocket by smashing his tormentor's head into a vertical stainless-steel pole. A problem solved, and at the next stop the failed pickpocket stumbled off the car holding his head. Before seeing this and becoming totally alert and prepared, on an earlier Metro my own wallet was plucked from my pocket. As I turned and pulled back my fist to hit a man (who appeared to be Algerian), he held up one hand in the signal to stop, he pointed down to the *quai* and lying there was my wallet. When it was being lifted from my pocket, I had grabbed his wrist, and he had dropped my wallet onto the Metro platform. I scooped up the wallet, we parted with a slight smile, and neither he nor his friend behind me had to threaten me with his unseen knife. Everyday European criminals do not carry pistols; this was not America.

Because of my height (being six feet, three inches tall), my clothing, and overall American look, I was a "mark," an obvious target when standing in the Metro car. But Donna would be sitting aside demurely, *toujours très chic* dressed in her standard *haute couture*[7] and imitating a *Parisienne*, wanting never to be seen as *Americaine*. To complete her disguise, strong-minded as ever and in no uncertain words, she had told me that—because I would never look French—never on the Metro to talk with her either in English or in my Baltimore-accented French. We communicated by nods and gestures, and that was enough. As for me, without achieving the look, yet after adopting the attitude of a Parisian, I watched the feeding frenzy. Voracious pickpockets routinely came unrecognized upon their bait, the unending stream of American tourists, who often did not know they had been robbed until after they had left the Metro and wanted to buy lunch. While I do not welcome that Paris seems infested with pickpockets, I came to realize that this was an everyday game mostly to be played with unwary tourists, and nobody was to be hurt if everyone played smoothly, gently, and within the rules of the game. The OECD economists would not approve, but it seems that with Paris having evolved a "pickpocketing market" that is free and fair, one might say that in this way too Paris has achieved a high level of sophistication.

In 1996 and for the first time in our lives, in the Metro cars Donna and I saw signs warning riders to report any abandoned package or luggage. Terrorism is not a game, and so in the Paris Metro we also saw the military guarding rail-transit stations, usually two young soldiers each carrying a semi-automatic weapon slung off his holder. Looking bewildered while trying to look tough, fortunately these kids were always accompanied and directed by an older, uniformed policeman, a *gendarme* who presumably would tell these youngsters when to start spraying bullets around inside the station. In 1996–97, Algerian dissidents did explode bombs in three Metro stations, including the station at Port-Royal, just one stop beyond my regular station at Boulevard Saint-Michel. In following years, there were fewer young soldiers and more heavily armed police equipped as if for combat.

Every weekday, happily I would take the Metro to work at Porte d'Auteuil in a satellite office of the OECD, not wearing a business suit but certainly wearing a jacket and necktie. While my clothing and overall look was American, I dressed in what today might be called "business casual." Even if a pollution fighter is not as I was an official representative of the United States, it is important to dress properly in a sophisticated, big city. Donna and I saw too many American visitors to Paris wearing T-shirts inscribed with almost anything, baggy, droopy trousers or summer shorts, black socks above white tennis shoes, baseball caps and fanny packs, talking loudly, and with the oversize cameras of the day videotaping their passage along sidewalks. I don't suppose these tourists had read Mark Twain, who humorously wrote, "In Paris they simply stared at me when I spoke to them in French. I never did succeed in making those idiots understand their language," but that seemed to be their attitude. And many Americans were tall like me—and also overweight. With some fright at the prospect of being stepped on by a massive American with a camera in front of his face while stumbling down the sidewalk, any French women would step aside or duck away to let the lumbering spectacle pass.

As you may know, in the spirit of *Liberté, Egalité, Fraternité,* the French love to have work slowdowns, strikes, and demonstrations that they call *manifestations.* These can become quite disrupting, but at times may be entertaining. One day in June I was walking in Paris near the Seine toward an open space where several roads converged. The time was about ten minutes before noon, the hour when the daily TV news would be beamed from Paris to all of France and *Outre-mer* to its overseas foreign *départements et territoires*. I began to hear wailing sirens of emergency vehicles approaching from every direction. I could see no fire, explosion, or airplane crash, all seemed normal, except that about 15 ambulances and several TV trucks at five minutes before noon arrived to the open space where I happened to be.

Wearing whites and scrubs, about 40 doctors, nurses, and medical techs assembled so quietly and smoothly that they must have done this before, and the TV cameras were readied. A few minutes after noon and on signal just before the TV lights came on, the medical professionals began to chant, shake their fists, and wave placards. A doctor made a very short speech about the need for better pay and benefits. After no more than two minutes of this *manifestation* of professional discontent, the TV lights went off. In five minutes more the place was empty, no sirens were heard leaving, and it was as if it had never happened. The organization and teamwork were outstanding, and no doubt so it would be also in their hospital operating rooms. But all of France had received the impression that many patients might die if there were not more money for medical professionals. This does not happen in America, and in decades past my wife, an R.N., like most nurses then was never paid what she was worth.

The French surely know how to create a scene, and in early July it was not an airplane crash that came to mind but bombs falling from airplanes. My small, windowed OECD office looked northwest near Porte d'Auteuil, and behind me about a mile to the southeast began the Avenue of the Elysian Fields in the 8th *arrondissement*. Being four floors up, my office window had a clear view of the northwestern sky in a direct line with the approach by air to the Avenue des Champs-Élysées. Shortly before noon on another OECD think-tank workday, my deep thoughts were interrupted by the sound of multiple aircraft approaching from the northwest. All at slow speed, first came a flight of fighter jets, then another, then flights of different bombers, light and heavy, then waves of helicopters, all heading toward the center of Paris to the southeast. I was panicked—had war been declared, were these French aircraft *en route* to fly on to bomb Russia? Had World War III begun? My colleagues were quite amused to have to inform me that these French forces were just practicing for the Bastille Day parade on July 14.

This *fête nationale* soon arrived, and we went to see the parade. On the ground, there were rows abreast of tanks, missiles on launchers, every other type of military vehicle, many ranks of the French armed forces, and interspersed marching military bands. From overhead came the endless roar of the air forces that had alarmed me on their practice day. Marchers included even the French Foreign Legion, traditionally comprised of French criminals who chose military service over prison, soldiers said by some to be so dangerous that these men could only be stationed in former French possessions overseas. They had come to Paris if just for the day, and proudly they too marched by. It reminded me of a parade through Moscow on May Day, but this was in Paris where revolutionary freedom began. It was so much more defiant than parades that I had seen in the USA, where the only weapons might be two—a rifle in the hands of each of the two soldiers who were the "color guard," marching on either side of the American flag. I leave it to my readers to contemplate what may be the basis for this cultural difference between the U.S. and France. I will say only that a knowledge of European history may help one to understand. Soon after Bastille Day, it was time to fly home to "fortress America."

Upon the collapse in 1989 of the USSR, in 1990 the OECD formed a Centre for Co-operation with Economies in Transition (since broadened to become the Centre for Co-operation with [OECD]

Non-Members). Working with Central European countries, it was essential to assist the newly independent states (NIS) in transition that had been under Russian domination from at least 1945 until 1991. The OECD has taken an important role in bringing former republics of the USSR into the governance norms and practices of Western European democracies. Many of these new Eastern European democracies would qualify for membership in the OECD, a first step along the road to perhaps qualifying to join the more consequential European Union (EU) or even the military alliance of the North Atlantic Treaty Organization (NATO). Eventually, some new democracies would achieve membership in all three, and western civilization would become larger and more secure.

Russia (the Russian Federation) itself in 1996 requested OECD membership, and the OECD in 1997 acknowledged this to be a shared goal. In about 2004, the OECD took me to Moscow as a member of an OECD delegation working to help Russia to improve its pollution control. But since then, Russia's history has added one more tragedy. Many hopes have been dashed by Russia's backsliding into a tyrannical kleptocracy. Today it is a police state seeking to undermine and destabilize Western European democracies, civilization, and all that the OECD stands for. Today Russian membership in the OECD seems unimaginable.

By 2002, it seemed that Western Europe's relatively "green" environmental values and politely consensual approaches to pollution control were not easily transmitted to some of the former USSR regimes that so recently had been totalitarian. Their formerly Communist state industries were still operating and polluting far more than was tolerable and safe. Western European nations, OECD members already, knew that the USEPA since 1970 had used strong enforcement to bring pollution under control. Everybody admired how this was accomplished without impairing the free-wheeling, immensely profitable economy of the U.S. A number of leaders in Western Europe and other OECD nations had seen cowboy movies about 19ᵗʰ-century sheriffs and the winning and civilizing of the American West. In short, to protect the environment in Europe's new "wild East," they wanted to learn more about the tough techniques of America's "Wild West," while considering also the polite experiences of other nations including the Netherlands, Poland, Sweden, U.K., and Australia.

So in 2002, this American pollution fighter was invited to return to Europe for 15 more weeks on official assignment to the OECD. My work was to draft guidance to newly independent governments wanting to enact, and then enforce, laws effective to control pollution. In the spring of 2002, I wrote more than 60 pages describing the fully matured USEPA approach. I described the full range of tools that I listed in the preceding chapter and more, ranging from the clenched fist of compulsion to the velvet glove of compliance incentives that a newly independent state should deploy.

For my return in 2002 to work again in the OECD's Environment Directorate, a friend had put me in touch with a former CIA operative retired from working under the cover of his position in a global business. This gentleman still maintained an apartment in Paris, and so Donna and I rented for almost four months what we jokingly called our "safe house." As the old quip goes, if I told you where it was located I would have to kill you. So let us just say that it was hidden behind a gate with a coded lock and beside the wall of a gatehouse with a watchful resident *guardienne*, in a very good and central part of the 16ᵗʰ *arrondissement*. It was less than two blocks from a Metro stop and much closer to the center of Paris than were the Marine barracks at the remotest end of the 16ᵗʰ *arrondissement*.

Paris has received many expatriates over the years, and in 2002 when I returned to the OECD I met many newly hired, younger colleagues from Eastern Europe who had been born and grown up under Russian domination. The OECD seemed reenergized by these new colleagues, all so eager to be outreaching to uplift their homelands. While their parents spoke as a second language mostly Russian, my new colleagues had experienced a generational shift. Since independence, English had become the preferred second language in their schools. With few good memories of their subjugation, they all spoke Russian, English, and French, and to be professionals employed by the OECD they had earned advanced university degrees.

With their diverse skills, they were working to transfer the good-governance tools of the OECD members to the newly independent states of the former USSR, including sometimes their own countries. I liked them all, but I will just name two, Krzysztof Michalak from Poland and Angela Bularga from Moldova, two of the finest people I ever hope to meet. While Angela is perhaps 30 years younger than me, in 2002 she oversaw my work with consummate skill, and we never had a moment's disagreement. Donna and I also renewed our friendship with Claudia Busch, a Californian who in the 1980s had worked in Washington at EPA. From there she had moved to work full-time at the OECD, where in 1996–97 we met, and I had worked with her on the German recycling project.

Within the Environment Directorate, the head of our unit was the delightful Brendan Gillespie, and after the end of the Friday workday in his office he held a staff meeting, for which attendance was only voluntary. Brendan and everyone else made me feel very welcome, and all said that input from the U.S. was highly valued because we Americans have a nation and a personal manner that is unafraid, optimistic, friendly, and can-do. Of course, the U.S. was not a society with social classes including nobility, we have not lived under Russian domination, we have not been the major battlefield for two world wars, and in 2002 we had not yet invaded Iraq.[8] All of my OECD colleagues were of the best sort, and if I am ever so fortunate as to see them again, there would be the warmest feelings all around.

Friday's staff-meeting refreshments included an endless supply of vodka and wine that were gifts from visitors or brought by staff back from missions to the East. (The OECD separately maintained an official and capacious wine cellar, used to fuel the warmth of high-level, diplomatic meetings.) I also learned that the OECD had organized an after-work-hours wine-tasting club. Such staff meetings and such a club are practices impossible to imagine within the monastic U.S. government as I know it. At the OECD in the offices I saw no liquor during working hours. Although attendance was only voluntary at this staff meeting to end the week, the office morale and attendance was as good or better than I have ever seen elsewhere. So to Brendan and all my former colleagues, from far across the sea when my memories come flooding back, I lift a glass and say *"Santé!"* and *"Vive l'OCDE!"*

In late May 2002, after I finished my writing to describe an effective environmental enforcement program, the OECD invited six or eight experts from interested member states and from the U.N. to review it. For a day and half, far more time than it takes to "defend" a thesis for a PhD, I presented and discussed each chapter. By July, I was back at EPA Headquarters, and the work at the OCED was continued by Angela Bularga. Very skillfully she converted my long paper into a shorter booklet published as the OECD's "Guiding Principles for Reform of Environmental Enforcement in Transition Economies of Eastern Europe, Caucasus, and Central Asia."[8] In October 2002, meeting in Almaty, Kazakhstan, representatives of the environmental enforcement authorities of Eastern Europe, Caucasus, and Central Asia endorsed and agreed to apply the OECD's principles as non-binding guidance. In retrospect, Angela and I do wish that the OECD had published my longer document with its many helpful details; they almost did, and perhaps someday the OECD will do so. Still, the "Guiding Principles" showed the way to real progress. Any nation can successfully apply these methods of environmental enforcement. As a pollution fighter, I take great satisfaction knowing that my efforts materialized as this guidance useful to help good governments emerging from Russian domination.

This work at the OECD introduced me to some experts from the United Nations Environment Programme, UNEP (*le Programme des Nations Unies pour l'Environnement, PNUE*). This would lead to an invitation in July 2003 from the United Nations Institute for Training and Research (UNITAR) to be a Special Fellow of UNITAR in 2004, and invitations to collaborate from time to time with UNEP. Until then, it seemed to me that UNEP had mostly just been the custodian for environmental treaties but without much attention to their effective national implementation. I was so pleased that the U.N. was taking up the issue of treaty Parties' environmental-law enforcement, took note of my work at the OECD 2002, and saw USEPA to be a very good model. As I was the EPA expert available to help, I was able to contribute to several training events and international publications, as I related in the earlier chapter "Saving the Earth."

But from the U.S. State Department I saw no awareness or appreciation that UNEP and many nations were looking to the USEPA as the best model for environmental-law enforcement. Because it rankles, again I express my dismay that State provided so few outreach opportunities and had to be asked for even minimal financial support for my foreign-assistance work to improve environmental-law enforcement. In the future, because the entire world must organize, learn, and work in partnership to effectively implement national laws to protect the climate, the State Department must greatly improve its appreciation for and collaboration with EPA's Office of Enforcement. I hope this will begin by no longer ignoring the substantial body of work contained in the several guidance-to-governments documents that the OECD and UNEP published from 2003 to 2007.[9] If we are ever to have an effective climate treaty that is enforceable, State should discover this trove of materials and work with also with the OECD and UNEP to revive and apply them to enforce climate protections.

Donna and I made our last, and partly official, trip to Paris in 2004. Considering both the OECD's focus on economics and the economic sophistication of EPA's Office of Enforcement, it is not surprising that the OECD requested from EPA a speech on the economic justifications for environmental enforcement and on the economic tools used within the enforcement process. For its high-level Global Forum on Sustainable Development, the OECD invited EPA's Deputy Assistant Administrator for Enforcement, an excellent top manager and lawyer, Phyllis Harris, to make the presentation. Considering my unique assignments from EPA's Office of Enforcement to work inside the OECD in 1996, 1997, and 2002, Phyllis asked me to write the speech, and she was thinking that I should accompany and assist her. I had chosen her hotel, and as she was a high-level official I had arranged for her to meet with the American Ambassador to the OECD.

But again there was inadequate EPA money and no State Department interest in or financial support for this foreign travel by EPA enforcement officials. Phyllis did not think that she could justify my travel costs in addition to her own. Though disappointed, after so many years in the impoverished EPA "monastery," I did like that Phyllis was prudent in managing EPA's limited funds. Compare her admirable frugality to what we have seen starting in 2017 from very recent U.S. political appointees who travel too often and too far with vast entourages. As if on a continuous celebrity tour, these self-entitled narcissists have carried off even short-distance stunts like traveling from Washington to Philadelphia, not by Amtrak, but by private charter jet costing perhaps one hundred times more and taking at least twice as long.

With my planning and advice for Phyllis, including warning her to beware of pickpockets, I felt that she should not have difficulty navigating the most sophisticated city in the world. Then a solution came to mind that could allow me at minimal government expense to accompany Phyllis. I proposed to her that I would receive no government travel money whatsoever and no pay for my days of vacation, but I would be paid for the several days in Paris when I would be working with her, the OECD, and UNEP. For my unpaid weekends and tourist days, I would use "vacation days" and personally pay all travel expense for Donna and me. We had frequent-flier miles to cover our flights, and of course we knew by then about saving money by renting Paris apartments. Considering also that I could be her French-speaking guide to a foreign country that I believe she had never visited, she quickly approved my plan. So very near to the Jardin de Luxembourg, Donna's favorite place to read on a bench amid the flowers in the sun, we rented an apartment for ten days.

In Paris with Phyllis, I was pleased to escort her everywhere, including to her meet-and-greet with the OECD's American Ambassador Connie Morella, a former outstanding Republican Congresswoman from Maryland. I knew that the Ambassador long before had been a State legislator and that her last year in the Maryland House of Delegates was 1974, just before my first year there in 1975. I told her that I too was a "graduate" of the Maryland General Assembly, though our years there did not overlap. We laughed about it being a small world, bonded immediately, and enjoyed talking about our experience as lawmakers. Phyllis relaxed and did not seem to mind that I may have talked too much with the Ambassador. The next day, Phyllis presented the speech[10] in the meeting held at the International Energy Agency, an autonomous intergovernmental organization affiliated with the OECD that was established because of the 1973 oil crisis, in its office very close by the Eiffel Tower.

Afterwards, in the early evening Phyllis and I walked outside to meet Donna as planned. We strolled under the Tour Eiffel shining in the sky, and with our OECD mission accomplished made sure that Phyllis enjoyed dinner with companionship and wine on her last night in Paris. At the end of our evening, after we had taken Phyllis for a ride on the Metro to see the Arc de Triomphe, I put her into a cab and told the driver the address of Phyllis's hotel. Donna and I were not tired, and we strolled down the Champs-Elysées. While I rarely saw Phyllis again, and while she left EPA too soon, I believe to go work for Walmart, that corporation in many ways has been very "green"—meaning progressive environmentally. I am happy for her and pleased to know that Phyllis Harris went through the revolving door to do more good than harm to the environment.

Phyllis flew home the next day, while we three stayed a few days longer as tourists, on my own time and wallet. Also according to my understanding with Phyllis, on paid, government time alone I visited the office in Paris of UNEP's Division of Technology, Industry, and Economics (DTIE) to meet the staff and begin more collaboration with EPA. My expanding relationship with UNEP would prove to be fruitful. In addition to my research and writing that contributed to UNEP publications (as I related above), during the next six years UNEP would invite me to bring the expertise of EPA to help to plan and conduct UNEP/DTIE enforcement training events in the Republic of Georgia, the Dominican Republic, and El Salvador. Usually UNEP paid to bring me in, but for other invitations U.S. government financial support typically was absent. So for EPA there were missed opportunities because official travel funding was unavailable even though I was invited and could have provided U.S. government assistance through UNEP to other nations needing our help.

After the gratuitous and ill-considered U.S. invasion of Iraq in 2003, I felt a chilly *froideur*.[11] In my work I saw firsthand that some foreign and international colleagues came to view the American government coldly with suspicion as possibly becoming a blundering and unwise bully. These colleagues told me that to see in Iraq the great U.S. repeat its fiasco of 1960s Vietnam was sorrowing. The formerly admired U.S. was no longer to be so automatically everywhere invited, welcomed, and trusted. When I write this in 2019, while enemies are laughing at the U.S. government, our allies are fearful as the U.S. is withdrawing from the family of civilized nations. And it is all too clear that a greedy ruling U.S. elite of fossil-fuel fanatics have been speeding the dismantling of the U.S. Environmental Protection Agency. It was once the biggest, best, and most respected environmental ministry in the world. Today EPA has been reduced to a hollow shell, while the possibility of human extinction from climate change is like an oncoming train speeding toward to us—while too many Americans simply stand in our dark tunnel of ignorance and apathy.

The last time Donna and I saw Paris was in 2004. We were always sad to leave behind our charming little rented homes and our new friends and colleagues. But our many beloved family members and our permanent jobs were not in Europe. Fortunately, our happy memories are portable, savory and sustaining. We have found to be true these words of Ernest Hemingway, who wrote, "If you are lucky enough to have lived in Paris…, then wherever you go for the rest of your life it stays with you, for Paris is a moveable feast."

For the pollution fighters of the future, solving the air-pollution problem causing climate change can only be done with global cooperation. The entire world needs you and will be welcoming your help in a wide range of professional fields—just as you have read that I was welcomed for bringing my particular expertise from the U.S. to the international level. To my youngest readers I say, if you too learn French and get good grades, you may well study in France. And after you have passed through an American university or a *université en France*, you too may work in France or beyond in the wider world, as I did so happily as a professional pollution fighter. If ever you create for yourself or out of the blue receive such an opportunity, seize it and move outward and upward into a big world awaiting you.

---

1. To navigate Paris, one often has to know the locations of the *arrondissements*. The city is divided into 20 *arrondissements municipaux*, numbered municipal administrative districts each with a mayor, and one often travels from one to another by its number.

2. To read the report online, google "ENV/EPOC/PPC(97)20/REV2," or visit www.sourceoecd.org where OECD publications are available. The report states that it "...is mostly developed from a draft report initially prepared [in 1996 and 1997] by Richard Emory, a U.S. Environmental Protection Agency specialist in international environmental policy and law." A reader of this report will likely share my view that to recycle routinely and well is to behave ethically and responsibly toward our planet, or God's creation, call it what you will. Few of us will be full-time, professional pollution fighters, but every one of us who recycles properly has joined the fight against pollution.

3. Prostitution is said to be the oldest profession, and lawyers too have always served mostly in the halls of the rich and powerful, historically beginning with tribal chieftains and kings. Although the appellation "Esquire" may not exist today in England and is perhaps going out of style in the U.S., some American lawyers still use "Esq." after their name. A thousand years ago in England, the term "squire" described the young nobleman who carried a knight's shield, and the word also may refer to or derive from the knight's shield itself, for which the word is "escutcheon."

Today, lawyers are often scorned as selling themselves to defend the rich and powerful from the justice they deserve for their evil misdeeds. Yet all persons do have the right to an ethical defense within the rule of law. A lawyer who chooses to be a pollution fighter must also guard against injustice. This can mean being sure that a rich and powerful person is not charged criminally for an offense that is not so serious and should be on an administrative or civil track. It can mean also not failing to do the hard work of trying to convict personally a rich and powerful corporate officer, even though surely he will be very well defended by lawyers who may be more numerous and will earn many multiples more money than do government lawyers.

4. *From Beirut to Jerusalem*, by Thomas L. Friedman (Farrar, Straus & Giroux, 1989).

5. *The Nightingale,* by Kristin Hanna (MacMillan, 2017), one of many stirring books about the Resistance, is an historical novel of two French sisters. They are estranged and during the German occupation take different paths, with one sister helping downed Allied pilots hide and escape to Spain.

6. *Is Paris Burning?,* by Larry Collins and Dominique Lapierre (Penguin, 1965), well describes the liberation of the city, including the secret diplomatic negotiations that enable Paris to survive the war without destruction.

7. High-style tailoring or fashion. In low-level English, this has become "hoity-toity"!

8. This is document CCNM/ENV/EAP(2003)6, OECD, Paris, 2003, available at www.sourceoecd.org.

9. The document "Guiding Principles for Reform of Environmental Enforcement Authorities in Transition Economies of Eastern Europe, Caucasus, and Central Asia," OECD, Paris, 2003 (document CCNM/ENV/EAP[2003]6), was based on the underlying draft that I prepared while resident at the OECD in 2002, with added international and OECD secretariat input. This led directly to "Assuring Environmental Compliance—A Toolkit for Building Better Environmental Inspectorates in Eastern Europe, Caucasus, and Central Asia," OECD, Paris, 2004 (ISBN 92-64-01492-6), which was based on the above guiding principles, again with input contributed by me and

others. This was followed by "Manual on Compliance with and Enforcement of Multilateral Environmental Agreements," UNEP, Nairobi, 2006 (ISBN 93-807-2703-6, at www.unep.org/dec/docs/ UNEPManual.pdf), that named me among contributors, and by "Environmental Non-Compliance: What Response in OECD Countries?", OECD, Paris, 2007, that also named me among contributors. This work led to "Guide for Negotiators of Multilateral Environmental Agreements," UNEP, Nairobi, 2007 (ISBN 978-92-807-2807-1). There may be later additions to this list, but your author in retirement has not followed all developments.

10. "Combining Legal Mandates with Economics in the Application of Environmental Law," Proceedings of the Seventh International Conference on Environmental Compliance and Enforcement (OECD, Paris, 2004) is reprinted as an addendum to this book. I was the principal author of this speech for the outstanding former Deputy Assistant Administrator who delivered this speech at this conference organized by the OECD. An important part of this talk was to inform many nations about EPA's sophisticated penalty policies. Starting in the 1990s, these were developed by a wonderful EPA colleague, Jonathan Libber, also of Baltimore. By including economic incentives in setting the outcomes of enforcement cases, EPA's penalty policy encouraged reforming violators to mitigate their environmental damage and to enhance the environment. A corporation valuing its public image would often choose to perform a supplemental environmental project and thus to resolve its violation(s) in the best light possible to its customers and stockholders. Until abolished in 2017 or 2018 as part of the present Administration's effort to dismantle EPA, this wise and innovative policy—at no taxpayer expense—achieved environmental benefits in addition to the punishment and deterrence that are all that is possible with only traditional command-and-control penalties.

11. After the U.S. invasion of Iraq in 2003, which many Europeans consider to be a colossal mistake by a U.S. straying into arrogant adventurism, a chill did develop. It intensified with the U.S. role in plunging the world into the 2008 financial collapse. Since 2017, the U.S. President has abandoned America's role of leadership to achieve economic cooperation, the advancement of social welfare, and other global goals of WWII's Atlantic Charter that led to the creation of the U.N., NATO, and the OECD. Instead, the U.S. has reverted to isolationist

nationalism that is weakening the traditional Western Alliance against domestic and Russian autocracy. And in the U.S. the wealth gap between rich and poor has grown to be like that of today's Russia. Today in Europe, the U.S. is as much silently feared and suspected as it is publicly welcomed.

Chapter 9—Climate Change

IN 2005, AFTER HURRICANE KATRINA hit New Orleans, Louisiana, killing over 1,800 people, the U.S. public was stunned by governmental incompetence. The national flood control and emergency management agencies had failed to plan well in advance, and after the storm the federal response was confusion. Displaced persons were even put into formaldehyde-contaminated, toxic trailer homes, there to be poisoned. So much bungling distracted national attention from climate change, and this ocean flood was a wake-up call not heard in America.

Today in 2019, we can all see now that the weather is more threatening. Weather events worldwide are becoming abnormally extreme, damaging, and frequent.[1] Most obvious are hurricanes that are increasing in size and intensity. Even a routine coastal rainstorm may now sit for several days constantly pumping moisture over the land—for which we have new terms, an "atmospheric river" producing a "rain bomb" bringing unprecedented inland flooding on top of coastal flooding. The U.S. experiences about 85 to 90 percent of the world's tornadoes, and these too are coming earlier and later and to places where rarely or never seen before. In other places the problems are wildfires and drought, usually appearing not as daily weather events but within altered weather patterns continuing for weeks or months or longer.

Had we been paying attention before now, this would not have come as a surprise. In 1896, Svante Arrhenius, a Swedish scientist who won the Nobel Prize for Chemistry in 1903, first successfully hypothesized that burning fossil fuels would warm the climate in what he called the "hot-house theory." Today we call it the "greenhouse gas effect," and there is no scientific uncertainty or controversy about how the GHG effect works. Most ultraviolet radiation arriving from the sun is absorbed by the Earth, warming it enough to sustain life. Some incoming solar energy is reflected back into space as infrared radiation. Some of this is trapped in the troposphere where greenhouse gases (GHGs)—mostly CO_2—reflect the radiation downward as heat. A natural "blanket" is good because it keeps what we might call the "body" of the Earth's surface from being too cold for many living things. But now on top of this natural "blanket" we have added another, man-made "blanket" of GHGs, mostly as the result of burning fossil fuels. The result is overheating, but we cannot just toss the extra blanket on the floor and quickly be comfortable again.

Globally, there is no question that average temperatures, like CO_2, are steadily rising. Because there can still be locally cold weather, lest anyone find the term "global warming" confusing or inaccurate, scientists suggest we say instead "energized atmosphere." When the air is pumped full of too much atmospheric energy from CO_2 and other chemicals released and emitted by the hand of man, this makes for a wide variety of more highly energized and strange weather events, also including intervals of very cold, Arctic weather farther south than normal.

Today, scientists can measure directly back about 800,000 years by sampling and testing air bubbles trapped in glacial ice cores and in limestone stalagmites and stalactites in caves. They can measure the actual isotopic ratios of the elements in air; natural greenhouse gases like CO_2, methane/natural gas (CH_4), and nitrous oxide; water, volcanic dust, etc. Scientists can distinguish the carbon in the air naturally from today's decaying plants and respiration, and they can measure it separately from combusted fossil-fuel carbon emitted from our chimneys and exhaust pipes that has the unique isotopic ratio of ancient, fossilized carbon.[2] In addition to the excess CO_2 (put into the air after burning fossil fuels), man's activities have also caused the large-scale release of CH_4, as this chapter will soon discuss. And man has intentionally manufactured (synthesized) and emitted a set of other unnatural chemicals that are both sun-shield (ozone)-destroying and powerfully climate-changing. These synthetic ozone-depleting chemicals, not existing in nature, are mostly refrigerants and propellants that on a per-molecule basis can be thousands of time more climate-killing than CO_2.

We know that since about 1750 (the start of the fossil-fuels-based industrial revolution) average global temperature has increased about one degree Celsius (almost two degrees Fahrenheit). And we know that man-made CO_2 emissions to the air have increased atmospheric CO_2 from about 270 ppm in 1750 to a level in 2019 of about 415 ppm. Some scientists tell us that this much CO_2 is the highest ever measured in 800,000 years, and has probably not been this high since about three million years ago before the end of the Pliocene epoch.[3] Then and earlier, giant camels roamed the Artic, more than a third of all land-based ice had melted, and the global sea level was about 80 feet higher. Other scientists tell us that 415 ppm has not been found in the atmosphere of Earth since at least 10 million years ago, when the sea level was about 100 feet higher than today because almost half of all land-based ice had melted. On top of the 415 ppm of CO_2, in the air today also are roughly another 100 ppm of man's cornucopia of self-generated greenhouse gases other than CO_2. Yes, there are natural cycles to the Earth's temperature caused by slight changes to the Earth's orbit, but at these GHG levels the man-made impacts are far greater than any other cause.

Now, CO_2 and temperature are rising at a rate 50 to 100 times the historical record, and with business as usual this astonishing rate of increase is accelerating. Here it bears repeating what I wrote in the first chapter, that of all CO_2 and heat from burning fossil fuels that man has pumped into the air, we are lucky that about 92 percent of this has been absorbed into the dense and absorbent sea. Were all this heat to have remained in the air, today average global air temperature would exceed

120 degrees Fahrenheit and on land we would be dying like flies. But the impact on the sea is terrible, and whenever a new scientific update appears, it reports that the sea is rising faster to levels higher than earlier measurements and predictions. If today we were to stop emitting GHGs into the air, still at least 1,000 years—a millennium—will be needed for CO_2 to come down to its natural level or equilibrium. This is why many scientists agree that it is now inevitable—unavoidable, we might say "already baked in"—that soon, by no later than 2100, humanity must begin abandoning cities at sea level and vast coastal areas, and that it is now too late to completely "fix" the climate before the disaster we have made is upon us.

Whether the sea eventually will rise 65, 80, or 100 feet does not really matter. With the geologic record indicating and many scientists telling us that it is too late to save vast coastal areas and all our seaports from being permanently under the sea, probably the only big question now is when. Yet it is likely that the timing and extent of inundation (and how much time remains to prepare for it) can be deferred or extended when the U.S. and the world take responsibility and act decisively to prevent 220 feet or more of sea level rise if we melt all the ice on Earth.

The United States, with 5 percent of world population, over many decades has put much more CO_2 and other climate-killing GHGs into the air than any other country. On an annual basis, today the U.S. still pumps out about 20 percent of these GHGs, and recently has been surpassed by China as the world's biggest economy and biggest emitter of CO_2. It is important that the U.S. wake up to the reality, because this is an issue of morality and accountability both to our own citizens and to the many other people in the less-developed world who will suffer even more. Even self-centeredly considering only ourselves in the United States, it is an existential issue that the entire, low-lying coast from Texas to Massachusetts is imperiled by imminent sea-level rise that will also extend far up the Mississippi River.

Now with scientific certainty regarding the causes, the dynamics, and the effects of climate change, research is shifting to the uncertainties that will determine the timing and extent of the inevitable climate catastrophe. While each assessment of the U.S. government and of the world-wide Intergovernmental Panel on Climate Change (IPCC) is more dire, these official forecasts have been just "lowest common denominator," the least to which almost all scientists can agree, and only extending to 2100. Most unsettling is that these conservative predictions have tended to ignore possibilities that cannot easily be modeled or predicted, the so-called "wild cards," all of which would raise the sea sooner. Yet in 2010, the U.S. National Academy of Sciences did present a new element—the nightmare vision of points of no return from an enormous disaster. In "Advancing the Science of Climate Change," the Academy wrote that

> There may be tipping points or thresholds that, once crossed, lead to irreversible events. Some of the physical and biological feedbacks triggered by climate change can become irreversible when they pass a certain threshold or tipping point.... Human systems [also] can experience tipping points, such as the collapse of an economy or political system. Because of the possibility of crossing such thresholds, simple extrapolations of recent trends may underestimate future climate change impacts. Given the complexity of coupled human-environment systems, it is difficult to predict when a tipping point might be approaching, but the probability of crossing [a tipping point] increases as the climate system moves outside the range of natural variability.

Reasons why disaster could be coming very soon, even in a few decades and in the middle of this 21st century, include the following:

- Black soot from ordinary air pollution that is accelerating icemelt in Greenland. Deposited on the ice, the black soot catches the sun's heat and speeds the melting of the ice. If all ice on Greenland melts, the sea will rise about 20 feet.

- Similarly, with the Arctic floating sea ice now often gone, there is reduced albedo/reflectivity or increased darkness in the open Arctic Sea, which is now absorbing more of the heat of summer.

- The global temperature increase is highest in the Arctic, and in a dangerous feedback loop, heat from the warming Arctic Sea is melting the permafrost on land around the Arctic in Siberia, Alaska, and Canada. Here the vast deposits of methane (natural gas, CH_4) are no longer frozen in place but are seeping, leaking, and even erupting from the tundra and from bubbling from the bottoms of far-northern lakes. To be explained below is that a molecule of methane is much more climate-damaging than a molecule of $C2O_2$.

- In Antarctica, there are seven enormous glaciers standing in ocean water that now are being undermined by the warming Southern Ocean. In this century, any one or more of these glaciers could slip into the sea and melt. Together, these glaciers are about the size of Texas and California combined, with ice about two miles thick, enough if all melt to raise the sea about 20 feet. Furthermore, if all the ice on land in Antarctica melts, the sea could rise about another 175 to 200 feet.

Another blatantly man-made cause, not in official models or predictions, for why disaster could be coming sooner is hydraulic fracturing—commonly called "fracking"—to release natural gas from deep underground. By now its local victims are well aware that fracking can create local earthquakes, explode a home, poison groundwater, cause drinking water from wells to become flammable, and bring on cancer. To liberate fracking from federal regulation, in 2005, at the instigation of then Vice President Cheney, the U.S. Congress took away EPA's authority since 1974 under the Safe Drinking Water Act to regulate fracking's chemical-injection wells. Compare Europe, where there has been movement to increase groundwater safety so that drinking water is not poisoned by fracking.

All U.S. Presidents since about 2001 consistently have encouraged changing from coal-fired power plants to natural gas, and in 2017 the bewitched EPA even rolled back the Clean Air Act's late and minimal regulation of fracking's escaping emissions. Residents breathing near leaking fracking installations can be sickened by smelly whiffs of a very toxic gas emitted with the methane. This gas is hydrogen sulfide, the very same chemical expected to cause human extinction if reckless fracking continues. While fossil-fuel promoters say that natural gas is a bridge to renewable energy, the truth is that it is a bridge to disaster by delaying the uptake of renewable energy and accelerating climate chaos. The problem is "fugitive" methane that inevitably escapes from industrial fracking's ruptures or fissures in the earth, from leaky on-site installations, and even from some intentional venting at the well source. More methane escapes from the thousands of miles of piping all the way to cities where the local, natural-gas pipes are notoriously old and leaky.

Over about 25 years, the climate-damaging effect of CH_4 is about 70 times that of one molecule of CO_2.[4] To comprehend the danger, now we can do the math, multiplying methane's relative potency factor of 70 by the 3 to 8 percent of methane that is lost into the air. The interim result is that the climate-killing effect of escaping natural gas is at least twice, and maybe more than five times, worse than CO_2 from combustion.[5] To this we must add a factor of 0.5, because when piped methane is burned as natural-gas fuel it produces climate-changing CO_2, though only about half as much as burning coal. The result is that generating electricity by switching to natural gas has a climate-destroying effect that is roughly three to six times worse than continuing to burn coal. Rather than a bridge to a good future, natural gas is a one-way gangplank off the side of a pirate ship at sea.

The National Oceanographic and Atmospheric Administration (NOAA) in 2017 suggested officially that by 2100 the world may suffer 8 feet of sea-level rise, enough to flood the docks most of the seaports of the world. But a worst-case scenario by 2100 for sea-level rise of 10 to 30 feet is predicted or seen as very possible by some top scientists, including Harold Wanless, Chair of Geological Sciences of the University of Miami, and James E. Hansen, formerly of U.S. National Aeronautics and Space Administration (NASA). Now retired, from 1981 to 2013 Dr. Hansen headed the Goddard Institute for Space Studies in New York City. He had studied planetary atmospheres, and unlike so many other astrophysicists entranced by space travel, he realized that we must take care of our own planet first. In 1988, now more than 30 years ago, his testimony before a Senate Committee was the first to try to alert the U.S. Congress. He was pivotal at least to move the global-warming issue from academic into governmental policy circles.[6] And there in the U.S. Congress the debate in the U.S. died, killed by the special interests thriving from fossil fuels and by the indifference of the first President Bush.

Former Vice President Al Gore was ridiculed when his 2006 film *An Inconvenient Truth* showed an animation of seawater flooding the World Trade Center's 9/11 memorial in New York City. Yet very soon, on October 29, 2012, exactly this happened when Superstorm Sandy also flooded the subways. Because Gore's early climate predictions have proved accurate, let us find courage in his explanation in 2013 of his optimism about stopping climate change. He noted other, constructive "tipping points" in public opinion leading to historic social change and new laws. His examples include ending first slavery, then segregation in the U.S.; ending apartheid in South Africa; and freezing the nuclear arms race with Russia and destroying excess weapons (though this may now be reversed by Putin). We have ended smoking on airplanes, then in restaurants and even in bars, and we have reduced ridicule and discrimination against gays, lesbians, and others in the "LGBTQIA community."

Al Gore tells us that ridicule once directed against himself is being retargeted against deniers of climate change. He says that more big-business leaders tell him privately that as we are already paying costs of excess carbon, it makes sense to put a price on carbon. He predicts that, as we saw happen with cell phones, flat-screen TVs, and tablet computers, with the proper incentives the uptake of clean energy technologies may come much more quickly than in early projections. In a final chapter, we will look at solutions to climate change, including creating new economic incentives. But reform will require widespread popular understanding and will to change. Within the notoriously short-term attention span and "infotainment" emphasis of U.S. popular news media, only at last in 2019 are some of the more thoughtful news outlets reporting the link between worsening weather and the deteriorating climate. Al Gore does foresee coming soon a tipping point when the public will demand climate protection. This cannot happen soon enough.

By the late 1990s, to protect the climate EPA had begun steps to address CO_2, CH_4, and other GHGs as air pollutants under the existing Clean Air Act. But with the 2000 election came political change. EPA fell under the control of the second Bush Administration, and its Office of General Counsel came to be led by the type of politically appointed lawyers to be expected. In 2003, they decided that the Clean Air Act, for the purpose of climate protection, does not provide the legal authority to regulate vehicular ("tailpipe") emissions of CO_2 and other GHGs. Ignoring the recommendations of government scientists, the Administration also decided that EPA as a matter of policy would not act to protect the climate even if again and more explicitly handed by Congress the authority to do so.

While climate-change predictions may seem so overwhelming and solutions so daunting, it helps to realize that to EPA this is just another air-pollution problem, and that the U.S. Supreme Court in 2007 narrowly agreed. In a 5–4 decision reversing the Bush Administration, the Supreme Court held that the Clean Air Act as written does give EPA the authority to regulate tailpipe emissions, and that EPA must do so absent any reasonable explanation why not.[7] EPA then found that CO_2 and five other GHGs "in the atmosphere may reasonably be anticipated to endanger public health and to endanger public welfare," and in 2012 the U.S. Court of Appeals for the D.C. Circuit upheld this scientific finding.

Since 2009, the regulatory roller-coaster moved up until 2017, then swooped down again. Meanwhile, the situation is dire and getting worse by the day, and to almost all scientists (if not paid by fossil-fuel companies) it is imperative that climate-killing air pollutants must be brought quickly under control. At the same time, since 2017 judicial appointments have shaped a Supreme Court seeming less inclined to uphold our national government's legal authority to protect the environment. Enormously powerful, these Justices are not scientists but lawyers with the majority typically inclined to rule that corporate America should be free to do as it will. During the future lifetimes of these Justices sitting so grandly on this bench, which is about all the time that we have left to avert climate chaos, the future may be threatened by just one man too many voting 5–4 against the planet.

By now it is inevitable that sea-level rise will stop international trade as seaports go underwater, and will destroy vast coastal habitat of dense human populations. Since 2003, the U.S. military in its constant contingency planning has been well aware that the U.S. Navy risks soon losing all its docks and bases on the shoreline. The Pentagon also has been studying the possibility of climate change causing wars from cross-border invasions, seeing that refugee migrations are already occurring as people have streamed out of drought-ravaged Syria and sub-Saharan Africa to cross into Europe. A surprising possibility is that the changing climate may alter the Gulf Stream and plunge Europe into bitter cold.

Looking back from today, we see that World War II burned through enormous amounts of fossil fuel, and after 1945 industrial development and populations erupted around the world and intensified in every decade. From 1750 until today, about 85 percent of the human-caused rise in CO_2 has occurred since about 1939. Of this 85 percent, about half the increase occurred in the 50 years from 1939 to 1989, and the other half since 1989 until today. This means that during just the last 30 or 40 years—after the science was clear in 1979 and Dr. Hansen warned Congress in 1988—we accelerated and doubled the human-caused rise in CO_2 of the previous 50 years (1939–1989).

While the evidence was steadily accumulating, we proceeded in ignorance and denial and lost the opportunity to cut in half the coming impacts. We have behaved like happy passengers partying on the next-to-last train to paradise in 1935.[8] Chugging from Miami down to Key West, on our train propelled by coal and funded by oil money, we did not see that nature was about to push us off the rails. From this colossal failure by our generation, we have doubled the burden on our children and grandchildren, who now are riding on the last train to paradise.

The generations that follow us will be abandoning ports and coasts flooded permanently under the sea, and then living in urban ruins resembling Warsaw or Berlin in 1945—homes burned out by wildfires, blown away by tornadoes and hurricanes, or inundated repeatedly by three-day rain bombs causing river and coastal flooding, followed by black mold. Their working lives will be weighed down with the tasks of rebuilding many cities on high ground while at the same time reengineering their entire economy to be climate-friendly. Assuming that the generation now in power continues to fumble internationally, our descendants also will have the difficult work of constructing an effective global climate regime with forceful and effective international and national laws. Amid deteriorating social order and with their economy in crisis, our descendants must become very tough pollution fighters indeed to implement these new national laws and treaties.

To close this chapter, by reading it slowly let us reflect upon this short poem written in London in the year 1631 by John Donne, entitled, "No Man Is An Island":

> No man is an island, Entire of itself.
> Each is a piece of the continent, A part of the main.
> If a clod be washed away by the sea,
>
> Europe is the less.
> As well as if a promontory were [washed away],
> As well as if a manor of thine own,
> Or of thine friend's were [washed away].
> Each man's death diminishes me,
>
> For I am involved in mankind.
> Therefore, ask not to know for whom the bell tolls...
>
> It tolls...for thee.

---

1. In 2012, the Intergovernmental Panel on Climate Change (IPCC) wrote that "A changing climate leads to changes in the frequency, intensity, spatial extent, duration and timing... and can result in

unprecedented extreme weather and climate events." We see the key point: small changes in average temperatures create big changes in extremes of weather.

2. "Light carbon" (carbon 12) is the stable, residual carbon isotope with six protons and six neutrons found in fossils after carbon 14 has decayed for epochs buried underground. In contrast, carbon 14 is formed constantly at the Earth's surface as cosmic rays collide with other atoms in the atmosphere, releasing energetic neutrons that form carbon 14 atoms (six protons, eight neutrons). Carbon 14 with a half-life of about 5,700 years decays very slowly to carbon 12, emitting radioactivity that can be detected, and this rate of decay is used as "carbon-dating." The ratio of ancient "light" carbon 12 to carbon 14 in today's atmosphere signifies and proves, by the increasing concentration (presently about 35 percent) of light carbon in the atmosphere, that this much of the recent increase in CO_2 is from extracting (unburying) and burning ancient fossil fuels—and that the increase is not of modern carbon 14 created daily at Earth's surface by continuous natural causes. In 2007, in its fourth scientific assessment the IPCC reported, using 2005 data, that "warming of the planet is unequivocal," and that "most of the observed increase...since the mid-20th century is very likely [meaning 90 to 95 percent] due to the increase in anthropogenic [meaning man-made] greenhouse gas emissions concentrations." Since then, this conclusion has become even more certain.

3. In an Addendum is my table summarizing environmental conditions and mass extinctions throughout geologic time since 500 million years ago when the first forms of life appeared on Earth.

4. Methane—natural gas—is a far more potent GHG than CO_2, which has a climate-changing rating per molecule of just 1. The climate-changing rating per molecule of natural gas exceeds 100 in the short term and then (unlike CO_2) declines toward zero in about 100 years. Here we use the rating of 70, its approximate potency over about 25 years, because one generation is perhaps all the time humanity will have before passing a climate tipping point of no return.

5. The multiplied impact of escaping, "fugitive" natural gas was identified in about 2010 by Prof. Robert Howarth of Cornell University. Studies by NOAA, driving instrument-equipped vehicles though

natural-gas well fields, showed that from 3 to 8 percent—and sometimes much more—of methane is leaking uncontrolled into the air. Though the natural gas producers dispute the rate of leaking, this research has never been refuted either with facts or in theory.

6. James Hansen since retiring has become an activist, and his first warning to Congress in 1988 has since been multiplied by reports and books, including his own book in 2009. The latest (2018) and upcoming reports of the U.N.'s International Panel on Climate Change are at https://www.ipcc.ch/. The latest (2018) U.S. National Climate Assessment is at https://nca2018.globalchange.gov/. Books include the following:

- *The End of Nature*, by Bill McKibben (1989 and many subsequent republications)
- *Earth in the Balance: Ecology and the Human Spirit*, by Al Gore (Penguin Random House, 1992); also *An Inconvenient Truth: The Planetary Emergency of Global Warming and What We Can Do About It* (Penguin Random House, 2006); and *The Future: Six Drivers of Global Change* (Penguin Random House, 2013)
- *Field Notes from a Catastrophe: Man, Nature, and Climate Change*, by Elizabeth Kolbert (Bloomsbury Publishing, 2007)
- *Under a Green Sky: Global Warming, the Mass Extinctions of the Past, and What They Can Tell Us About Our Future*, by Peter D. Ward (Smithsonian, 2007)
- *Storms of My Grandchildren: The Truth About the Coming Climate Catastrophe and Our Last Chance to Save Humanity*, by James Hansen (Bloomsbury USA, 2009)
- *High Tide on Main Street: Rising Sea Level and the Coming Coastal Crisis*, by John Englander (The Science Bookshelf, 2nd edition, 2013)
- *The Madhouse Effect: How Climate Change Denial Is Threatening Our Planet*, by Michael E. Mann and Tom Toles (Columbia University Press, 2016)
- *Ends of the World: Volcanic Apocalypses, Lethal Oceans, and Our Quest to Understand Earth's Past Mass Extinctions*, by Peter Brannen (Harper Collins, 2017)

- *This Is the Way the World Ends: How Droughts and Die-Offs, Heat Waves and Hurricanes Are Converging on America*, by Jeff Nesbit (Thomas Dunne Books, St. Martin's Press, 2018)
- *The Uninhabitable Earth: Life After Warming*, by David Wallace-Wells (Tim Dugan Books, 2019)

7. *Massachusetts v. EPA*, 549 U.S. 497 (2007)

8. *Last Train to Paradise: Henry Flagler and the Spectacular Rise and Fall of a Railroad That Crossed an Ocean,* by Les Standiford (Crown, 2002). A co-founder with John D. Rockefeller of Standard Oil Co., Flagler built the impressive Florida East Coast Railway. But on Labor Day of 1935, what today we would label a "category-five" hurricane pulverized the rail line extension from Miami to Key West into oblivion, when the Florida Keys were hit by a 20-foot tidal wave and winds of perhaps 200 mph. It is perhaps reading too much into this history to see it as a metaphoric harbinger of what is to come from climate change...but your writer could not resist.

Chapter 10—Herr Professor Doktor: Lessons from Germany

In 1999, I was awarded a fellowship that took Donna and me to a different culture and assignment that gave the opportunity to teach formally for the first time in my life. As a visiting professor sponsored by the U.S.-German Fulbright Commission and invited by Professor Thomas Lundmark, I would receive a living stipend and university housing, and again EPA would not have to dig into its pocket to pay. With the Faculty of Law at the University of North Rhine–Westphalia, in Münster, Germany, I would teach U.S. environmental law and U.S. constitutional law. So as not to be gone from Washington for most of a year, I opted for only the spring semester of 2000. As in the earlier chapter on Paris, this chapter about the business of working will also inform and entertain regarding the culture, sights, and adventures to be enjoyed by a pollution fighter on an official assignment abroad.

Before the spring semester, the Fulbright program invited us to come to Berlin in September 1999 to three days of orientation. Between classes in how to be a proper Fulbright award recipient, we were taken to visit the Reichstag, home of the German parliament. It had burned mysteriously in 1933, just one month after Adolf Hitler had been sworn in as Chancellor of Germany. The Nazis blamed the fire on Communist agitators, and Hitler used the fire as a pretext to impose emergency powers. Germany's self-created emergency under Nazi rule ended 12 years later in utter devastation by 1945.

After more than 60 years in ruins as a reminder of the folly of allowing a democracy to fall to an autocrat, the Reichstag was beautifully restored from 1995 to 1999, and it had just reopened earlier in the very month of September when we were there. Our Fulbright tour took us walking up curving ramps inside the top of its glass dome atop the parliamentary hall. This dome is a physical embodiment of transparency, because from here a visitor looks straight down far below to see parliament at work. The openness of the dome symbolizes that lawmakers will be held accountable in elections, as the people are watching. Coming down to sit for a lecture in the balcony of the hall, on the wall behind the speaker's podium we saw a large version of the double-headed eagle, traditional symbol of Germany (and Austria) that must constantly look both east and west. But this new eagle was not screeching and threatening France and Poland into submission. Today's German eagle looked more like a fat and docile chicken, a comforting thought indeed considering what the Germans have shown themselves capable of doing—both to as well as for—Western Civilization. We also visited the Pergamon Museum, housing extraordinary Greek and Middle Eastern antiquities, that for so many years had been inaccessible, sequestered in East Berlin because of Communist domination.

In March 2000, Donna and I arrived in Münster, Germany, for the spring semester at the University of North Rhine–Westphalia. While Americans may know Münster cheese, were you to ask for it by name in this town in northwest Germany near the Dutch border, you would get a puzzled look. Either there is no Münster cheese, or all the local cheese of any variety is Münster cheese! In World War II, the city of Münster was a gestapo regional headquarters, and as the last German city flying west, Münster was a target for Allied bombers returning from Berlin dropping any remaining ordnance. From photos we saw, except for some thick church walls, every building was obliterated down to the stubs of its walls, standing at most about three feet tall. Amazingly, by about 1960 the resilient people rebuilt the old town along the old street lines, with new buildings to historic dimensions. We would find that today Münster's attractions are many, including its large university in a town of perhaps 300,000 people. Formerly surrounded by a fortified wall (once very necessary in such flat land), this medieval wall was leveled. Atop what was rubble is now a park with a wide walking path among trees, and to the outer side below in the remains of the moat often there is water attracting ducks and swans. In this circular park, one can easily bike or in a healthy walk tour the entire old city, and today again Münster is magnificent.

Upon first arriving in the railroad station, we took a taxi to our little apartment one floor up in a complex of about 75 apartments. This was university housing for foreign graduate students (many from China) and visiting professors like me— Herr Professor Doktor Emory. Our apartment was very energy efficient. Before taking a shower, one had to turn on a water heater that otherwise stayed off, the sinks had instant hot-water coils controlled by the faucet handles, and the refrigerator was tiny.

We were hungry and would have to eat and go shopping, and we hardly knew a word of German. Fortunately, almost directly across the street was a neighborhood Italian restaurant, with its menu in German and Italian, but I was able to speak only French and Spanish. Hearing that my efforts in Italian sounded much like Spanish, the owner brought out the dishwasher—a man from Central America—to translate. Everyone was amused, he helped us to order our meal, and from that day we could not walk by the restaurant without been greeted with *"Hallo und Willkommen, Herr Professor Doktor und Frau Professor Doktor!"* They were so kind, the food was *delicioso*, and we ate there often.

To buy groceries, we went regularly to the cathedral square, the Domplatz, where perhaps twice a week a convoy of splendid trucks would arrive direct from farms and other vendors. These were not shabby old panel vans with little side windows selling tacos like we see in America, but polished and elegant makes such as Mercedes Benz, and each one opened up into an entire little store with an awning or hard side overhead sheltering the customers standing before the gleaming glass counter. All was brightly lit and scrupulously clean.

Timidly we approached the first van, a vendor selling chocolates. Upon first meeting any vendor, I would say *"Ich bin hier ein amerikanischer Professor. Ich spreche kein Deutsch,"* so that he would know that this American professor did not speak German and accept some confusion on our part. We sampled the chocolate, bought some, and after our first visit or two, when seeing us coming he would be holding a sample out to us and with a big smile saying, *"Professor, probieren Sie meine Schokolade."* He offered a sample also to Donna whenever she— welcomed as *Frau Professor Doktor*—might shop alone. Most of the merchants were just as cheerful and obliging. Considering the formal "titles" we found ourselves carrying and the reputation of many Germans as "stiff," we had thought that Germany might be reserved or unwelcoming. But compared to Paris, where an unsmiling face is to be worn perhaps even after formal introductions, this seemed the friendliest place we had ever been, and we were just getting started.

Of course, on our humble academic stipend from the German Fulbright program, Donna and I ate most meals in our apartment, and we produced the normal amount of household trash. We found in our apartment's desk two or three dense pages of the university's instructions for recycling, helpfully written in both Chinese and German, neither of which could we read. But this was a moment I had been anticipating for years, because during 1996 and 1997 at the OECD in Paris, as described in chapter 8, my task had been to study the details of Extended Producer Responsibility (EPR), the then very new German approach to recycling that is called the "Green Dot" or "Grüne Punkt" program.[1] Coming from America, the "throw-it-away" land, I was so ready to experience the German "take-it-back" method. I already held the admittedly dogmatic view that to recycle routinely and properly is to behave ethically and responsibly toward our planet, or God's creation, call it what you will. Not all of us will be full-time, professional pollution fighters, but every one of us who recycles properly will have joined the fight against pollution.

On our first walks in Münster, Donna and I had contemplated at scattered central locations the placement of three giant bins or "bells" for disposing empty bottles, one for each color of glass, whether clear, green, or brown. Just outside our apartment, we had seen large, multi-resident roll-to-curbside bins—green, blue, yellow, brown, and gray—with pictures showing residents what waste is to go into each. Even without understanding our apartment's pages of recycling instructions in Chinese and German, our role became clear. As consumers and residents in Münster, we were expected to begin the process by sorting or separating and then putting the right items in the right containers. And so we did, sometimes sheepishly lest neighbors count the accumulation of empty wine bottles that Donna was placing in the green-glass bin and the number of empty beer bottles that I was placing in the brown-glass bin.

A full-service grocery store in Münster was not within walking distance, so in our car we would drive about two miles to a store. Here we experienced the retailer's role in the Green Dot program. On arrival, we would hand our recyclables to the attendant in a special room by the entrance. He would value them while we were shopping and have ready for us at checkout a recycling credit to reduce the cost of our new purchases that day! This store credit was a free-market incentive to customers to both recycle and to shop there and be rewarded. While our grocery store participated in this way to attract customers, this was not so everywhere. Many retailers chose to avoid the space and extra employee required for the work of retail take-back. I believe this required from them a higher level of financial support for their private trade association that runs the Green Dot program of curbside collection in all neighborhoods.

During World War II in America, such retail-store recycling was a patriotic duty and everyone participated. Even after WWII, as a young boy in Baltimore I would return empty soda bottles to the corner store for the cash refunds. In those days, I could buy "penny" candy, and three nickels added up to serious money, enough for a ticket into the Saturday morning children's show at the movie theatre. With 14 more cents, I could make the round trip to the movies on the public bus. But perhaps by the 1960s, in every state the beverage companies began a campaign to repeal most or all deposit mandates and since then to defeat any new "bottle-bill" legislation. They considered their campaign successful; I consider it antisocial and a typical corporate move that should not be tolerated.

On the supply side, too often the private sector will maximize profits by off-loading—economists call this "externalizing"—their products' costs and impacts onto society, governments, and the environment. Businesses naturally minimize their responsibility for litter and pollution, and keep production costs low, so that their sales cannot be undercut by competitors. The result is what economists call "a race to the bottom." So while shopping in Münster, we were surprised to find the aluminum and glass containers of products including those of the Coca-Cola company stamped with the Green Dot logo and thus participating fully in effective European recycling! Then the sad thought dawned that these same American companies would only do this to gain EU market access, while at the same time in the U.S. still aggressively opposing all attempts by state and local governments to increase recycling in our homeland. I daresay that few Americans know of this unadvertised example of transatlantic duplicity and freedom without responsibility. Within the U.S., the bottlers' resistance to effective recycling has continued for decades and in almost every state. Nevertheless, in recent years, slowly and on a state-by-state basis and always fighting the beverage-companies' lobbyists, a few states have managed to legislate mandatory deposits to increase recycling, even sometimes including plastic as well as glass bottles.

When an entire business sector coordinates a race to the bottom to destroy a functioning market (as the bottlers destroyed most recycling after World War II in America), or when there is no free market able to create some "public goods," we must look to government for solutions. For police and fire departments, the U.S. Marines, National Park Service, the Environmental Protection Agency, and modern "turnpikes" and highway river crossings—public goods all—the private sector shows no interest because they cannot make income or profits except by receiving tax dollars as government contractors. For "public goods" that cannot made profitably, only government can provide them. This is not a radical theory—why, even in America all governments impose gasoline taxes to pay for roads, and charge tolls on big public bridges and tunnels, and many Americans can understand that those who use such a "public good" should pay the government for providing it when no private interest can or will do so correctly. We also agree in America that most, perhaps 75 percent, of an economy should consist of "private goods" —saleable products from shoes to cars to beverages and whatever—as these are best created by capitalism.

In addition to "pay as you go" user fees and tolls for public goods, libertarians and most economists agree that privatization and the use of market instruments very often can achieve a public good or social goal more efficiently and effectively than taxes and government. This is well understood in Germany, where a well-designed program for waste management since 1994 has blocked German manufacturers and retailers from what they would ordinarily do (as is done in the U.S.), which is to "externalize"—or impose on local governments and the environment—the costs and impacts of trash pollution caused by their products, containers, and packagings. Germans call this program "Extended Producer Responsibility" (EPR). Soon after EPR began in Germany, a Directive of the EU required all citizens and private enterprises to manage their waste on the German model, and today at least 29 countries use the program.

New legal obligations undergird the Green Dot program. Consistent with the name "Extended Producer Responsibility," national governments impose high recycling rates as legal responsibilities on their manufacturers and retailers. And manufacturers at all times—even while their products, containers, and packagings are out circulating in the hands of consumers—by law through endless life cycles always own the materials in them. To finance the manufacturers' and retailers' collective legal responsibility to fund and organize private curbside and retail-store collections, the manufacturers must pay to have the "right" to license and apply the unique Green Dot emblem or logo on all their containers, packagings, and many consumer products that must be recycled after they are used.

This Green Dot licensing-fee money "internalizes" the cost of trash control and disposal up-front in the market price of Green Dot items. These fees to the manufacturers' and retailers' trade association fund the private curbside and retail-store collections. This association zealously reclaims the valuable secondary materials in the trash that its members own. Then (to reduce Green-Dot licensing fees) the association makes money by selling the recycled and recovered materials back to its members, who use these ingredients to manufacture new products, containers, and packagings. These producers do not have to buy so much virgin material that would be more expensive and that would impose environmental cost or damage during extraction and often long-distance transportation being imported from far away. Also, to keep their costs down, many manufacturers design less wasteful packaging, and some large products (including German cars) are designed for easy dismantling of parts and sorting by the material that is in them.

While U.S. opponents of recycling falsely label EPR as "socialism," in fact it is the exact opposite—it is privatization. EU governments wisely have stepped out of trash management (and reduced residents' property tax bills accordingly), because the private sector can handle trash so much more efficiently than local governments. The result is that most Western Europeans recycle at the highest rates in the world, about twice the rate of the U.S. Another benefit—because Germans value highly their personal health and love their land—is that Germans have to endure relatively few ugly landfills and smoky waste incinerators. EPR is just one outstanding example of how, by government market formation and wise regulation, an entire business sector can be brought to doing the right thing for society and for the environment. All competitors share and are treated equally, there has been no loss of business profits, and the value of little Germany's export economy is as big as that of the huge USA. As a policy instrument, the Green Dot licensing fee to suppress trash pollution has its exact analogue in a carbon tax effective to internalize in fossil-fuel pricing the cost of its CO_2 air pollution that is destroying our climate. Indeed, EPR contains many lessons that can be applied to protect the climate pollution, as we shall see in the next chapter.

But in the U.S., the "land of the free, and the home of the brave"—sometimes called the "throw-away society"—we do not seem to understand the wisdom in using government-mandated privatization to create a highly efficient market that would not exist naturally. In too many states, we seem incapable of re-creating a natural market that a conspiracy of capitalism destroyed after WWII (when the beverage makers killed recycling of their bottles). So we too often just dump and bury or burn household and municipal waste. We pile up massive and ugly landfills, sometimes called "mount trashmores," on increasingly scarce land near urban areas. We build dicey municipal incinerators, emitting hard-to-control toxic smoke, and hard-to-get-rid-of toxic ash that goes into landfills that may leach chemicals that contaminate drinking water. I am not saying that these waste "management" facilities cannot possibly be operated almost or perhaps cleanly. But at best they are ugly permanent blights on the landscape, and they may threaten the health of people and nature. They are symptoms of and monuments to ignorance and greed. Little or none of this is tolerated in Germany.

After WWI, out-of-control suburban sprawl began in the U.S. because of the rapid conversion of factories from making war machines to making cars for the popular market. To increase sales, a different capitalist conspiracy of General Motors, Firestone Tire, and a subsidiary of Standard Oil of California bought up and shut down in America many of the urban trolleys or "street cars" (which Europeans call "trams"). But a key quality of German culture is the respect for farmland and public transportation. In Germany, farmland is regarded as national patrimony, not as in America a commodity to be paved and roofed over at will with suburban sprawl amid scattered landfills and municipal incinerators. Germans do not lack the self-control and good taste to strictly protect their land. While Münster today expands far beyond the former wall and moat of the old city, in most places the line between development and open land is very sharp. Münster's suburban city limit is often a long line of rear yards, beyond which are to be seen lovely views with no structures except historic and working farms and barns. After traveling (best by bicycle) out perhaps five to ten kilometers through the farmland, eventually one arrives at the next outlying town or village. Its boundaries also are delineated sharply, and each is served regularly by a municipal bus running between the town or village and Münster's central rail station. At this *Hauptbahnhof* there is a large parking lot and garage for thousands of vehicles, but only for bicycles—I saw no garage for cars. While a traveler is away on the train, in the bike garage there is a mechanic's shop where a bike can be fixed and cleaned for the traveler's return to Münster.

In Münster I taught two classes, both in English, commuting on my bicycle in 15 minutes, the only time I have ever had the fun of riding a bike to work. For this bike I can thank Natalie Meier, a German law student completing her studies who by chance had also been my international legal intern in EPA Headquarters in the previous summer of 1999. From her family home about an hour away from Münster, she also loaned us a German television, and during the semester she was often our local guide and companion on walks about the city and its lakeside park. After my classes, she would often appear at the right time to drink a beer, meeting in an outdoor café as I unwound from some tension of being a stand-up professor. She remains our friend to this day, and Donna and I call her "our German daughter."

German students have an additional year of high school, like a 13th grade, then the top 15 percent who qualify on national tests proceed with free tuition to a university. Law school combines with college and takes four years, followed by two years encompassing four mandatory and rotating six-month internships, rather like a medical residency in the U.S. At a few German universities including North Rhine–Westphalia, a student may opt for a two-year certificate in French law taught in the French language, or in Anglo-American law taught in English. Speaking English, I taught two classes, a small classroom elective in U.S. environmental law, and in an auditorium a large class of perhaps 60 students studying U.S. constitutional law and government. This may not seem like a heavy load, but I was very busy writing my own courses from scratch, and I found it challenging to become as very well prepared for a class as I knew would be necessary.

My classes were scheduled for afternoons just after the university-provided free after-lunch German lessons, and I quickly found that I was exhausted from the language lessons and then not at my best teaching my classes. I could not change the schedule, and I dropped the German lessons to which I had been so looking forward. Before becoming a language-school dropout, while attending the first lessons I saw that most of my classmates were Chinese graduate students who already in China had learned some English. With their young brains, they were picking up German quickly, and they probably saw it as an antique English dialect, which to some extent it is. To my lasting regret, I learned little of this half of the English language (the other half being Latin coming through France).

My small class in environmental law was very personal and easily interactive. I really came to know these students, and several of them visited Donna and me in the U.S. the following year. The large class in the U.S. Constitution was more challenging, and each session required many hours of preparation. Naturally, in the U.S. I had practiced law always within the framework of the U.S. Constitution, but I had not applied it every day for many years as I had done with environmental law. And German students in a large hall seemed to expect lectures to which they listen obediently. But in the U.S.—because the goal is not so much to transmit the law itself as it is to transmit the ability to think about the law—the law is taught by a more interactive and Socratic method. Very different from preparing a lecture, preparing for an interactive class is like writing a play, though I could only plan my Socratic questions and would need to be able to respond to all students' answers which could be almost anything. My classes would be mix of both methods of instruction.

In the large class, from the start I also had the problem of three uninterested boys who arrived late and then sat chatting rudely in the back. By the third session I was ready for them. I called them out, told them to stand up, and either to leave now and get no grade, or next time to arrive on time, keep quiet, and pay attention. During my "friendly advice" to the miscreants, the rest of the class just stared silently at the three standing boys. At the end of that class, I was surprised that most students rhythmically slammed or pounded on their desktops for about five seconds before leaving the room. Not knowing what to make of it, I asked one of the girls, "Does that mean 'Yankee go home'?" She said, "Certainly not, Professor, it means that we like you, you are keeping good order, and you are teaching us well."

This praise inspired me to even greater preparatory effort to create a participatory exercise. As we were studying the Bill of Rights including the Second Amendment to the U.S. Constitution, in the next week I asked the class to divide into two halves, boys and girls mixed. To encourage the girls to speak up more, I called one half of the class the "Pistol-Packin' Mamas" and the other half the "Mothers Against Handgun Death" (MAHD). The Pistol-Packin' Mamas seemed somewhere between amused and aghast at being asked to play the part of Americans whose behavior with firearms seems so angry and irresponsible in Germany where civilians may not carry pistols. Regardless, their role was to wave their pencils as imaginary pistols and to argue the legal principles supporting the right to keep and bear firearms. The MAHD group had the easier role, to argue what I consider to be proper interpretation of the Constitution's Second Amendment— that there is no unlimited right to possess or carry firearms. There are exceptions for traditional pistols used for home protection and for long guns used for hunting or by members of a government militia who are trained and trusted to carry military weapons.

The MAHD group became mad enough, showing some anger at horrific mass shootings everywhere in America resulting from the glut of military weapons designed only to kill as many enemy soldiers as fast as possible. Enjoying some freedom to be irresponsible, which is quite rare in Germany, the "Pistol-Packin' Mamas" seemed to enjoy their flirtation with the means of instant death. Both sides argued the issues well enough. But, as I had expected, my students' arguments were limited to right and wrong considering today's social policies and the need for personal vs. public safety. Before class ended, I went into my law professor's *persona* to demonstrate why the Constitution's framers' or founders' intent in 1791 is key and must not be overlooked. I ended the class explaining that their intent can be reconstructed by knowing the historical context in which they were living and by an 18th-century linguistic analysis of the words they used, especially "keep" and "bear."[2] The class seemed to appreciate their unique, interactive experience, and even my short closing lecture showing them key parts of a proper constitutional analysis that they had missed. At the end of this class, the desk banging was loud and long.

Excepting the three uninterested boys who remained surly and distant, my students thanked America for crushing Hitler and saving them from the Russians, but on the issue of firearms loose throughout society, the same America was confounding to them. Even the "Pistol-Packin' Mamas" after class could not fathom why "the land of the free and the home of the brave" had slipped to become notorious world-wide as the land of worsening gun violence, uncontrolled by freedom run amok. They asked how such a powerful nation could, on this issue, have such a passive government, unable to keep good order like Germans expect and enjoy. I share their bewilderment, augmented by my exasperation and anger that reform seems impossible.

My students' natural tendencies favored the cohesion and stability of their post-war, well-planned society. There is so much that Germany can teach America about apprentice-training programs, mandatory union membership on the boards of large corporations, how Germany manages business cycles with limited unemployment and without total layoffs, why German exports are equal to those of the U.S. which has four times the population and 28 times the land area, etc. I urge my readers to experience this difference in national cultures that makes Germany one of today's most progressive and yet self-regulating democracies. On the spectrum between good order and liberty, the large and diverse U.S. lies much closer to liberty. A nation with weak social norms and little respect for decency and the rule of law—a nation with too much freedom—can fall into chaos. No democracy is ever to be taken for granted or assumed, but each is a work in progress in which its every good citizen must take a lifelong, constructive role.

Of course, Germany's modern history until 1945 shows that too much obedience and order also can cause a fall into chaos. From the heights of 19th-century scientific, technical, and artistic achievement, Germany fell to the absolute depths of Nazi fascism and to utter devastation by the Allies. In my class on American constitutional law, all of my German students knew the name of Konrad Adenauer, the first Chancellor of the Federal Republic of Germany that emerged from the ashes of World War II. From 1949 to 1963, he led his country back to be again a prudent and prosperous nation, building close relations with former enemies France, the U.K., and the U.S. Some of my law students knew the name of George Washington, but I was surprised that they could not name the originator who orchestrated the constitution of modern Germany before Adenauer's leadership began in 1949. Probably my students were surprised to learn that an American could be said to be the "Founding Father" of modern Germany.[3]

Four-star U.S. Army General Lucius D. Clay was the American military governor in Berlin from the end of World War II. With other Western authorities, he assembled *émigré* and surviving German scholars and civic leaders who had opposed Hitler. To write the constitution for the new Federal Republic of Germany, they considered the U.S. Constitution to be a very useful model. Unlike the British constitution which is unwritten, and the French constitution which has changed several times, the U.S. Constitution has relative certainty and permanency. Perhaps the most significant feature taken from the U.S. is that the new Germany elevated the sovereignty of the 16 German states (*Bundesländer*). By their decentralizing the new Germany into a *federal* government, we all can hope that another Hitler may not so easily come to national power.

In 1948, the Russians blocked land access to Berlin. Unfazed, General Clay organized the Berlin airlift to supply Allied forces inside the surrounded city. Then, without permission from headquarters in Washington, he continued to supply all people in West Berlin. News pictures flashed everywhere of very thin but happy German children grabbing for candies on tiny parachutes dropping from incoming American planes (the "candy bombers") moments before the planes landed to offload food and coal for the winter. Germans began to warm to the Western Allies who had conquered them, and Clay's superiors in Washington dared not stop the risky rescue. Moscow, seeing that German and international opinion was building against its bullying, in 1949 lifted its land blockade. When General Clay died in 1978, the free people of Berlin placed a footstone at his grave at West Point. It reads: *"Wir danken dem Bewahrer unserer Freiheit"* ("We thank the defender of our freedom"). After my students learned the story of General Clay, at the end of class they pounded and banged their desks as loudly as ever.

During my time in Münster, I was invited to give a lecture at the University of Bremen, and I attended an environmental conference in Arnheim in the Netherlands. The best extracurricular opportunity to be a good-will "ambassador" was when our State Department sent me to speak at the annual celebration of the U.S. Army's liberation of Pilsen, a small city in the western Czech Republic. You will recognize the name as the home of a great beer; Pilsner lager was born here. I was amazed that the U.S. was so highly esteemed by Pilseners, because—by prior agreement with Stalin—at the end of the war the liberating American forces had retreated, and Pilsen languished for more than 40 years, stomped under the Russian heel. Happily, apparently assisted by their great beer, the Pilseners remained cheerful and seemed to have forgotten or forgiven completely. Their annual observance is to remember their joy to have been liberated by American forces, and our welcome in Pilsen was a celebration. Afterwards, our State Department escort drove us to Prague to stay three nights (at our expense) in a well-located hotel she selected for us. And so we explored yet another gorgeous European city. From Prague on Sunday we went to its airport, Donna flew directly back to work in the U.S., and I flew across Germany back to work in Münster. Monday morning came too soon.

Before we depart from Münster, leaving untold so many more stories of sights seen and adventures taken, I must tell you why Münster itself is important to world history. We had been to its town hall and seen inside the 10-foot-high symbolic sword, hundreds of years old. On medieval market days, this sword was placed out in front, in view of all would-be pickpockets and vendors who would put their fingers on the scale, as a warning that justice would be swift and hard. But I had wondered why I was seeing many Dutch tour buses coming to the town hall, especially on weekends. Just this sword—though an interesting symbol of fair play or else—could not have been enough to attract them. Of course, I knew the importance in Philadelphia of the former Pennsylvania State House, now called "Independence Hall," as the home of both the U.S. Declaration of Independence and the U.S. Constitution. I was about to learn that the Münster Town Hall contains a back room also called the "Independence Hall" of the Netherlands, and that this hall is one of the two venues for the signing of the Peace of Westphalia in 1648.

This international agreement concluded many decades of horrific war in which about eight million people had died. It

201

ended the brutal domination by Catholic Spain of the Protestant Netherlands, which then became free. Unless you are of Dutch background, you may find this only mildly interesting. But if you are headed for a career in diplomacy or international work of any kind, including working somewhere else in the world as a pollution fighter, you should know this: the Peace of Westphalia by treaty is the basis for today's system of global political order based on co-existing sovereign states. It established a balance of power in an attempt to prevent aggression across borders. Most important is that it established new norms, including one against interference in another state's domestic affairs and one for the immunity of diplomats. Since then, without fear of arrest, credentialed diplomats may travel to negotiate to prevent and to end wars. As European influence from the 17th century was beginning to spread across the globe, the Westphalian principles since 1648 became the foundation for international law[4] that undergirds today's prevailing world order. Today, your consular officers will be available to assist you should you have difficulty almost anywhere in the world.

Before I learned this history, my German law students would have known it. With so much to talk about, sometimes I would take them for lunch or beers after class, and Donna with a glass of wine would join us. Because the German government informs schoolchildren fully about Germany's terrible behavior and tragic history in the 20th century until 1946, around the table my students all said that they abhorred the history of Nazi Germany. Several said that the years of support for Hitler can only be understood as a time of national insanity, and that their grandparents' attempted explanations never were convincing. My students expressed gratitude to the USA first for crushing the Nazis and then for keeping West Germany safe from Russia. They told us that they liked our American music, movies, and talking with Donna and me because we are Americans.

Walking back to our apartment, often Donna and I passed through a cemetery that many residents enjoyed as if it were a park. In one corner was a haunting section of a perhaps 30 very dark crosses at the graves of German soldiers dead in war. This contrasted with the many white crosses and monuments, perfectly maintained amid flowering plants and many offerings of cut flowers. It seemed that even if no family member survived, every grave was well cared for by both cemetery staff and by townspeople, some carrying in brooms, rakes, and shovels. The cleanliness, the quiet peacefulness, the polite respect among neighbors strolling together—Donna and I often chose to walk through the cemetery.

Most remarkable was the grave of Sister Maria Euthymia, a nun born Emma Üffing in 1914 as one of 11 children in a farm family. The site around her grave had expanded to contain uncountable offerings of flowers, candles, and prayer cards. Several prayerful people were always in attendance, and we were told that for her life of heroic virtue by the Pope in 1988 she had been venerated in the first step to sainthood. We learned that as a baby she had suffered from rickets that stunted her growth, and she was always in poor health, yet she entered the order of Sisters of the Congregation of Compassion (*Klemensschwestern*). She studied and became an excellent "sister" (meaning medical nurse in German) of clemency. Throughout World War II, she nursed prisoners of war and foreigners—many being British and Ukrainian people, Poles and Russians—trapped in Germany during the war and often having infectious diseases. With her warm and quiet sympathy, she gave them hope in the midst of total war. In 1955, at the young age of 41, she died of cancer in Münster.

For most of her adult life until age 31 in 1945, Sister Euthymia lived under the evil tyrant who had seized political power and destroyed her country. She had only the power of goodness and mercy despite her hard and constricted life, and she felt herself sustained entirely by God's love. Though raised respectively in the Catholic and the Episcopalian churches, neither Donna nor I today are religious, yet we came frequently to stand silently and usually among others also visiting her grave. We considered this merciful Sister of Compassion to be the very antithesis of Hitler, and we were pleased to see that so many townspeople also came to remember her. The year after we left Münster, Sister Euthymia was beatified, which in the Catholic Church puts her one step away from being Saint Euthymia. We think of her still.

By mid-July 2000, law-school exams had been taken and graded. Donna and I were sad to leave when our time in Münster ended. We knew that, if in a future year were we ever to return to Münster, all my students would have moved on, never to be seen again. So how pleased we were that during the next year four students asked to visit us in Baltimore, and at three different times they did so. Two came together and then went on to stay in Washington in international student lodgings that I found for them there. All found surprising and somewhat disturbing that American flags seemed to fly in so many places—small American flags on many blue-collar homes and giant flags over auto sales lots. One visiting student memorably said, "In Germany, we do not have these religious, patriotic expressions."

Indeed, it is good that in Germany today to present a Nazi flag, song, salute, or greeting is a crime, though all these expressions in the U.S. are allowed as a First Amendment freedom. Today's Federal Republic of Germany, and modern Germans themselves, "walk on eggshells" to avoid militaristic displays and actions. As Germans are a superbly competent and well-organized people, this is a very good thing for them, for the U.S., and for all of Europe. The many good qualities of my law students, some to be future leaders, leaves me happily feeling that Germany will remain among the most civilized and successful nations on our planet.

The Peace of Westphalia, signed in Münster, was the foundation for my opportunity for 17 years, between 1994 and 2011, occasionally to leave America to provide environmental expertise in sovereign, foreign countries other than France and Germany, and especially in Latin America. Many of these nations were parties to modern environmental treaties, and they all wanted to learn U.S. methods to control pollution without damaging their economies. Though some were hopelessly corrupt, despotic, and dangerous, I would work safely as an invited and honored visitor, provided I was very careful. I remember one elegant hotel with a lovely garden and a sign at the garden entrance warning that guests should not leave the outdoor dining area to enter the garden after dark! This meant after dinner walking for fresh, night air only outside the hotel's front door but not beyond the heavily armed guards at the ends of the street fronting the hotel. I would politely greet them each with *Hola, buenas noches*—and similarly also greet the armed guard at the hotel's front door. I would only get in a taxi from the front door of a hotel or ordered up by a dinnertime restaurant, and not from anywhere in the street.

In Western Europe, of course many countries are safe, with good governments, clean, green, and very protective of environmental and cultural resources. By now you will have surmised correctly that—from my European perspectives—I think that sometimes the U.S. seems relatively uncivilized, a place where too many uncaring misbehaviors are tolerated in the name of unbridled freedom. Indeed, were my family and employer not in America, I might have preferred living in France or Germany. My foreign assignments there were never more than three or four months, but it was enough time to make some comparisons in which the USA frequently does not measure up. Fortunately, in the U.S. we have not fallen to the point that every *hotel, farmacia, restaurante elegante,* and *gasolinera* requires a private guard with a pistol if not a machine gun.

In late summer 2000, from the Fulbright Professorship in Germany I returned to Washington to work in EPA's International Compliance Division in the Office of Federal Activities. After 13 months there, on September 11, 2001, terrorists flew two hijacked airliners into the gigantic Twin Towers of the World Trade Center in New York City, killing over 2,600 people in a few minutes. Of course, it was a colossal failure that several U.S. governmental agencies were not exchanging bits of information about the plotters that each agency secretly possessed before the attack. So that supposed teammates would "share the basketball" in the future, Congress created the Department of Homeland Security. Immediately after the attack, "hide or hog the ball" continued with another botched "headquarters" decision of the U.S. government like the one that had killed my grandfather in World War I.[5] Ignoring scientific advice to proceed with extreme caution, high-level politicians in Washington showed callous disregard for the safety of the first-responders and cleanup workers. After the Towers collapsed into a dusty pile, the scientists of EPA were warning the EPA Administrator, Christie Todd Whitman, that nobody should be allowed to even be there, much less work there, without bottled oxygen or full respirator masks. The site was contaminated with jet fuel, dioxins, PCBs, heavy metals, asbestos, and incredibly high levels of cement-dust alkalinity, and they wanted her to declare it unsafe without the appropriate protective equipment. Unfortunately, the National Security Council in the White House of President George Bush blithely overruled her and allowed workers on the site with only flimsy paper face masks. EPA Administrator Whitman acceded to the White House order that EPA public relations spokespersons declare the air at the site to be "safe." Then the White House classified (declared secret) the accumulating evidence that the toxic-waste "pile" was making the unprotected workers very, very sick.

As of 2019, about 2,000 on-site workers have died painful, lingering deaths from working without proper protective equipment on what should have been declared a "Superfund" toxic-waste site. In a few more years, the cancer and respiratory death toll of the tens of thousands of exposed 9/11-site workers will exceed the number of people kinetically killed in the actual attack and collapse of the World Trade Center. Like Colin Powell, who testified incorrectly to the U.N. that Saddam Hussein had a nuclear weapons capability, Christie Todd Whitman also is a fine American, and any good person can make a big mistake. I would imagine that today she too feels shame and wishes that she had resigned on the spot when ordered to ignore the EPA scientists. They were the experts in the field with eyes on the problem, just like my grandfather with eyes on the enemy who was ignored by the headquarters artillery commander sitting safely far from the danger—and just like the climate scientists whom politicians in high office ignore or accuse of perpetrating a hoax when the scientists are just trying to warn us.

Following 9/11 and the collapse of the World Trade Center towers, bungling in Washington at the highest level continued and was compounded by official deception leading to the White House scheme to falsely blame and subsequently invade Iraq in 2003. From then I observed international sympathy for the 9/11 attack melt away. A new frostiness impaired our foreign-assistance efforts abroad that were no longer quite so warmly invited and welcomed. Aggressive U.S. meddling threw the Middle East into turmoil, and climate neglect caused drought there that even contributed to the ensuing Syrian civil war and eventual outflow of refugees into Europe. Destabilizing Syrians flowed into modern Germany, a nation contrite and welcoming. They followed the Turks, who in 2000 stood in line with me at the *Ausländeramt* (immigration office), for permission to reside in Germany. Fleeing drought and famine in sub-Saharan Africa, more refugees come by boat across the open Mediterranean Sea into southern Europe.

It has become evident to the world that U.S. adventurism and self-absorption has inflicted unnecessary death on too many people and damaged the reputation of the United States. Our ham-fisted and trigger-happy White House of George Bush and Dick Cheney wasted many lives and over $1 trillion in public money. With our bellicose self-esteem, the U.S. maintains almost as many members of military marching bands and orchestras as we do diplomats or foreign-service officers. We have taken in very few of the refugees of forced migrations that our reckless and climate-damaging policies are generating. But these wrong-headed decisions are almost insignificant, and the number of deaths miniscule, compared to the future ruination that official, highest-level scorn for climate science will cause many average Americans—and the people of the world—to suffer in coming decades. So I have come fully to share my German law students' fears of excessive, unilateral, and misdirected nationalism. I have admired since 2000 how clear-headed Germany encouraged wind and solar energy, and in recent years took in more than its share of Syrian refugees. In 2019 when I write this, while enemies are laughing at the decline of U.S. influence in the world, our loyal allies are fearful. To young people reading this: I wish it were not so, but today my generation of negligent American grandparents has created and then handed you a mess.

Rather than end on such a sour note, and hoping that some of my readers will follow me and my German law students into the practice of law, I offer these reflections on the legal profession. After the end of my career and nearing the end of this book, it should be clear that I feel thoroughly satisfied having made the huge effort to go to law school and to rummage about in the profession until I found my passion working in public service as a pollution fighter. While I have criticized many a lawyer, and have joked about lawyers as the "second-oldest profession," I am not alone in observing that the average lawyer is more ethical and rules-based than the average businessman. For young people, the law is only one of many professional pathways into the fight against pollution, yet it is an essential one. I do hope that some of my readers will follow this path and become shields to preserve the blessings both of democracy and of the gifts of nature on this planet.

Of the 55 framers of the U.S. Constitution, 35 were lawyers, and these Founding Fathers designed our republic with a legal framework having mechanisms to block an unstable populist who might become an autocrat from coming to absolute power. I concur with Alexis de Tocqueville in seeing the great value and importance of lawyers in serving as a barrier or brake to the "unreflective passions of democracy."[6] In the 1830s through 1850s, writing after both the French Revolution and the ascendance of Napoleon, de Tocqueville remained conservative in fearing the leader of a mob. He wrote, "I cannot believe that a republic could subsist if the influence of the lawyers in public business did not increase in proportion to the power of the people." As to the attributes of lawyers that qualify them for a special influence in public affairs, he wrote, "Men who have made a special study of the laws...derive from the occupation certain habits of order, a taste for formalities, and a kind of instinctive regard for the regular connection of ideas, which naturally render them very hostile to the revolutionary spirit and the unreflecting passions of the multitude."

Beyond this conservative aspect, beyond serving as shields and champions in conflict resolution, the best lawyers implement a culture of civic wisdom based on respect for legal rights. This is founded in their belief in first knowing the facts, and then applying the rule of law, then assuring accountability of all citizens including those most empowered and elite. As de Tocqueville also wrote, "Lawyers belong to the people by birth and interest, and to the aristocracy by habit and taste; they may be looked upon as the connecting link of the two great classes of society." Lawyers may work in private practice for clients of wealth and high status, and the best of even highly paid lawyers will represent some worthy cases or causes *pro bono publico* (without charging a fee). Other lawyers may be employed by governments or volunteer to assert the public interest across social boundaries in work to assert the rights of the poor and disadvantaged. To end their careers, we often see that many of the best lawyers take up public service to become the courtroom judges of us all.

---

1. The OECD would eventually publish the fruit of my work as "Extended and Shared Producer Responsibility—Phase 2 Framework Report," OECD, Paris, 1998. The Report was finalized by my OECD colleague Claudia Busch, and it states that it "...is mostly developed from a draft report initially prepared [in 1996 and 1997] by Richard Emory, a U.S. Environmental Protection Agency specialist in international environmental policy and law". To read the report online, google "ENV/EPOC/PPC(97)20/REV2," or visit www.sourceoecd.org where all OECD publications are available.

2. The Founding Fathers' 18th-century use of the word "keep" may be a reference to the "castle keep," the central tower in a fortress that is the place of last retreat—and the place to keep the government's store of weaponry. "Keep" thus may refer to an armory where the militia would safely keep its piles of weapons, just as National Guard armories do today. To "bear" arms in 1791 also meant to collectively do so in a military sense, as when trudging along in a military column bearing a very heavy load of weapons and ammunition that will be needed in the battle ahead. (This is not to exclude that at the same time "bear" could mean to possess a weapon individually.) This linguistic analysis is consistent with the historical context that the Second Amendment was intended to assure the passage of the Bill of Rights by guaranteeing that a new national or "federal" standing army would not mean the elimination of the state militias that had fought and won independence from the British King. This interpretation was given life and credence

by invocation of the Second Amendment to authorize the continuation in each of our 50 states a militia force that we call "the National Guard."

3. *Lucius D. Clay: An American Life,* by Jean Edward Smith (First Glance Books 1990). He wrote many superb books, including *John Marshall: Definer of a Nation* (Henry Holt and Co. 1998), which any would-be lawyer must read. My favorite American is John Marshall, who served as one of Washington's officers, was briefly Secretary of State, and then became--not the first Chief Justice of the Supreme Court—but in the opinion of many the greatest Justice.

4. The Dutch jurist Hugo Grotius, though he died in 1645, is considered the intellectual father of international law and of the Peace of Westphalia. This treaty gave concrete expression to Grotius's concept that international relations should be governed not by threats and war, but by laws and mutual agreement to enforce those laws.

He was important also for applying the Roman concept of "corporation" to limit the civil liability of Dutch ship owners to the value of one wrecked ship and its lost cargo. This encouraged risk-taking voyages by the Dutch East India Company, trading of its shares on the original Amsterdam Stock Exchange, and the surge of colonial capitalism. Unfortunately, as we have seen in my chapter "Speaking Truth to Power," the "corporation" has since been expanded by the U.S. Department of Justice to become what Grotius never intended, a *de facto* shield to criminal culpability, and a vehicle for big money to have undue influence in U.S. elections and threaten our very democracy.

5. Arrogance and imprudence in any headquarters can be very destructive, and to me obviously it is a sensitive subject. A personal reason that I feel this way is because of the end of the life of my paternal grandfather. In 1918, he was a major commanding a battalion of U.S. Army infantry on the most dangerous part of the front line in eastern France. He led from the front, and seeing with his own eyes that U.S. artillery was overshooting the German machine guns, he asked the artillery to lower their sights. The Army headquarters artillery officers, sitting in comfort and safety far in the rear, ignored the "eyes-on" request of my grandfather to properly target their artillery to hit the German machine guns. The next morning, on November 1, he and many of his men charging the Germans were machine-gunned to death—just because headquarters typically thinks

it knows best. Until two weeks after the Armistice on November 11, my grandmother thought her husband would come home alive. This family shock is remembered more than 100 years later.

Because EPA Special Agents routinely report to toxic-waste spills and dump sites, along with the rifles in their car trunks they also carry chemical-protection suits with full-face respirators, commonly called "moon suits." I believe that they were the only federal law-enforcement officers so equipped to properly respond to the site of the collapsed towers.

6. *Democracy in America*, p. 252, by Alexis de Tocqueville (University of Chicago Press, 2000).

Chapter 11—Clean Energy from Here to Eternity

LIKE ALBERT EINSTEIN TALKING ABOUT THE ATOM BOMB, Rachel Carson also told us that the fate of all life on Earth is in the hands of man, and so it is. In 1962, Rachel Carson wrote that, "only within the moment of time... [of] the present century has one species—man—acquired significant power to alter the nature of the world." Putting aside nuclear war, among the multitude of other ways that humanity is threating life on the Earth, climate change now is clearly at the top of the list. Our planet has begun a new epoch of geologic time, the "Anthropocene," an invented word now gaining scientific acceptance as the name for the new epoch.[1]

The Anthropocene epoch began either with the Industrial Revolution, or certainly by the second half of the 20th century when it had become clear that humanity is now the force of nature with the biggest impact on our planet. If in the future the air temperature rises by four or five degrees Celsius, if CO_2 exceeds 1,000 ppm, and all of Earth's ice melts—the sea level will rise by at least 220 feet. There is uncertainty about the timing, but this could happen perhaps during the 23rd century or earlier. Either then or soon to follow is the worst-case scenario, extinction of most life on Earth, as the anoxic ocean first destroys marine life and then emits hydrogen sulfide that could completely poison the atmosphere. The longer humanity continues business as usual, burning fossil fuels and emitting other climate-damaging air pollutants, the sooner and more likely is this fate.

In the short term for behaviors that can no longer be tolerated, achieving reform can be painful. Defeating fascism by 1945 required a U.S. big government's national mobilization and a global alliance of nations.[2] To stop slavery in America by 1865 required a bloody Civil War. Stopping business as usual that is destroying the climate will not require a war, but it is being and will be opposed by the rich and powerful owners of obsolete technologies that threaten life on Earth.

Humanity is now at tipping point where a 19th-century poem (that is also a Protestant hymn) is timely:

> Once to ev'ry man and nation
> Comes the moment to decide,
> In the strife of truth and falsehood,
> For the good or evil side;
> Some great cause, some great decision,
> Off'ring each the bloom or blight,
> And the choice goes by forever
> 'Twixt that darkness and that light.[3]

To make the right choice sooner rather than later, consider the tools of environmental protection that will save us. They are already here, all around us, floating like life rings or rafts—we just have to just grab onto them. The U.S. Environmental Protection Agency created and used these tools to clean up abandoned toxic-waste dumps, protect the stratospheric ozone sun shield, stop acid rain killing forests and lakes, take the lead out of gasoline, and reduce many forms of water and air pollution. The U.S. was not alone among nations taking effective action, and many of these problems also have been addressed globally with environmental treaties.

We have two old, familiar, toolboxes, both tried and true. One toolbox is labeled "adaptation," and the other is "mitigation," or "decarbonization." First, consider the toolbox "adaptation," meaning to strengthen our defenses, build "resilience," and to buy time. We all know that since medieval times the people of the Netherlands have been adapting to the sea. Now they have built enormous berms and water gates, some each as wide as the Eiffel Tower is tall. Dutch adaptation includes enormous pumps to remove seawater, powered by rows of giant wind turbines often standing in the sea. Generating electricity to remove seawater flooding the land, these devices do the same work as did their medieval windmills turning mechanical lifts. After Superstorm Sandy in 2012, Dutch experts came to consult and to help redesign the entrance to New York Harbor. They produced design drawings of a five-mile-wide water barrier from Sandy Hook in New Jersey to Rockaway on Long Island. While it would cost about $30 billion, this is only about one-third of the cost of the storm damage in 2012. But since then, there have been no steps toward its construction, even though everyone knows that New York City and its coastal region will flood again soon enough. And the next time the cause may be a landfalling hurricane, not merely a landfalling tropical storm like Sandy.

But for New York City and everywhere it will not be enough to construct adaptive defenses such as water gates. The harsh reality is that mitigation is essential. Mitigation may include both preventing the emission of greenhouse gases (GHGs), and retrieving or recapturing carbon already in the air and "locking it away" by sequestration in plants (including kelp in the sea and forests on land), soil, and deep underground. Sequestration is a little toolbox that holds some promise, and new technologies are being discovered. But sequestration alone will not remove large enough volumes in the time we have left. Without preventing new emissions of GHGs, both adaptation and sequestration in coming decades and certainly in the next century will prove to be futile as putting a Band-Aid on a cancer without treating the disease. They will be as futile as rearranging the deck chairs on the *Titanic* without also changing the ship's course safely to the south. After Superstorm Sandy, we saw on the New Jersey shore that a roller-coaster had fallen into the sea. It should be clear by now that our carbon-fueled "fun ride" has ended and cannot be restored with Band-Aids and other half measures. Without stopping new emissions, we will suffer more unplanned coastal destruction and abandonment. So now let us put aside both adaptation and sequestration.

Let us move on to consider the essential climate "mitigation" technologies that stop pumping carbon and other GHGs into the air. Among these technologies are new "fun rides," most being electric cars with rechargeable batteries. (Of course, these cars are only so clean as the fuel used in each power plant making electricity to charge the cars' batteries.) Hydrogen fuel is an alternative being piloted in demonstration buses first made in Europe that operate on hydrogen fuel cells. The first hydrogen-powered production car—the 2016 "Mirai" ("future" in Japanese)—was made by Toyota, famous for the Prius. Totally clean, a hydrogen vehicle's only exhaust is water mist or drops of water. Germany and China are building the first "wind-to-hydrogen" plants in the world using wind turbines to make electricity to electrolytically split H_2O—water—into oxygen and hydrogen. Hydrogen fuel made with renewable energy will support 100-percent combustion-free transport from fuel production to its consumption on the road. Norway, France, U.K., India, China, and other nations seeing the future are incentivizing clean-energy vehicles and have goals soon to limit numbers or make it illegal to buy a new gasoline or diesel-powered car.

In 1973 and 1974, the Organization of Arab Oil Exporting Countries (OPEC) embargoed oil shipments to nations that had supported Israel after the surprise attack by Egypt and Syria in the Yom Kippur War. Americans of a certain age will remember standing in long lines at gasoline stations, sometimes unable to buy gasoline even at a very high price. The people of Sweden and Denmark were also standing in lines at gas stations during OPEC oil shock. But they were not asleep. The Danes realized that 94 percent of their fuel was imported oil, and decided that gasoline was an addiction. Without any then-known domestic source of fossil fuels to subvert their government's plans, the Danes freely chose to develop renewable energy sources. They imposed the first carbon tax, and it funded generous national government subsidies to transition to renewable energy. The Danish company Vestas began to make modern wind turbines, and today it is a global leader with manufacturing plants in Germany, India, Italy, Romania, the United Kingdom, Spain, Sweden, Norway, Australia, China, and the United States. With less than six million people, tiny Denmark brings in huge amounts of money and creates many good jobs making many of the best wind turbines in the world. Danish carbon pollution has been cut by more than half.[4]

Vestas is only one reason that the Danes (like neighboring Nordic nations) regularly are rated among or at the top of the list of the happiest people in the world. Denmark and Germany were among the first to discover that solar energy works very well even in rather cloudy, cold weather. Solar energy also has been incentivized and is installed in many of the right places. But energy sourced from the wind and the sun are not constant, and their intermittency raises a most important question: on cold nights with no wind blowing, how can the world best make climate-friendly baseload electricity? How can the world be like Sweden, where 100 percent of its electricity is generated by a combination of hydro, wind, sun—and nuclear? Putting aside geothermal and water power that in some places can be helpful locally, for most of the world there is only one power source that is not intermittent—new "fourth-generation" nuclear reactors of advanced design.

These will not be the conventional, "light-water" nuclear reactors that were conceptualized starting during World War II, These primitive reactors were commercialized to make electricity starting in the 1960s, in part because some also produced material for nuclear weapons. After WWII, the U.S. at the same time also developed—but then mostly ignored— advanced-design reactors. These cannot melt down, and they can be made much more proliferation-resistant than conventional reactors. Another advantage is that the advanced reactors will consume as fuel much of the radioactive waste stockpiled at today's aging, primitive nuclear-power plants.

After WWII, the Argonne National Lab developed the advanced design of the integral fast reactor (IFR), built a prototype IFR power plant that operated at Idaho National Lab successfully from 1964 to 1994, and the Department of Energy (DOE) built a second prototype in the 1980s. So in the U.S. it was a presidential debacle in the mid-1990s to abandon DOE's advanced nuclear-power reactors. Mismanagement has continued since by trying to bury in deep geologic disposal the waste from today's power plants that can fuel advanced reactors.[5] Now the flood of climate-damaging, cheap natural gas is undercutting climate-friendly nuclear power. The U.S. government is compounding the tragedy by doing nothing as even existing nuclear plants shut too early, while no new and advanced nuclear plants are being built in the U.S.

This ongoing official ignorance and blundering reflects public hysteria arising from the power-plant incident at Three Mile Island (Pennsylvania) in 1979, and the disasters at Chernobyl (formerly within the USSR, today within the north of Ukraine near Belarus) in 1986 and at Fukushima (Japan) in 2011. Yet in the public mind in the U.S., Japan, and Germany, and probably the minds of many politicians, these conventional plants have been confused with and have unfairly tainted the advanced designs that are quite different, being more efficient and much safer. Some internationally active environmental groups have been totally confused and to this day are spreading fear about nuclear power. In fact, it is impossible for even a conventional nuclear reactor to explode like a bomb or a nuclear weapon.

From the accident at Three Mile Island there was no radiation leakage or death. The Fukushima nuclear plant in 2011 embodied the risks in old-design, conventional reactors, but disaster came only for being sited too low to the sea. With only a 19-foot seawall protecting the power plant, it and the town were hit by tsunami at least twice as high. Here is the human death toll:

- 18,000 in town killed in a natural disaster caused by an earthquake under the sea

- Perhaps 1,000 killed in the frantic and botched evacuation

- More than 10,000 killed since by air pollution from coal burning after Japan's panicked response that was to replace all nuclear with coal plants

- 0—zero—killed in a nuclear-power industrial accident

The conclusion: "Radiation rarely kills anyone, but fear of radiation kills a lot of people."[6]

At Chernobyl in 1986, operator errors caused a steam explosion and fire, made worse by the shocking absence of a containment vessel, and radiation did kill many responding workers (47 by the official count). Deaths in the general population were increased by the Soviet government's secrecy, so that lifesaving iodine pills were not quickly distributed before radiation spread over a wide area. It is certainly good that the area around Chernobyl was evacuated, and studies by the World Health Organization and International Atomic Energy Agency have shown that radiation deaths would be "very difficult to detect" among the dispersed and general population. They can only estimate that radiation-caused cancer someday may—or may not—kill up to "several thousand" people. Radiation levels have declined greatly in 30 years; and today the evacuated zone is a very healthy, natural ecosystem.[7]

Nuclear-power opponents should consider that since the 1960s even the commercialized, primitive reactors have caused far fewer deaths and environmental harms than the many foul and varied impacts of burning coal. Air pollution (especially sulfur, heavy elemental metals, and particulates) from coal plants causes emphysema and cancer that kill at least 13,000 people per year just in the U.S. Global estimates range from one to three million people each year killed by coal, disproportionately children. Even much more radiation is emitted by coal-burning plants than from nuclear reactors operating normally without smokestacks that cause no air pollution of any kind. Many coal miners also die each year, but it seems that in the U.S. no worker has ever been killed by the nuclear elements of a nuclear power reactor. To date, of all sources of power, world history and many studies show—without even considering the climate destruction coal causes—that coal is by far the most deadly source of energy, and even conventional or primitive nuclear plants are definitely the safest. France and Sweden understood early this benefit of nuclear power, and today a growing number of nations agree.

An open question is, will the advanced nuclear reactors invented in the U.S. be "made in USA"? Not if we maintain our irrational fears about nuclear power, and not unless we wake up. Our continued ignorance and mismanagement may cause another major industry to be lost to other countries with governments capable of perfecting and bringing advanced designs online. Russia today leads the world in supplying turnkey nuclear plants to many nations, and it is perfecting its advanced designs. South Korea may be joining in this trade. As with cell phones, laptops, flat-screen TVs, and solar panels, the Chinese are taking steps to be able in coming decades to manufacture and export advanced nuclear reactors to the waiting world. Without the cost overruns of constructing massive reactors on a distant site, these Chinese exports likely will be small modular reactors (SMRs), made in shipyards, and exported widely in China's "Belt and Road Initiative." Anywhere in the world, the customer will just line up and connect one, two, or however many little reactors are needed, and then plug them in to the electric grid. For use in the U.S., when the wind is not turning the blades for our turbines bought from Vestas, or the sun is not shining on our imported Chinese solar panels, soon safe and cheap SMRs imported from China will be available. To buy them, the U.S. will increase our debt or send ever more of our dollars to China, while too many of our citizens lack manufacturing jobs.

The public-health, economic, and geophysical bottom lines are this: Coal, all fossil fuels, and their resulting climate change are far more life-threatening than the advanced nuclear power that can stop climate change. So today it is urgent that the U.S. DOE reopen the program that President Clinton killed, and generously fund the development of advanced designs such as the IFR and molten-salt reactor. As quickly as possible, advanced reactors should be licensed for mass production or for construction on site under strict supervision to prevent outrageous cost-overruns. In particular, DOE in collaboration with the Department of Defense should place an initial order of about 50 SMRs perhaps first to be installed at U.S. military bases, a number large enough to make it worthwhile to build the plant to mass-produce them. Unlike the reactors at Fukushima and at many existing sites operating conventional reactors, the new reactors should be installed only above where the sea too soon will be flooding, whether from the tidal waves that at times may be caused by earthquakes or worsening hurricanes, or by sea-level rise coming during the century or more that a reactor may operate. And no more U.S. reactors ever again should be placed on earthquake fault lines. Done correctly, this infrastructure program is key to human survival on this planet.

Let us turn now from overviewing our technological tools of GHG mitigation to our tools of social policy that can bring effective mitigation into life. Many economists and experts agree that—as we saw happen in Denmark and now is happening in countries going greener like China—of course we can enjoy both a strong economy and a clean environment. It is not a choice of one or other, the economy and the environment are not enemies, and both can rise together. It is not "bad economics" to end the fossil-fuel business. Instead, it is devastatingly bad economics not to realize that "the economy is a wholly-owned subsidiary of the environment,"[8] and not to see that the benefits of acting now far exceed the costs of waiting for the enormous disaster coming soon enough if we continue to wander down our present path.

Most economists also take the correct and conservative position that the switch to renewable energy can be done more efficiently not by governments, but by profitable private business enterprises. As we have seen with the uptake of modern TVs and electronic personal devices, progress can be very rapid when private profits are big. Two key questions are these: Who can correct the free market's disastrous failure to bring in climate-friendly energy sources fast enough, even though the social benefits are great beyond measure? By what new social policies or rules can we create big profit incentives for businesses so that reform comes quickly? The answer to both questions is that national governments must write new marketplace rules to make reform very profitable for businesses.

It helps to remember some simple, rather recent examples. Consider airbags and seat belts. Starting in the 1970s, many national governments used command-and-control to require that all new cars have these safety devices. The law applied also to imported cars, so no domestic auto maker would be undersold by non-complying imports. Only new cars were regulated, so there was no required retrofitting, and old, relatively unsafe cars could be used until scrapped. As a result, more cars have been sold than ever. Today in the U.S. with more than twice as many cars on the road, half as many people die in auto wrecks as they did 40 years ago when cars were not so safe. Social benefits far exceed incremental costs.

The rules requiring these upgrades in new cars are a familiar example of basic "command-and-control," or "do-it-or-else," traditional regulation. Such regulation began long ago, when sleepy citizens of medieval towns were prohibited from throwing their night soil and urine out the window into the street (yet we still allow massive industries to throw their waste CO_2 up into the air). Starting in the 1970s, polluting factories and power plants have been required to get permits to pollute (allowed only up to levels that EPA scientists deem tolerable). The total number of permits to pollute can be "capped" or limited where necessary not to overload the environment. Like driving a car without license, it can be a criminal offense to operate without a pollution permit after the date required to get one. (Of course, some activities, like toxic-waste dumping, are so horrific that they can only be banned, and after the effective date of a command-and-control ban any intentional violation will be criminal.)

It has been said that "if the only tool you have is a hammer, then every problem is a nail to be pounded." But every problem is not a "nail" requiring the hammer of command-and-control regulation. Many problems can be fixed with tape or glue and without pounding with a hammer. And so it was that a conservative, "free-market" think tank during the 1970s conceptualized a new type of regulation called "cap-and-trade." Polluters liked it—at least compared to traditional rules, and EPA adopted this private-sector-recommended social policy. To implement the "trade" element of cap-and-trade, starting in the 1980 in the U.S., a very big innovation has been for the EPA to create new free markets for some *tradeable* pollution permits. Like stocks and bonds in securities markets, and even more like grain and cattle futures in the commodities markets, some pollution permits can be bought and sold as commodities under government oversight to ensure market integrity. More than 35 years ago in the 1980s, EPA used capped and tradeable lead permits to facilitate refineries removing from gasoline the lead causing brain-damaged city children. More than 25 years ago in the 1990s, EPA used capped and tradeable permits to reduce air pollution (primarily sulfur) from coal-fired power plants causing acid rain. Today the EU, parts of China, Canada, and a growing number of U.S. states have created starter markets for tradeable carbon-pollution permits. And on January 1, 2013, to protect the climate, trading of carbon permits began in the world's fifth or sixth largest economy—the State of California.

To protect the climate, the mechanics of a national cap-and-trade decarbonization program would be these: EPA scientists first determine as a starting point the total carbon that can be emitted by all polluting sources in each regulated business sector. At that level, EPA puts a cap or upper limit on the number of carbon permits. Then EPA issues, freely or at a set price or at auction, permits—often called pollution "allowances" or "credits." To continue to operate lawfully, each source must have enough permits for its amount of pollution. EPA creates and oversees an honest, free market for trading permits issued, a public place for each polluting source to buy and sell the permits it needs to continue to operate. Over time, EPA will gradually reduce the cap (total pollution allowed for the business sector) and correspondingly reduce the total number of allowed permits; these permits may become more expensive as the cap is reduced.

A polluting source that early in the cap-and-trade program has depreciated, dirty equipment needing replacement will quickly switch to clean, non-polluting fuels and technology. Not only will this source not need to buy tradeable permits, it will be rewarded by being able to sell its unneeded, unexpired permits to a source still polluting using dirty fuels and aging technology. To recover some of the capital cost to modernize is a nice reward for being among the first to come "clean"! A polluting source still using old fuels and dirty equipment need not immediately scrap it all, but can buy permits and continue to operate the dirty equipment until it is fully depreciated—or until it becomes too expensive to buy carbon-pollution permits becoming more scarce as EPA shrinks the cap. Over time, as everywhere "dirty" old equipment eventually wears out and must be replaced anyway, as each year passes more sources will switch, each spending its money to modernize instead of buying permits. When the cap falls to zero, all sources still using dirty, old fuels and equipment must immediately switch to climate-friendly operation.

With a trading market for pollution permits, each factory, refinery, power plant (and whatever may be a polluting source in a regulated business sector) has the time and the freedom to decide for itself when to modernize, and to do so only when it costs less. As we saw with seat belts, airbags, and air-conditioning equipment under the Montreal Protocol, a cap-and-trade program allows existing equipment to wear out until it would need to be replaced anyway. Unfortunately, industries may find that their climate-change denial and obstruction over the last few decades have squandered years that could have made possible such a gradual and easy way to reform. With so little time now to save the climate from dirty fuels and equipment with a long life span, EPA may have to more quickly reduce the cap to force early retrofitting or replacement before old equipment is fully depreciated.

With climate change now taking on the aspect of a global emergency, attention is turning to another old tool that also is not a command-and-control hammer, but may be faster and simpler to administer than cap-and-trade. More than 100 years ago, the British economist Arthur Pigou wrote that social cost should be "internalized" in product pricing by a so-called "sin tax" on each troublesome product sold. These avoidable taxes send price signals to buyers either (1) to select another product instead that is cheaper (being tax-free) and cleaner (or without sin), or (2) when buying a troublesome product to pay the sin tax to cover the damages that the product will "externalize" or cast off onto society or the environment. In the EU, they call this "The Polluter Pays Principle." If using taxes to send price signals in the marketplace sounds radical, consider that many, indeed most, U.S. states use "sin taxes" to raise revenue while suppressing troublesome products that remain mostly tolerable with necessary state oversight. States happily tax cigarettes, liquor, state lotteries, and most recently marijuana. Environmental "sin taxes" familiar to all Americans include town or municipal charges for sewer (and the clean water that humans turn into sewage) and the fee at the landfill to take what the garbage truck will not accept from your curbside. To repurpose and apply this familiar, same old public-policy tool to climate mitigation will not in any way be radical.

Very recently, this trusty old tool has been applied to reduce to throw-away, blow-away, flimsy plastic market-shopping bags. While they are banned outright in some progressive places like California, New York State, and France, a softer approach is to tax this offending product. Today Britain, Denmark, Hong Kong, and South Africa are among many nations that require retailers to collect a small tax or fee on each throw-away bag. In the U.S., some states and cities are also requiring this. Smart shoppers are happy to switch to reusable cloth market bags, now available everywhere and often given away to the public. Only shoppers who still want the nuisance bags pay the blow-away-bag tax. Each shopper has a market choice, freely made. The European Polluter Pays Principle—the full-cost "internalization" principle—is also applied in the "Green Dot" program described in the previous chapter on Germany. Here the "sin tax" takes the form of the small licensing fee included in the retail price of each container, packaging, and product marked with the "Green Dot" logo and covered by the Extended Producer Responsibility program. The collected fees are used to fund private waste management that recycles twice as much as public authorities, upon whom can no longer be offloaded or "externalized" the cost of waste management.

Let us move on from blow-away bags and consider sin taxation regarding a runaway climate. Lacking a sin tax to support the U.S. Federal Emergency Management Agency, in 2012 FEMA already was in great debt in 2012 when Superstorm Sandy devastated New York and New Jersey. To pay for Sandy's cost, Congress with a federal "bailout" borrowed about $60 billion, mostly from China, and U.S. taxpayers must pay this back. Since 2012, up and down the East and Gulf Coasts there have been major floods, caused by "rain bombs" from "atmospheric rivers" —three days of heavy rain in air flowing in from above the warmer sea. These floods have sunk FEMA further into debt, and in the future it will be worse. But as of 2019, the U.S. has no financing plan for FEMA other than to borrow more money from China.

Imagine a much better way to fund FEMA fully and in advance—a national "sin tax" on carbon emissions that only the polluter pays. A Pigovian carbon tax, like the Danes and later the Swedes use to help achieve both their great national prosperity and superb environmental management, could fully fund a new "U.S. Climate Security Social Insurance Fund." With this money, FEMA would be prepared to both respond to storms and to do much more—to plan ahead by funding new public projects of adaptation, abandonment, and relocation to higher ground. Done correctly, this infrastructure program also will have many benefits. If this sounds radical, consider that many, indeed most, U.S. states by law mandate payments into insurance funds for workers' compensation insurance, unemployment compensation insurance, and automobile insurance for each driver.[9] Required insurance protects ordinary people from some forms of economic devastation, and these long-standing state programs are in no way controversial. Again, there is nothing new here—a new "U.S. Climate Security Social Insurance Fund" would just be the repurposing of a trusty and proven policy tool to sensibly address a new problem that must be managed at the national level.

In addition to social insurance, an attractive new policy tool might be called "free money"—100 percent tax rebates! The Province of British Columbia in 2008 instituted a popular carbon tax that is rebated 100 percent by reducing other taxes on payrolls and incomes. British Columbia has the lowest payroll and personal income tax rates in Canada and one of the lowest corporate tax rates in North America. Gross domestic product (GDP)—the economy—is up and climate-changing pollution is down compared to the rest of Canada. In 2019, Canada imposed a nationwide carbon tax on fossil fuels and industries emitting carbon. The Canadian government expects from the tax money to rebate more cash benefits to the average household than it paid as carbon tax.

Recently in the U.S., some well-known, even famous leaders and economists[10] calling themselves "The Climate Leadership Council" have proposed a national "Carbon Tax and Dividend" that would be 100 percent rebated to the people. In the "Conservative Case for Carbon Dividends," these statesmen proposed a "...new climate strategy [a carbon tax, rebated—with revenue neutrality, that] can strengthen our economy, reduce regulation, help working-class Americans, shrink government, and promote national security." By making fossil fuels comparatively more expensive, with rebated "free money" for consumers to spend in the marketplace, the advantage of these plans is doubled. A fully rebated carbon tax will drive down fossil-fuel use at the same time it that stimulates the uptake of electric or hydrogen vehicles and clean electrical power. To "tax the bads to free the goods" is beautifully conservative, and in no way radical or socialistic.

In a world of globalized trade, to prevent competitive disadvantage, a climate-friendly nation will impose its carbon fee or tax on imported, carbon-intensive goods—and on all goods it imports from a foreign nation not having a carbon tax or a comparable climate-saving regime. A climate-friendly nation also will protect its exports from competitive disadvantage. For goods being shipped to a foreign nation where a carbon tax is imposed on these imports, the exporting nation will refund its internal carbon tax so that it is not paid twice. The device of a tax refund on exports is already familiar to many American tourists who routinely receive a refund of the European value-added tax (VAT) when returning home with consumer goods bought in Europe. A scheme of such carefully crafted border adjustments to the carbon fee or tax, affecting both imports and exports, is the starting point to protect climate-friendly nations from unfair competition in trade with climate-damaging nations. When the slumbering World Trade Organization awakens to the existential threat of climate change, the WTO will create such a globally harmonized regime for all member nations, and it will allow and better yet will require national trade sanctions upon nations that are not climate-friendly. Then international trade will proceed with little confusion and maximized climate protection.

With all tools of technology and policy in hand, when enough people decide to keep the fossil fuels in the ground, we will live under national climate-protection laws required by an effective treaty. Parties to the treaty will be reciprocally obligated by international law to enact national laws to reduce greenhouse-gas emissions, to employ pollution fighters to combat GHG-tax evasion and fraud in trading GHG permits, to self-report to the U.N., and to consent to U.N. monitoring and inspections. Governments that do not join the treaty or that fail to meet its obligations will violate international law and be subject to escalating trade sanctions, restrictions, and bans. This is not new or complicated. As children in elementary school, we were all told to play nicely with other children and to stay away from a mean child who plays dirty. Our teacher would keep the nasty bully inside during recess. As adults on a global economic playground or sports field, our shared international goal is that there be fun products and happiness (profits) for all, and that there be fair competition on a field that is green and level.

Nations that are dirty players will be benched and removed from the game.

These government-against-government trade sanctions are tried and true as the familiar enforcement mechanism of treaties. The U.N. and World Trade Organization (WTO) already use sanctions to control the global economic playground so that nations that do not fairly trade the goods they produce—hats, shoes, cars, and whatever—have to sit in the penalty box, isolated until they will play fairly. An effective climate-change treaty, like many other treaties already do, will do this and more so that climate-friendly nations can close their borders to climate-destroying nations. The rogue nations hurting the climate—the bullies—will enjoy no international trade, no international banking, no landing of their airplanes or ships in ports abroad, no visas for their citizens to visit or work abroad, and no visiting tourists bringing in hard money from climate-friendly countries. In recent years, we have all seen a variation of such sanctions placed on Iraq, Iran, North Korea, and Russia. These sanctions have been to encourage self-control and disarmament for chemical and nuclear weapons, and to punish Russia for invading and seizing parts of Ukraine. When the world realizes that climate chaos will be at least as damaging as military invasion and the misuse of weapons of genocide and mass destruction, these familiar policy tools will be made available in a new treaty strong enough for real climate protection.

Our planet is losing its life, our climate is crashing, and since 2017 our President has deconstructed our Environmental Protection Agency. Considering the dire situation we face, and how my generation has failed to rise to the challenge, nevertheless I do see reasons for hope. Devastating sea-level rise by at least five to ten feet will likely happen sometime in this century, and in the 22ⁿᵈ century it is inevitable that the sea will rise much, much more. We can hope that this disastrous inundation will happen at least a century before the oceans and then the air become deadly poisonous with hydrogen sulfide. While my generation still does too little, younger generations, who are more thoughtful and alert now see this danger and are marching in demonstrations for immediate action. Within a few decades, all of our grandchildren, then in adulthood, will see our port cities start to go permanently under ocean waves, and too many will find themselves living in or near routinely flooding or post-apocalyptic ruined homes. Wading in the problem, no longer will the threat be distant and deniable. Though the climate will be terrible, we can hope that our descendants will have at least another century, just enough time to prevent CO_2 from rising to 1,000 ppm, the threshold for human extinction. This will be the last chance for them and their grandchildren to act in time to stop more climate pollution, just before human extinction becomes real.

My generation's culture of "meritocracy" has become individualistic to the point of self-centeredness, consumerist to the point of excess, and capitalist to the point of domination and expropriation. Struggling amid social upheaval and in deprivation among the drowned and crumbling remnants of materialism, some among future generations will slip into thievery and villainy. Still I see hope too that this culture will change in our descendants, as we see in today's neighbors and responders after tornadoes and other natural disasters, when only a few steal what they can find in the ruins. Most people even when suffering themselves will not take from others, but will give of themselves to help others. When feeling that "we are all in this together," at least in most people a sense of community will replace self-centered individualism, and contributing often replaces taking.[11] Europeans call this "solidarity," a shared mindset united in helpful action. And as the Danes and other Nordics have long known from daily living in this way, more people feel happy even with less—in the case of the Nordics, with less after-tax income and little or no sun during some of nature's toughest winters. And let us be uplifted by the memory of Sister Euthymia of Münster, Germany, who—by giving her stunted life to the service of others—found bliss.

I expect that future generations, forced in hard times to labor communally to do right by nature and by each other, will uplift themselves and experience a spiritual reawakening of the soul. Though reduced in numbers, humanity will be better for having suffered. With remaining natural resources diminished to the point of scarcity, there will be a great need to preserve what remains and to prevent damage to the usable environment. Almost every person, in one way or another, will become a pollution fighter. The USEPA and UNEP will not remain puny and insufficient to the task. In far greater numbers, a larger proportion of society will come to do the work of fighting pollution, while feeling the same intense satisfaction that I enjoyed in my career in environmental protection.

We cannot roll back the clock to the reset the climate. Yet the very good news is that right now humanity has all the tools, both of technology and social policy or law, to very quickly stop more climate pollution. Today we lack only the necessary mass fear and popular will to reform our economy and to save our posterity. We can hope for the best, but we are long past overdue to prepare for worst, and I suspect that my generation of self-centered "meritocracy" may continue to fail humanity. By continuing to follow the same path ending in a disaster of our own making, many of today's grandparents, especially our do-nothing leaders, are on track to be scorned in memory and history like Nero who fiddled while Rome burned. Whether—and when—today's older generations and leaders will ever wake up to act decisively, effectively, and globally, will shape the memory of us and the planet that we will be leaving for our grandchildren to inherit.

To my young readers who have traveled this far with me, a final message: I do hope that my thesis has come through that you too can find great satisfaction in being environmental activists. Let my ending be your beginning. In this book I have tried to model for you the planet-protecting power of a law degree, as just one of the keys to a career that can help save our life on Earth. Many of you will be needed in many professions needed for pollution control and natural-resource conservation, yet perhaps more of you will be needed as engineers in the private sector. You will build in safe places the new, clean-energy equipment to mitigate the collapse of the climate. You will build—often relocated to safer ground—the civil infrastructure and private properties that will survive the harsh new environment. If you are about to enter a university, consider studying for a growing number of occupations where you can find real happiness and paychecks as full-time professionals working to save our planet.

At the same time, speak with and try to "wake up" your parents and grandparents so that they will better understand and support your goals. Ask them to read books like mine that credibly model the feasibility of a "green" professional career. Don't hesitate to join a climate march, and do invite your older family members to join you in the protest. They should remember how the marches of their youth helped to gain better rights for women, African Americans, and other minorities, and to end the U.S. government's unnecessary and tragic war in Vietnam. I hope that your older family members will come to share your passion and agree that getting the necessary education is worth the family or personal expense and the effort. For *your* grandchildren to follow, saving the planet will be the great mission of your time. You can do it, and I wish you well.

1. "Anthropocene" as a new term was created by Paul Crutzen, the Dutch scientist among those awarded the Nobel Prize for discovering the threat to the stratospheric ozone sun shield.

2. For a view of this future, read *The Collapse of Western Civilization: A View from the Future*, by Naomi Oreskes and Erik M. Conway (Columbia University Press, 2014). They foresee vast social disruption as all coastal habitats, including many of our most important cities, are abandoned, and all people and infrastructure must be relocated to upland areas inland. To attempt to handle the chaos, the authors predict that the U.S. necessarily will experience a big-government mobilization exceeding that of World War II. They also predict the collapse of free-market capitalism, not because it created the fossil-fuel menace, but because it has prevented our democratic government from acting in the 20th century and even now after the danger has become scientifically certain. See also *This Changes Everything: Capitalism vs. the Climate*, by Naomi Klein (Simon & Schuster, 2015).

3. "Once to Every Man and Nation" was written by James Russell Lowell of Boston in 1845. It was composed in opposition to the U.S. invasion of Mexico, and it was sung also by Americans who would abolish slavery. This poem is apt for any crucial turning point requiring that the right choice be made.

4. *The Almost Nearly Perfect People: The Truth About the Nordic Miracle*, by Michael Booth (Jonathan Cape, 2014). Yes, taxes are very high in most Nordic countries. But the payback is huge—assured health care and day care, educational opportunity, upward social and economic mobility, thriving free-enterprise, low inequality, strong social cohesion (high levels of trust), little corruption, and low crime rates. With some of the darkest and coldest winters, Nordics may not be joyful each day, but they are rarely miserable and usually well satisfied. A Nordic nation is almost always rated as the "happiest" in the world.

Capital in the Twenty-First Century, by Thomas Piketty (Harvard University Press, 2014) states that the real story of today's global capitalism is that, far beyond the right amount of economic inequality, it is concentrating wealth and income to the point of social dissatisfaction and instability. Without such enormous economic polarization, Nordic nations stand in sharp contrast to many other nations, whose 26 plutocrats have the same wealth as the bottom half ($3.85 billion) people of the world, and in the U.S. the top three wealthiest men possess wealth equal to the entire bottom half of the U.S population. Yet in many capitalist nations following the social mobilization of WWII, from 1945 to about 1975 there was a brief time when gross inequality declined. This was particularly true in Anglo-American countries including Canada that briefly had very progressive national tax systems. Even despite to the social turmoil of the 1960s and Vietnam War, for Americans these were mostly happy and productive years with increasing paychecks for average workers and compensation for CEOs that was not exorbitant.

5. *The Power to Save the World: The Truth About Nuclear Energy*, by Gwyneth Cravens (Penguin Random House 2017, Knopf 2007); *Prescription for the Planet*, by Tom Blees (Amazon's Booksurge Company, 2008) www.prescriptionfortheplanet.com; *Beyond Fossil Fools*, by Jos. M. Shuster (Beaver's Pond Press, 2008); *Plentiful Energy: The Story of the Integral Fast Reactor*, by Charles E. Till and Yoon Il Chang (Amazon's Create Space Company, 2011).

6. *A Bright Future: How Some Countries Have Solved Climate Change and the Rest Can Follow*, page 91, by Joshua S. Goldstein and Staffan A. Qvist (PublicAffairs, 2018).

7. *Ibid.*, page 92.

8. This memorable line has been attributed to Senator Gaylord Nelson and to former Senator Timothy Wirth when he was at the State Department. *Apollo's Fire: Igniting America's Clean-Energy Economy*, by Jay Inslee and Bracken Hendricks (Island Press, 2009; *Unstoppable: Harnessing Science to Change the World,* by Bill Nye, "The Science Guy" (St. Martin's Press/Macmillan, 2015).

9. Other U.S. examples of mandated social insurance are national— Social Security, Medicare, and Medicaid. The Europeans and Canadians are among the highly civilized people who have long since accomplished universal health care for all as a right of citizenship or just of common humanity. But in the U.S., "the land of the free and the home of the brave," the availability of universal health care

("Obamacare," enacted in 2010) has been under constant attack in Congress, the federal courts, and national political debate.

10. James A. Baker III, Martin Feldstein, Ted Halstead, N. Gregory Mankiw, Henry M. Paulson, Jr., George P. Schulz, Thomas Stephenson, and Rob Walton are among the first prominent Americans to promote this. The list has been growing steadily. According to the *New York Times* (1/20/19), on January 17, 2019, "The last four people to lead the Federal Reserve, 15 former leaders of the White House Council of Economic Advisers, and 27 Nobel Laureates signed a letter endorsing a gradually rising carbon tax whose proceeds would be distributed to consumers as "carbon dividends." These leaders are among the many economists who would "internalize"—include in product pricing—the social and environmental costs that capitalism without adequate regulation will naturally offload or "externalize" as burdens on society and the environment. In the U.S., a grassroots and effective group calling itself the "Citizens' Climate Lobby" now is focused on achieving a national "carbon fee and dividend" law.

11. *The Second Mountain*, by David Brooks (Random House, 2019).

Addenda

History of Earth Science and the "Big Five" Mass Extinctions

Improving National Enforcement for Better Governance
Implementing Multilateral Environmental Agreements

Combining Legal Mandates with Economics in the Application
of Environmental Law (Phyllis P. Harris)

Partial List of the Author's Publications

History of Earth Science and "Big Five" Mass Extinctions

Date	Results	Source	Cause	CO₂; SLR
6th Extinction, now ongoing; now in Anthropocene epoch	After 2200 CE in 23rd century; possible completion of 6th Extinction if BAU continues	Humanity burning through fossil fuels 10X faster than end-of-Permian	CO_2 causing global warming, ocean anoxia, releasing hydrogen sulfide; also destroying ozone shield	1,000 ppm
After 2100 CE in 22nd century				up to +220'SLR with all glaciers melted
2019 CE (now) – end of Holocene epoch, start of Anthropocene epoch				**ca. 415 ppm**
Before about 1750 CE, start of the modern Industrial Revolution using fossil fuels				270–280 ppm
11.7K years ago, end of last ice age, start of Holocene epoch in Cenozoic era				200 ppm
11.7K to 2.6M years ago – Pleistocene epoch, characterized by repeated glaciations alternating with pleasant climate. By about 200K years ago, modern man emerges. During greatest glaciations, CO_2 bottoms out at about 180 ppm.				
2.6–5M years ago, Pliocene epoch (within today's Cenozoic era, meaning "era of new life" or the "age of mammals" that follows the end of dinosaurs)			Temperature about 2–3°C or 4–5°F above today	400–450 ppm; SLR +65–85' (or 25 meters) above today
5th Extinction, 66M years ago at "End of Cretaceous period" (at end of Mesozoic era) – 75% of species extinct	Extinction of T-Rex and all non-bird dinosaurs, many mammals, marsupials, and birds	6-mile-wide asteroid hitting near Yucatan; proven by iridium layer of this element found in space rocks, but rare on Earth	Instant local death from a fire of radiation; ejecta returning as worldwide blizzard of meteorites causing great heat, then global freezing from dust dimming sunlight. Impact may have caused earthquake, starting volcanic lava flows in today's India that then caused global warming. CO₂ ppm in dispute	

History of Earth Science and "Big Five" Mass Extinctions

Date	Results	Source	Cause	CO₂; SLR
Jurassic period (middle of Mesozoic era) – dinosaurs recolonize Earth				
	4th Extinction, 201M years ago at "End of Triassic period" (in beginning of Mesozoic era) – 80% of species extinct	Volcanoes and magma burning though accumulated fossil fuels	CO_2 & methane causing global warming, ocean anoxia, releasing deadly hydrogen sulfide & chemicals destroying ozone shield	2,000 ppm
First dinosaurs, crocodilians, and mammals appear				
	3rd Extinction 252M years ago "End of Permian period" (at end of Paleozoic era) – in "The Great Dying," about 95% of marine species extinct, and up to 75% of species extinct on land (that was the super-continent Pangaea)	Several causes possible, including volcanoes burning though fossil fuels accumulated in the Paleozoic era	CO_2 & methane causing global warming, ocean anoxia, hurricanes of deadly hydrogen sulfide & chemicals destroying ozone shield	3,000 ppm
	2nd Extinction, 374M years ago at "End of Devonian period" – 75% of species extinct	Multiple extinction mechanisms over about 20M years; research is incomplete, but likely global warming was involved		
	1st Extinction, 445M years ago at "End of Ordovician period within the Paleozoic era" – 86% of species extinct	Slow glaciation followed by sudden warming and extreme SLR		
ca. 500M years or about ½B years ago – complex life emerges and begins on Earth				
4.6+B years ago – formation of Earth				

Disclaimer

The chart on the preceding pages is an attempt by your author, a nonscientist, to help any other layman to take a very quick overview of enough history to fill a library. This attempt to reduce 500 million years of life on Earth to two pages may not be pleasing to all. My apologies to any trained geologist or paleontologist who finds errors in it, and I do not dispute such a trained person who holds a different opinion.

Abbreviations and Acronyms in the Chart

"BAU" is business as usual poisoning the atmosphere by burning fossil fuels.

"Big-Five" is those events when more than half of Earth's species went extinct. The current, sixth extinction may reach this level of devastation in 200 or 300 years with continued BAU.

"Epoch" is the smallest unit of geologic time. From shortest to longest, these units are epoch, period, era, and eon.

"CE" means "common era," equivalent to *anno domini* (AD) but used in science as a term without explicit religious connotation. BCE refers to before the common era. "Common" refers to the most commonly used calendar system, the Gregorian Calendar, which made adjustments since but did start with the nativity of Jesus.

"SLR" means sea-level rise.

"PPM" means a concentration measured in parts per million of a contaminant in a medium, here carbon dioxide measured in air. Actual measurement by isotopic ratios of the elements in air itself, and natural GHGs (methane, nitrous oxide, and carbon), water, volcanic dust, etc., goes back about 400K years in ice cores and about 800K years in stalagmites and stalactites (from caves) where minute air samples are also found. For the more distant past, measurement is done by studying fossils.

"Carbon-dating" also measures PPM, though not with accuracy before about 60K years in the past. This process involves measuring two forms of carbon, carbon 14 and carbon 12, and the ratio carbon 14 to 12 that declines over time as carbon 14 degrades to 12. Carbon 12 ("light carbon") is the stable, residual, and ancient carbon isotope with six protons and six neutrons found in fossils—and found also released into the air after fossil fuels are extracted (unburied) and burned. Carbon 14 is formed continuously in daily life at the Earth's surface as cosmic rays collide with atoms in the atmosphere, releasing energetic neutrons that form carbon 14 atoms (six protons, eight neutrons). Carbon 14 with a half-life of about 5,700 years decays very slowly to carbon 12, and after millions of years all buried fossil fuels are carbon 12. Carbon 14 emits radioactivity that can be detected, and this rate of decay is used as "carbon-dating."

Of most interest is the modern ratio in the atmosphere of light carbon 12 to carbon 14. It signifies and conclusively proves, by the increasing concentration (presently about 35 percent) of ancient light carbon in the atmosphere, that this much increase since about 1750 of atmospheric CO_2 can only have been caused by extracting and then burning fossil fuels.

Improving National Enforcement for Better Governance Implementing Multilateral Environmental Agreements

Recommendations for Meeting of Experts Called by the Division of Environmental Conventions of the United Nations Environment Programme, Sri Lanka, January 21–22, 2006

Richard W. Emory, Jr.[*]

ON THE TOPIC OF IMPROVING NATIONAL ENFORCEMENT as a key tool to better governance under multilateral environmental agreements (MEAs), I have the honor to offer this short paper of recommendations. The views expressed here are entirely my own and do not represent those of United States Environmental Protection Agency (USEPA) or the U.S. Government. While I regret that I am unable to attend the meeting, I hope that this paper will contribute to useful discussion and outcomes.

Here I address "enforcement" by national governments applying national law against regulated enterprises (including "persons" of any type) to achieve compliance with national law to implement MEA obligations. More specifically, I recommend steps by which (1) Conferences of the Parties (COPs) to MEAs and (2) MEA Secretariats may support and strengthen

---

[*] For the past 14 years, Mr. Emory has served as a senior attorney in the international compliance assurance unit of the U.S. Environmental Protection Agency. A 1967 graduate of Harvard Law School, he has 29 years of government experience in both civil and criminal environmental enforcement. He has worked at the state, national, and international levels, and in all three branches of government. The views expressed herein are his own and do not represent the USEPA. This article is based only on information previously published officially or reported publicly. Since 2006, only a very few revisions have been made.

"enforcement" by national governments to this end. (I do not address related topics such as assuring "compliance" by national governments with their MEA obligations, the role of the WTO, international law, or trade measures.)

In what follows, paragraphs 1–3 describe structural and institutional measures to enable MEAs to better support national enforcement. In addition, for the topic of import/export control, paragraph 4 offers a number of solutions addressing mostly systems, process, and operations.

I. ESTABLISH AN ENFORCEMENT COMMITTEE OF THE PARTIES

If the Parties to a MEA have the vision or goal that as national governments they want more MEA enforcement, the Parties should form an Enforcement Committee of the Parties. National representatives to Enforcement Committees of the Parties should be persons who have had hands-on, on-duty enforcement experience. This means that their expertise and identities should not or will not be the same as that of:

- The high-level policy makers who are the National Focal Points for MEAs,
- Persons who serve on chemical-selection, wildlife-listing, and other such committees where scientific research, environmental monitoring, and standard setting are done, or
- Persons, often with diplomatic or trade expertise, who serve on Compliance Committees and address on a state-to-state basis questions of national compliance and the application of MEA compliance-assurance mechanisms to other nations.

While an Implementation Committee of the Parties may address enforcement, "implementation" is a very broad word, and Implementation Committees have not produced sufficient progress in enforcement. The most undiluted, immediate, and effective enforcement results will be obtained by forming Enforcement Committees of the Parties.

II. HIRE MORE STAFF WITH ENFORCEMENT EXPERIENCE

If the secretariat of a MEA has the vision or goal that, as an international civil servant, he or she wants to support more MEA enforcement, hire staff with the relevant experience. Such personnel would not enforce. They would credibly interact with and support national authorities actually doing the enforcement. MEA secretariats staffed with more enforcement experience should proactively propose and (within their authority) take supportive actions, and raise issues of enforcement policy for decisions by Enforcement Committees of the Parties and by COPs.

III. DESIGNATE AND EMPOWER ONE UNIT OF UNEP TO BE THE COORDINATING LEAD INTERNATIONAL AGENCY FOR SUPPORT TO NATIONAL ENFORCEMENT

If the United Nations (UN) system and the COPs of the MEAs have the vision or the goal that MEA enforcement should be more synergized, collectively designate one unit of UNEP to be the coordinating lead agency for cross-cutting enforcement issues affecting all or many MEAs. The unit that is "UNEP Lead for MEA Enforcement Support" will need some new (but limited) powers and duties, including:

- Institutional responsibility for ongoing work to address and offer synergistic solutions to improve national enforcement and international cooperation supporting it for MEAs,"

- Authority to convene and to present for consideration new, systematic approaches, and some new means to encourage integration as may be needed among currently quite autonomous individual MEA secretariats, and

- Representational authority to meet regularly with InterPol, the World Customs Organization (WCO), the U.N. Centre for Trade Facilitation and Electronic Business (CEFACT), and other public (and non-governmental, as appropriate) international organizations, to coordinate on behalf of all MEA secretariats on cross-cutting issues.

IV. SOLUTIONS TO ILLEGAL INTERNATIONAL TRADE

The remaining solutions are focused on import/export control (I do not address the many aspects of national enforcement that are domestic or internal). To combat international trafficking that undercuts MEAs, there is enormous potential for improved measures that are simple and effective. An ultimate goal should be comprehensive data management with automated inter-ministerial data linkages to assure real-time approvals and interdictions. Where today national regulatory action is failing, it can become quick and accurate.

For constructive change to occur, directors of MEA secretariats and concerned Parties should provide more vision and leadership. First, develop a comprehensive vision of the prerequisites needed to enable effective *national* enforcement— such as a more uniform and integrated *inter*national system and the other steps or solutions offered in this paper—and a vision of what constitutes effective national enforcement (some indicators or measures of enforcement success). Second, establish more leadership to implement the steps to the vision—leadership to cause steady, regular action on solutions offered in this paper. Implementation of the following solutions usually would follow the same process,

1. Propose to all Parties,
2. Pilot among willing Parties, and
3. Prescribe by decisions of COPs that successful measures become treaty obligations.

A. Designate and Empower One Unit among each Nation's MEA Focal Points to be "National Lead for MEA Enforcement Coordination"

MEA secretariats individually and the "UNEP Lead for MEA Enforcement Support" should encourage each Party to designate one unit among the MEA Focal Points of a national government to be the lead agency for coordinating with the national customs ministry on common (or "cross-cutting") enforcement issues affecting all or many of the MEAs to which the nation is a Party. The Party's unit that is "National Lead for MEA Enforcement Coordination" will be responsible at the national level for moving toward integration and uniformity, to reduce the fragmentation and confusion within and among national ministries that multiple MEA Focal Points have created for customs officers.

Below the level of MEA Focal Points, in most countries the operational national programs for approving and monitoring international trade are complex, varied, and dispersed among and within ministries. It is essential that these national programs organize themselves both to streamline operations and present one window to front-line customs officers who need to know where to request quick environmental assistance to implement MEAs at borders. National ministries that are responsible for MEAs yet unable or unwilling to reform may need a presidential order or legislation.

B. Link each Nation's Customs Ministry with the Nation's Environmental (and other MEA Focal-Point) Ministries

MEA secretariats should suggest to or encourage Parties to focus on linking customs ministries with environmental (and other MEA Focal-Point) ministries in each Party nation. For example, to integrate and channel all trade-data communications in the U.S., Customs and Border Protection and each U.S. national ministry wanting its help for trade control must create what is called the "single-window." This data linkage will be a good foundation to enable full-scope cooperation in all aspects of the inter-ministerial working relationship.

For delivery to each "National Lead for MEA Enforcement Coordination" of a Party, the UNEP unit that is the "UNEP Lead for MEA Enforcement Support" should develop a Model National Inter-Ministerial MEA Cooperation Agreement. This document would provide a framework and offer generic details of effective intra-governmental, domestic working relationships. Within any

Party, its "National Lead for MEA Enforcement Coordination" would negotiate such an agreement with the national customs ministry. Such agreements should make arrangements for routine inter-ministerial information sharing, and should organize these diverse ministries around the shared goals of permitting and tracking (i.e., monitoring compliance of) international shipments effectively (with speed and accuracy).

Arrangements for inter-ministerial information sharing must be appropriate to the state of development of any Party. A Model National Inter-Ministerial MEA Cooperation Agreement should arrange for information to move by paper and fax. As for Parties to an MEA (at least those that are advanced countries) that have the vision or goal to use computers to achieve speed and accuracy in permitting and tracking of international shipments, a Model National Inter-Ministerial MEA Cooperation Agreement will establish the means for comprehensive data management with automated inter-ministerial data linkages to assure real-time approvals and interdictions.

C. Require Product-Specific Codes so that Modern Methods Including Computers can be Used

If the Parties to an MEA have the vision or goal that modern methods including computers should be usable to achieve speed and accuracy in permitting and tracking of international shipments, with the assistance of MEA secretariats, Parties should move to develop and, by decisions of the COPs, to require as MEA obligations that Parties use chemical-specific and other-product-specific codes. In addition, codes should be explored and as soon as feasible required both for business entities and "persons" of any type, and for physical plants or facilities subject to regulation to implement MEAs.

As the WCO's HTS codes often are too broad or general to assure accurate compliance monitoring, they can be supplemented by more detailed codes sometimes called "qualifiers". For example, for chemicals the required coding could well be the HTS code hyphenated to the CAS code. The WCO may facilitate and accommodate such product-specific qualifiers, but it is not likely to require them for environmental (non-customs) purposes. This is likely to be the responsibility of MEAs. Achieving this overdue measure is a prerequisite to using computers to manage MEA data needed for national approvals and interdictions.

D. Propose/Pilot/Prescribe More Standardized Licensing Schemes and Movement Documents

Within MEA secretariats, design and propose to the Parties systematic approaches to compliance monitoring for imports and exports. Presently, most MEAs allow and (where lacking detailed models or standards) do little to discourage a plethora of discordant national approaches. The burden on customs officers to comprehend and recognize MEA requirements and covered trade is too great. As examples:

- Even where licensing is required as a treaty obligation, the details of any scheme may be whatever a nation imagines—or fails to imagine properly.

- It is worse for shipping documents. For example, a customs officer, instead of just one or perhaps 5 or 10 movement-documents formats, may be faced with hundreds or a thousand or more (*e.g.*, 5 MEAs X 200 countries = 1,000 different movement documents).

To customs officers, MEAs may be analogized to satellites in space. Both seem unreal—impossibly remote, mysterious, and disconnected. Let us compare to MEA secretariats the operators of television satellites in relation to their customers, television owners wanting satellite programming. Like front-line customs posts, individual television sets will fail to operate without having essential and highly complex connections that their individual operators can scarcely imagine or create for themselves. For this reason, satellite signal providers carefully design and offer one system with the best means to make all linkages (see para. IV(B) above on linkages), including dishes and cables all properly coded (see para. IV(C) above on codes) to connect with end users.

Customs officers should enjoy an MEA system presenting a comprehensible uniformity and connectedness from top to bottom, from MEA secretariat to customs post. An MEA compliance-monitoring *system* would include an international model or standardized (1) notification/application form, (2) licensing/approval process, and (3) accompanying documentation form. In addition to a paper process, there would be a parallel paperless process available for advanced countries. The result of good MEA systems design for any customs officer also could be a seamless "plug-in-and-play" experience, almost as ordinary and simple as switching on a television properly connected to a satellite!

The system of passports (for humans exporting and importing themselves) also is ordinary, routine, and unremarkable. It is also a useful vision for what may be achieved for shipments controlled by MEAs. For human travelers, Parties have agreed to prescribe national passports that are highly standardized. Customs officers instantly recognize human passports, and— because of their commonality and compatibility—they know exactly what they mean and how to read them. The shipment (a human) is recognized by two unique identifiers (the individual's picture and file number or code), and for immediate verification usually there is an automated inter-ministerial data linkage (a bar code) by which the customs officer can check instantly with the approving ministry. At national option, visas can be required to document prior informed consent to import a traveler.

For chemicals and other products, MEA secretariats could well move to offer more detailed legal elements and programs for national compliance monitoring for imports and exports, both for notification/approval/licensing schemes and for movement documents. At least for electronic messaging, CEFACT provides an existing forum bringing together industry (see para. IV(G) below), customs, and environmental professionals. This work is similar to and may encompass standardization for MEA import/export messaging processes. The "UNEP Lead for MEA Enforcement Support" (see para. III above) could well join in the CEFACT work. As models or proposed standards are developed for MEAs, during any piloting or testing phase, Parties may choose to take up (plug in to) a proposed model or standard. As these are refined and proven successful in testing, COPs should convert them to become required elements of national law within increasingly standardized international systems. As Parties adopt international standards, they would reduce the confusion of discordant national schemes.

As with human passports and CEFACT, for chemicals (and other products regulated by MEAs) the purpose of adopting an international system for compliance monitoring would not be to diminish but to bolster national sovereignty to deal with violations. These occur mostly in international travel and trade between nations, when only briefly may violators (whether human passengers or chemicals) be within the grasp of a nation's jurisdiction. Good systems design will enable any nation—during the moment when a violator is present at the national port or border—to enforce effectively. More international standardization will not mean supra-national "world government." It will mean that MEA secretariats and leading Parties will have done more to enable all Parties to fulfill their treaty obligations to effective national enforcement.

E. Develop an Intelligence Capability to Anticipate Illegality and Assess Threats

The Montreal Protocol on Substances that Deplete the Ozone Layer (Montreal Protocol) failed to anticipate illegality, assess threats, and foresee that its implementation would give rise to black markets and rampant smuggling by organized and entrepreneurial criminals. This failure now should not be repeated.

For example, while probably there will be little trade for most chemicals covered by the Stockholm Convention on Persistent

Organic Pollutants (Stockholm Convention), for this and the Rotterdam Convention, each chemical and its market should be studied. Analysts first would look domestically or internally for black markets. If a black market is found, the analysis would extend to possible foreign sources and users. If there are any, this finding would implicate international trade. Some seaports or transit nations that are suspected smuggling *entrepots* should be studied and be the subjects of intelligence threat assessments. This work could be undertaken by key Parties on behalf of all, or perhaps by the unit of UNEP designated to be the coordinating lead agency for cross-cutting enforcement issues.

The resulting MEA risk assessments and inspection targeting criteria will be welcomed by customs ministries. With this information, they will be able to expedite apparently legitimate trade, and have a rational basis for focusing their scarce inspectional resources only on shipments most deserving close scrutiny. For customs ministries, success will be finding more environmental violators by better applying front-line resources that are not increasing.

F. Require that Criminal Penalties be Available

If the Parties to a MEA want to maximize deterrence ("voluntary" compliance) and (where there are serious violations) to interest prosecutors and judges, they should enact explicit *criminal* penalties, including prison time. (It is not enough to use "illegal," a word that at least includes minor infractions but does not necessarily extend to what is "criminal.") The most serious punishments are appropriate for many import/export violations, where usually there will be criminal intent and culpability, for several reasons:

- Persons involved will have great sophistication (knowledge) to be in the business of shipping in commercial quantities internationally,
- Groups of smugglers often are organized as criminal enterprises,

- The large risk of harm and therefore wrongfulness, such as contributing to species extinction, or mishandling of chemicals globally recognized as most environmentally hazardous, it is or should be obvious to persons involved, and
- The illegality of the conduct is known and intended, as proven by evasive or clandestine behavior.

COPs should require as an MEA obligation that national law provide available criminal penalties for appropriate cases.

To maintain balance, MEA secretariats and Parties should not speak only of concern for investigating illegal trafficking and crime fighting. Of equal concern should be promoting and monitoring compliance for all shipments, and for expediting clearance of the majority of shipments that are legitimate. Front-line, uniformed customs inspectors first must be enabled to succeed (in the routine compliance monitoring and detection of suspect shipments) before there will be many cases for law-enforcement officers who are criminal investigators. For routine infractions that do not rise to criminality, Parties should be encouraged to provide administrative processes and penalties.

G. Engage Legitimate Industry as Partners

Here and in other import-export measures, when designing national regulatory programs, MEA secretariats and Parties should engage legitimate industry (*e.g.*, trade associations of importers and exporters). The leading stakeholders will:

- Know much (have useful intelligence) about their unlawful competitors who are undercutting the stakeholders' legitimate businesses,
- Use modern methods, including computers [available] commercially, to achieve speed and accuracy in tracking of their international shipments,
- Understand and apply systems design to their production and transportation processes,

- Engage in international standardization efforts and organizations, and
- Cooperate with governments to combat illegal enterprises and to assist governments to develop information technology systems to achieve on-line (computerized) notifications, applications, and tracking of international shipments.

For example, to support the implementation of the Montreal Protocol by the U.S. government in the enforcement of the U.S. Clean Air Act, the private sector provided key assistance including intelligence and sampling equipment. The result was the detection and criminal conviction of many smugglers of ozone-depleting substances. This fruitful collaboration can be repeated. With outreach to private stakeholders, secretariats and national governments can join with legitimate industry to achieve as shared goals expedited clearance of proper shipments and real-time detection and investigation of suspect shipments.

V. CONCLUSION

In conclusion, this paper has described solutions by which MEA secretariats and concerned Parties may support and strengthen "enforcement" by national governments. Paragraphs I–III described U.N. structural and institutional measures to this end. For the key *inter*national topic import/export control, this paper offered a vision of a more integrated system. To realize the improvements described, MEA secretariats and concerned Parties should exercise more leadership in a regular course of action to:

1. *Propose* models and possible standards to all Parties,
2. *Pilot* these measures among willing Parties, and
3. *Prescribe* by decisions of COPs that successful measures become international standards and MEA (treaty) obligations.

Combining Legal Mandates with Economics in the Application of Environmental Law

Phyllis P. Harris

Principal Deputy Assistant Administrator, Office of Enforcement and Compliance Assurance United States Environmental Protection Agency, harris.phyllis@epa.gov

SUMMARY

It has been the experience of United States Environmental Protection Agency (EPA) that strong environmental protection has helped, not hurt, the U.S. economy. EPA does not see the economy and the environment as being in conflict; instead they are mutually supporting. This paper discusses the role of monetary penalties in improving compliance with environmental requirements, analyzes how the 'polluter pays' principle has been implemented in the United States, and presents case studies on both civil and criminal penalties.

1 INTRODUCTION

This paper briefly describes the environmental enforcement challenges faced in the United States. We use sound economic approaches to apply the "polluter pays principle." Today EPA achieves very high compliance rates without being unduly punitive and usually without closing enterprises or causing unemployment. We see this linkage of law and economics as a key ingredient for our success in the U.S.

In the United States, this economic competition and resulting environmental degradation resulted in the creation of United States Environmental Protection Agency (EPA) in 1970. Since then, in the world's biggest economy, the EPA has been able to control pollution while at the same time allow our industries to be economically competitive in a global economy. Likewise, nations across the globe are privatizing, democratizing, transitioning, and rapidly developing. In many respects, the United States is a microcosm of all of these characteristics. Science and technology are key to solving or improving most environmental problems. Knowledge is also widely shared as to what makes good environmental law. Many nations, however, lack the political will to enforce environmental laws. This lack of will arises from the perceived conflict between economic goals and the desire to protect the environment.

Responsibility for successful enforcement of environmental standards is in my office within the EPA, the Office of Enforcement and Compliance Assurance. In the enforcement of our environmental laws, we follow a philosophy of "Smart Enforcement," which is using the most appropriate tools to address the most significant problems to achieve the best outcomes. We also build in human economic motivators. As a result, we have made good progress toward including economic incentives within the effective enforcement of the law.

This paper is about pollution control, which we handle very effectively in the United States. EPA applies sound economic approaches by using the "polluter-pays principle." We see this linkage of law and economics as a key ingredient of our success in enforcing environmental law, and we recommend this approach to any nation.

2 ECONOMICS AND MAKING THE VIOLATOR PAY

In the United States, Congress created command-and-control statutory mandates that define prohibited acts and prescribe penalties. To execute this statutory intent, our core enforcement program has strategically focused on the "outlaws" or violators of environmental laws. EPA applies these laws with well-known rigor that creates the cognizance in the regulated community that violations are likely to be detected and followed by an enforcement response that imposes a heavy penalty or sanction. By making it unprofitable to fail to comply immediately, the government is able to get prompt, voluntary conformity or compliance from most companies. The rest we punish, deter or dissuade.

Our U.S. approach of large penalties, and sometimes imprisonment, may seem excessive today in countries where there is consideration of using economic instruments as the best way to encourage environmental compliance. Some countries enjoy a culture of greater cooperation, respect for government, and voluntary adherence to green values and laws. But in many parts of the world there is great poverty, corruption and chaos, for which only a very strong hand of government can exert any control. As a result, based on the experience of the U.S., it may be necessary to be very strong in command-and-control applications of economics-based enforcement instruments.

The goal of a pollution control economic policy instrument is to minimize unwanted "externalities" by having enterprises internalize all costs, including pollution control, in product pricing. Because the EPA is well known to be an effective enforcer, most regulated enterprises choose to pay for effective pollution control and do achieve compliance. As a result, fear of EPA enforcement is an important motivator for compliance. Whatever other motivation may be present, a small governmental expenditure on dissuasion or deterrence produces a huge investment in pollution control. In this way, the permitted and lawful polluter internalizes the cost of pollution control.

For violators, we make sure that the costs to be internalized and paid are even higher. In a limited way, we have done this under some of our laws that require the cleanup of sites and natural resources damaged by the release or improper disposal of hazardous wastes and substances. In an ideal or theoretical world, we would always price the natural resources—including air and water—damaged. But in most pollution control enforcement cases, it is neither necessary nor possible for EPA to price either the value of the natural resources damaged, or the cost of their clean up or restoration. Usually, violations of our laws do not involve catastrophic spills. Most violations result from routine operational mismanagement and everyday illegal pollution from chimneys, stacks and pipes from factories and other plant facilities. Indeed, it is very important to our overall success that EPA laws are applied early and preventively, usually before there is measurable natural resource damage or harm to public health.

For the EPA enforcement program, it is enough just to prove that the violating source discharged, emitted or released more pollutants to the environment than permitted or to prove that the facility operated outside of the law. Our source-based controls typically define the allowed parts per million or smaller for each chemical, and it is a violation to allow anything more to leave the chimney, stack or pipe. It is precisely because EPA does not either use ambient controls or try to measure environmental damage, but relies on source-based controls, that it has become possible for EPA to prove most routine violations. We do not have to prove the cost of the environmental damage or wrongful externalities. We look elsewhere. A starting point is the maximum penalty set by law; it provides the upper limit of the penalty amount. Under the typical EPA statute, each day of exceedance for each controlled chemical is a separate violation, and each day of violation may be penalized up to as much as $32,500 per day. Violations continuing for a period of time or for multiple pollutants can quickly reach tens or hundreds of millions of dollars. By referring to that maximum penalty, EPA quickly gets the attention of a violator.

The maximum penalty available by law often has little rational relationship to the facts and to economics. EPA's goal is not to use the highest possible penalties to cause unemployment by closing enterprises, but to keep enterprises open provided they operate in compliance. Assuming that a violating enterprise wants to remain open, EPA first requires the installation of all required pollution control equipment. Then, EPA takes the following three steps to provide economic incentives to violators to comply with the law.

2.1 Assessing "Compensatory" Penalty Component to Recover the Economic Benefit of Noncompliance

In this penalty calculation, EPA applies a very effective "economic instrument" by which "the polluting violator pays." In this regard, EPA's economic goal is to level the economic playing field in the enterprise sector of which the violator is a member. EPA sets the monetary penalty at a level that recovers from the violator the full "economic benefit of noncompliance," to recapture the violator's wrongful cost savings from not controlling pollution, and from undercutting non-polluting competitors. If this was not corrected, polluters would drive out compliers, and ultimately only lawbreakers would remain operating. To eliminate this unfair economic advantage, EPA calculates the wrongful savings by the violator as this "compensatory" element of the penalty. "BEN" is the name of EPA's model used to (http://www.epa.gov/oeca/datasys/dsm2.html) calculate the present value of the violator's failure to buy, install, and operate pollution-control technology. Because a violator should not be permitted to realize any illicit economic gain from a violation, this amount is almost always recovered and usually is not reduced in negotiations. EPA economists have testified in court in support of the efficacy of BEN calculations, and judges have regularly upheld EPA's penalty assessment method as based on sound economics, principled, and fair. BEN is a huge success for us.

2.2 Adding the "Punitive" Component of the Penalty

BEN is only the beginning. We have found that if all an enterprise has to do is pay a penalty to restore the level playing field, most will just wait until they are caught. Instead, to create a reason for business to comply voluntarily and to deter others from not complying with the law, EPA increases the monetary penalty by the punitive—what we call "gravity based"—element of the penalty. This is adjusted up by considering factors such as the extent of departure from required behavior and whether there was the potential or actuality of environmental harm. At this point, if we have any information as to the value of the natural resources damaged, this may be considered not as a matter of economic compensation but as justification for an additional penalty that is a punishment. Finally, we may also adjust penalties downward in consideration of the defendant's cooperation and lack of prior offenses.

2.3 Reducing Penalties by the Value of Voluntary Work to Go Beyond Compliance

Beginning in 1991, EPA began developing ways to reduce payment as punishment and to do more to encourage environmentally desirable behavior—while still using our traditionally tough enforcement processes and large penalty assessments. We now may agree to reduce the punitive component of the final penalty assessment by the amount paid by the violator for certain extraordinary actions that the violator agrees to take to protect the environment or to assure future good behavior. These refinements by EPA policy have been well received by the public and by companies found in violation. As a result, EPA now has "carrots to accompany the stick" These "carrots" encourage the right behavior, benefit the environment, and in many instances those communities that were impacted by violator's actions.

Supplemental Environmental Projects (SEPs) are actions that qualify for such a penalty reduction. These must (1) be in addition to required compliance with EPA's end-of-pipe or stack pollution control requirements; (2) "go beyond compliance" with EPA's pollution control requirements, and thus be extraordinary projects that are even more protective of the environment than is legally required; and (3) cost no less than the amount of the penalty mitigated. EPA will not reduce its penalty more than the amount of the violator's expenditure on a SEP. Because a violator should not be permitted to realize any economic gain from a violation, the economic benefit component of the penalty is always recovered and not mitigated. Penalty reductions for SEPs may only apply to reduce the punitive penalty, and usually at least some penalty must be paid so that no violation is "free."

Some types of SEPs are:

(1) production process (source reduction, waste minimization) changes to prevent pollution (not just control it);

(2) environmental restoration or clean-up activities upstream, where others caused contamination, or of damage not caused by the violation; and

(3) community emergency planning and preparedness assistance, such as providing hazardous materials control equipment or training to local governments that must respond to pollution emergencies. To calculate the cost of the SEP on economic principles, we use a computerized economic model.

2.4 EPA's Enforcement Policies on Environmental Auditing

In the United States, permitted polluters must self-monitor pollution control performance and report certain self-monitoring results. Beyond this, there is no legal requirement for companies to conduct comprehensive self-audits or to develop environmental management systems. EPA welcomes the activities of the industry-based International Standards Organization (ISO) that encourage environmental audits or environmental management systems (EMS).

However, because the ISO 14000 program does not address compliance per se, it does not fulfill EPA legal requirements. So, EPA by policy incorporated environmental auditing firmly within the enforcement process, an achievement that we believe to be highly significant and perhaps unique. Starting in 1986, a violator's voluntary agreement to do an environmental audit may be the basis for a substantial reduction in the punitive portion of its EPA penalty assessment. Additional penalty reductions may be given to government agencies or nonprofit organizations that are violators, provided they use their money to come into compliance and remain so. Also, small enterprises in violation now may receive total penalty credit and pay no penalty if they agree to perform continuous environmental self-audits to report and correct violations. EPA invites violators to "voluntarily" conduct an audit (which EPA cannot legally require), rather like a voluntary Supplemental Environmental Project that the government will reward in the same way. It is EPA's reputation for tough enforcement that has greatly increased the use of auditing. A 1995 survey showed that in the U.S. more than 90% of the responding enterprises that conducted environmental audits did so to find and correct environmental violations before they were found by government inspectors and punished! (While the cost of the audit is credited to reduce the penalty, the cost of correcting or achieving compliance based upon the audit's findings—which by law must be done anyway—is not credited.)

Even where EPA has not identified a violation, EPA's audit policy encourages companies to discover violations and disclose them to EPA. This must be done in a way that is systematic, prompt and independent. The company must agree to correct and remediate harm, prevent recurrence, make information publicly available and cooperate with regulators. EPA reserves to the government the right to protect the public health and the environment in cases of serious violation. EPA's audit policy does not excuse and does not apply where there are repeat violations or there is a pattern of violations, imminent or substantial endangerment or serious actual harm, criminal conduct or substantial economic benefit from noncompliance. There is no total amnesty.

2.5 Environmental Auditing in Relationship to Criminal Cases

Where a criminal case is filed, for many years it also has been the policy of national prosecutors and many national judges to encourage environmental auditing. A guilty environmental offender may receive a reduced sentence where there was already in effect a good faith environmental auditing or compliance program. Similarly, an offender can expect some leniency when, reasonably promptly after becoming aware of the crime, the offender reports it to government authorities, cooperates and accepts responsibility. Also, when sentencing an environmental offender, leniency may be shown to the offender who agrees to begin an effective environmental auditing program to prevent and detect future violations. In this way, criminal punishment, like civil penalties, is reduced to encourage and reward environmental auditing.

EPA by policy will not initiate criminal cases against companies that voluntarily and promptly disclose and correct violations and meet the specific conditions of the audit policy. But where an enterprise or its employees ignore audit reports of violations, are willfully blind to violations or conceal or condone continuing non-compliance, any audit report may become what we call a "smoking gun" or strong evidence of guilt. Then, the audit report may be evidence of knowledge of violations, intent to continue to violate, and thus actual criminal behavior of the most serious kind.

3 CASE STUDIES

These principles can be illustrated with two examples of U.S. cases. Usually EPA files a formal complaint with a court or administrative judge to begin the enforcement action based on violations. Civil court proceedings and administrative cases seek monetary penalties paid to the U.S. Treasury, and a court order, if needed, to stop an illegal or dangerous activity or to require a clean up. The filed complaint brings industry lawyers to the table to negotiate with the government over the resolution of the problems. Because EPA collects good evidence of violations, most cases are settled without trial.

3.1 Civil Case Example

The "Petroleum Refinery Initiative," is one of the most successful enforcement initiatives undertaken by the EPA (http://www.epa.gov/compliance/civil/programs/caa/oil/index .html). This initiative illustrates how "global" agreements (addressing major sources of pollutants at all of an enterprise's facilities at once) in a specific sector are economically feasible while improving environmental performance. Since 2000, EPA has entered into settlements for environmental compliance with petroleum refining companies that control approximately 40 percent of the nation's refining capacity in more than 20 of our 50 states. Negotiations are continuing with refiners representing another 40 percent of the nation's refining capacity. Taken as a whole, these settlements will (based on the settling companies' estimates) result in a reduction of atmospheric emissions of nearly 45,000 tons of nitrogen oxide, more than 95,000 tons of sulphur dioxide, and large reductions of benzene, volatile organic compounds and particulate matter. The companies agreed to invest nearly $2 billion in control technologies, pay civil penalties of $36.8 million, and perform Supplemental Environmental Projects valued at approximately $25 million. One SEP was the donation of an island for a county park, another to install pollution controls on public school buses.

The Petroleum Refinery Initiative applied an innovative, enterprise-wide approach, addressing major sources of pollutants at all of an enterprise's refineries at once, rather than taking a traditional facility- by-facility, violation-by-violation enforcement path. This approach enabled EPA and refining companies to efficiently and quickly address many environmental problems presented by this large and complex industrial sector.

By agreeing to address pollution problems in a coordinated, enterprise-wide basis, settling refiners were able to receive the first refinery-wide emission caps negotiated in a consent decree. By avoiding a chimney-by-chimney regulatory approach, these plant-wide caps enhance a refiner's flexibility for producing fuels. These caps are expected to help eliminate production problems that could limit fuel supplies and raise prices, to improve plant efficiency, and to significantly reduce emissions. The refineries also agreed to use the most modern control technologies. For example, detection and repair of leaking equipment and benzene waste will be controlled by measures exceeding what is required by national law. Moreover, in some instances, as permitted by law, settling refineries are partnering to develop new and better control technology.

These cases illustrate that there is almost always some penalty money paid to the government, even when an enterprise eventually cooperates. The U.S. approach to environmental enforcement which includes payment of penalties is a strong deterrent to future violations. Without penalties, even for the first violation, most companies would not comply until they are caught. Moreover, the government does not have the resources to prosecute all of those companies that are out of compliance. Therefore, the EPA almost always imposes a cash penalty. We find that this creates an atmosphere in which enterprises will chose to comply because they are "deterred" from committing violations, and because they believe that our system is fair. We estimate that in the U.S. the rate of compliance with EPA requirements is between 80% and 95% in various programs.

3.2 Criminal Case Example

In criminal cases, the government seeks prison time for individuals who commit environmental crimes. In the United States, while we have been developing economic incentives to encourage compliance, simultaneously we have strengthened our means to compel it using forms of dissuasion exceeding what can be achieved by economics and monetary penalties. Today we have a national force of about 225 EPA pollution control police officers. They increase the stakes for industry. Sending to prison those managers and workers who pollute intentionally is very popular with the American people, who regard environmental crime as unacceptable behavior.

For example, treatment as criminals is both appropriate and necessary for international businesses that smuggle chlorofluorocarbons (CFCs). Within the U.S. the market for illegal CFCs is as profitable to smugglers as illegal narcotic drugs. EPA's national environmental police, together with customs and revenue police, find these criminals and bring them to our Department of Justice for prosecution.

The case of AGA International Corporation and Barry Himes is one of many in the U.S. against smugglers who would undercut the Montreal Protocol on Substances that Deplete the Ozone Layer. Mr. Himes imported CFCs from Russia and China that were shipped through Canada into the U.S. Between 1996 and 1998, more than one million pounds of CFCs were imported illegally, falsely described as recycled. The criminals used various shell companies and offshore bank accounts in the Bahamas and Antigua to conceal their control of these transactions to defeat efforts by tax authorities to collect the substantial excise tax that the U.S. imposed to promote use of ozone-friendly replacement products.

Himes was charged as a criminal and pled guilty in a national court. In 2003, he was sentenced to six and a half years in prison and ordered to pay $1.8 million in restitution and a fine of $12,500. Mr. Himes had previously forfeited to the government more than $3 million in property including an expensive home, car and jewelry. His principal colleague was sentenced to a term of four years in prison and ordered to pay $1.2 million in restitution. Ten other persons pled guilty and each received an average of one and half years in prison.

This criminal case illustrates that sometimes deterrence fails. To an economist, it may seem crude or incorrect to say that such command-and-control enforcement illustrates the application of an economic instrument. To this I can only answer that surely criminal polluters "pay" dearly when they receive such sentences. A major advantage to society of having the criminal proceedings and penalties available is that this tool produces so great a deterrent effect that usually it seldom has to be used.

As economists observe, good information is essential to making rational choices. For this reason, EPA regularly issues announcements regarding significant enforcement case filings and conclusions. We are very transparent, even making available on the Internet the compliance records of violators. From anywhere in the world, you can visit our Internet site to see if an enterprise operating in the United States has performed within the law or is in violation (http://www.epa.gov/echo). If a violating enterprise is coming to your nation, we want you to know so that you may consider imposing special permit conditions and surveillance.

4 CONCLUSION

This paper has described how in the U.S. we use sound economic approaches to apply the "polluter pays principle." Today EPA achieves very high compliance rates without being unduly punitive and usually without closing enterprises or causing unemployment. We see this linkage of law and economics as a key ingredient for our success in the U.S., and we recommend this approach to any nation that would effectively enforce its environmental law.

The United States Environmental Protection Agency wants to cooperate with all nations seeking better environmental enforcement. We readily collaborate with all like-minded nations that ask our help to improve their domestic environmental enforcement capacity, and nations that want to develop cases against international environmental criminals. EPA is ready to be a partner in this effort.

5 REFERENCE

This paper was presented to the Organisation for Economic Co-operation and Development on December 1-2, 2004, at its Global Forum for Sustainable Development in Paris. Ms. Harris has served as the United States Environmental Protection Agency's number-two enforcement official since 2001. She is also a Co-Chair of the International Network for Environmental Compliance and Enforcement (INECE).

Partial List of Publications

by Richard W. Emory, Jr.
as author, co-author, a contributor, or "ghost writer"

"The Conservation Easement," *Maryland State Bar Journal* (Oct. 1974)

"Environmental Criminal Enforcement Priorities for the 1990s," *The George Washington Law Review* (April 1991)—principal author as "ghost writer" of this article for a former Assistant Administrator

"Extended and Shared Producer Responsibility: Phase 2 Framework Report," Organisation for Economic Co-Operation and Development (document ENV/EPOC/PPC(97)20/REV2, OECD, Paris, May 1998)—named as principal author of this study for the OECD's Environment Directorate on new approaches to recycling

"Probing the Protections in the Convention on PIC (Prior Informed Consent)," *Journal of International Environmental Law and Policy* (University of Colorado, spring 2001)

"Transposing to Enforceable National Laws the Obligations of the PIC and POPs Conventions for Imports and Exports," *Journal of International Environmental Law and Policy* (University of Colorado, spring 2002)

"Guiding Principles for Reform of Environmental Enforcement Authorities in Transition Economies of Eastern Europe, Caucasus, and Central Asia" (document CCNM/ENV/EAP(2003)6, OECD, Paris, spring 2003)—based on an underlying draft prepared by Mr. Emory, with international and OECD secretariat input

"Assuring Environmental Compliance: A Toolkit for Building Better Environmental Inspectorates in Eastern Europe, Caucasus, and Central Asia" (OECD, Paris, 2004; ISBN 92-64-01492-6)— based on the above guiding principles, with input contributed by Mr. Emory and others

"Combining Legal Mandates with Economics in the Application of Environmental Law," Proceedings of the Seventh International Conference on Environmental Compliance and Enforcement (OECD, Paris, 2004)—principal author as "ghost writer" of this speech for a former Deputy Assistant Administrator which she delivered at this conference organized by the OECD and INECE, reprinted as the previous addendum to this book

"Manual on Compliance with and Enforcement of Multilateral Environmental Agreements," UNEP (Nairobi 2006; ISBN 93-807-2703-6, at www.unep.org/dec/docs/UNEP Manual.pdf, which named me among contributors

"Environmental Non-Compliance: What Response in OECD Countries?" (OECD, Paris, 2007), which named me among contributors

"Improving National Enforcement for Better Governance Implementing Multilateral Environmental Agreements" —my recommendations requested by and submitted to the "Meeting of Experts Called by the Division of Environmental Conventions of the United Nations Environment Programme, Sri Lanka, January 21–22, 2006," as published by the Denver Journal of International Law and Policy (University of Denver, 2008); reprinted as an addendum to this book

"Principles for Customs and Environmental Cooperation— Toward Better Import-Export Control" (2008)—principal author of this USEPA course for international use, fostering effective national programs to control international trade under multilateral environmental agreements

"Negotiating Customs and Environmental Cooperation: Effective National Program Design" (2008)—author of this EPA international training course to assist foreign governments to organize national institutional relationships and establish programs to control international trade regulated for environmental reasons, first used successfully in El Salvador in 2009

"Ensuring Environmental Compliance: Trends and Good Practices" (OECD, Paris, 2009)—named among contributors, and managed U.S. input

"Bridging the Customs and Environmental Gap: Achieving Inter-Ministerial Cooperation for Effective Control of Trade Regulated for Environmental Threats" (International Network for Environmental Compliance and Enforcement, summer 2011)—http://www.inece.org/conference/9/proceedings/51_Emory.pdf (2011)

Bibliography

Benedick, Richard Elliot. *Ozone Diplomacy.* Cambridge, MA: Harvard University Press, 2nd ed. 1998.

Blees, Tom. *Prescription for the Planet.* Charleston, SC: Amazon's Booksurge Company, 2008, online at www.prescriptionfor theplanet.com.

Booth, Michael Booth. *The Almost Nearly Perfect People: The Truth About the Nordic Miracle.* London: Jonathan Cape, 2014.

Brannen, Peter. *Ends of the World: Volcanic Apocalypses, Lethal Oceans, and Our Quest to Understand Earth's Past Mass Extinctions.* New York: Harper Collins, 2017.

Brooks, David. *The Second Mountain.* New York: Random House, 2019.

Caputo, Philip J. *A Rumor of War.* New York: Henry Holt & Company, 1977.

Carson, Rachel. *Silent Spring.* New York: Houghton Mifflin, 1962.

_____. *The Sense of Wonder.* New York: Open Road Media, 2011.

Center for Science in the Public Interest (CSPI). *Nutrition Action Healthletter.* Washington.

Colburn, Theo, Dianne Dumanoski, and John Peterson Myers. *Our Stolen Future: Are We Threatening Our Fertility, Intelligence, and Survival? A Scientific Detective Story.* New York: Dutton, 1996.

Collins, Larry, and Dominique Lapierre. *Is Paris Burning?* New York: Penguin, 1965.

Cravens, Gwyneth. *The Power to Save the World: The Truth About Nuclear Energy. New York:* Penguin Random House, 2017; Alfred A. Knopf, 2007.

Darwin, Charles. *The Origin of Species.* London: John Murray, 1859.

de Tocqueville, Alexis. *Democracy in America.* Chicago: University of Chicago Press, 2000.

Eisinger, Jesse. *The Chickenshit Club: Why the Justice Department Fails to Prosecute Executives.* New York: Simon & Schuster, 2017.

Emory, Ben. *Sailor for the Wild: On Maine, Conservation, and Boats.* Brooklin, ME: Seapoint Books and Media, 2017.

Englander, John. *High Tide on Main Street: Rising Sea Level and the Coming Coastal Crisis.* The Science Bookshelf, 2nd edition, 2013.

Friedman, Thomas L. *From Beirut to Jerusalem.* New York: Farrar, Straus & Giroux, 1989.

Goldstein, Joshua S., and Staffan A. Qvist. *A Bright Future: How Some Countries Have Solved Climate Change and the Rest Can Follow.* New York: PublicAffairs, 2018.

Gore, Al. *An Inconvenient Truth: The Planetary Emergency of Global Warming and What We Can Do About It .* New York: Penguin Random House, 2006.

_____. *Earth in the Balance: Ecology and the Human Spirit.* New York: Penguin Random House, 1992.

_____. *The Future: Six Drivers of Global Change.* New York: Penguin Random House, 2013.

Graham, Katharine. *Personal History.* New York: Alfred A. Knopf, 1997.

Hanna, Kristin. *The Nightingale.* New York: St. Martin's Press/Macmillan, 2017.

Hansen, James. *Storms of My Grandchildren: The Truth About the Coming Climate Catastrophe and Our Last Chance to Save Humanity.* New York: Bloomsbury USA, 2009.

Hunter, David, James E. Salzman, and Durwood J. Zaelke. *International Environmental Law and Policy.* St. Paul, MN: Foundation Press 5th ed., 2015.

Inslee, Jay, and Bracken Hendricks. *Apollo's Fire: Igniting America's Clean-Energy Economy.* Washington: Island Press, 2009.

Kipling, Rudyard. "If," from *Rewards and Fairies.* New York: Doubleday, 1910.

Klein, Naomi. *This Changes Everything: Capitalism vs. the Climate.* New York: Simon & Schuster, 2015.

Kolbert, Elizabeth. *Field Notes from a Catastrophe: Man, Nature, and Climate Change.* New York: Bloomsbury Publishing, 2007.

_____. *The Sixth Extinction: An Unnatural History.* New York: Henry Holt & Company, 2014.

Lambright, W. Henry. *NASA and the Environment: The Case of Ozone Depletion.* No. 38 in the series "Monographs in Aerospace History" (NASA SP-2005-4538; May 2005), online at https://history.nasa.gov/monograph38.pdf.

Lear, Linda. *Rachel Carson: Witness for Nature.* New York: Houghton Mifflin Harcourt, 2009.

_____, editor. *Lost Woods: The Discovered Writing of Rachel Carson.* Boston: Beacon Press, 1998.

Little, Amanda. *The Fate of Food: What We'll Eat in a Bigger, Hotter, Smarter World.* New York: Harmony Books, 2019.

Lowell, James Russell. "Once to Every Man and Nation" (appears in many hymnals of the sects of Protestant Christianity), 1845.

Mann, Michael E., and Tom Toles. *The Madhouse Effect: How Climate Change Denial Is Threatening Our Planet.* New York: Columbia University Press, 2016.

McKibben, Bill. *The End of Nature.* New York: Random House, 1989 (and subsequent editions).

Neill, Peter. *The Once and Future Ocean: Notes Toward a New Hydraulic Society.* Sedgwick, ME: Leete's Island Books, 2015.

Nesbit, Jeff. *This Is the Way the World Ends: How Droughts and Die-Offs, Heat Waves and Hurricanes Are Converging on America.* New York: Thomas Dunne Books/St. Martin's Press, 2018.

Nye, Bill, "The Science Guy." *Unstoppable: Harnessing Science to Change the World.* New York: St. Martin's Press/Macmillan, 2015.

Oreskes, Naomi, and Erik M. Conway. *The Collapse of Western Civilization: A View from the Future.* New York: Columbia University Press, 2014.

Piketty, Thomas. *Capital in the Twenty-First Century.* Cambridge, MA: Harvard University Press, 2014.

Rich, Nathaniel. *Losing Earth: A Recent History*. New York: Farrar, Straus & Giroux, 2019.

Shetterly, Susan H. *Seaweed Chronicles: A World at the Water's Edge.* Chapel Hill, NC: Algonquin Books, 2018.

Shuster, Jos. M. *Beyond Fossil Fools.* Edina, MN: Beaver's Pond Press, 2008.

Smith, Jean Edward. *John Marshall: Definer of a Nation.* New York: Henry Holt & Company, 1998.

_____. *Lucius D. Clay: An American Life.* St. Louis, MO: First Glance Books, 1990.

Standiford, Les. *Last Train to Paradise: Henry Flagler and the Spectacular Rise and Fall of a Railroad That Crossed an Ocean.* New York: Crown, 2002.

Till, Charles E., and Yoon Il Chang. *Plentiful Energy: The Story of the Integral Fast Reactor.* Amazon's Create Space Company, 2011.

Vogel, David. *The Politics of Precaution: Regulating Health, Safety, and Environmental Risks in Europe and in the United States.* Princeton, NJ: Princeton University Press, 2012.

Wallace-Wells, David. *The Uninhabitable Earth: Life After Warming.* New York: Tim Duggan Books/Crown, 2019.

Ward, Peter D. *Under a Green Sky: Global Warming, the Mass Extinctions of the Past, and What They Can Tell Us About Our Future.* Washington: Smithsonian, 2007.

Wilson, Edward Osborne ("E. O."). *The Future of Life.* London: Abacus Books, 2002.

Wood, Mary Christina. *Nature's Trust: Environmental Law for a New Ecological Age.* Cambridge, U.K.: Cambridge University Press, 2014.

Index

The typeface used in this book is Cambria, designed by Jelle Bosma (with others) in 2004 for Microsoft's ClearType collection, a suite of fonts intended to render well both in print and on LCD screens. A very readable "new Times New Roman," Cambria is somewhat more condensed than most serif body text fonts, with even spacing and proportions. Described by Bosma as a "transitional slab-serif hybrid," the typeface has sturdy letter construction with heavy vertical serifs, retaining legibility at small sizes or displayed on a low-resolution screen, while Cambria's thin horizontals ensure the design remains crisp at larger sizes.